Praise for *AI and Information Access*

'Information access is vital for work, study, and daily life. Libraries, along with search engines and mobile phones, have provided this access. However, users face information overload, relevance issues, and disinformation. Large language models provide on-the-fly content creation but can hallucinate and raise ethical concerns. In nine chapters, *AI and Information Access* explores these issues, along with tools, processes, practices, and how they relate to everyday life, teaching, and research. It is a timely book for information professionals interested in using and promoting AI responsibly.'
Professor Naresh Agarwal, School of Library and Information Science, Simmons University, Boston, USA

'In *AI and Information Access*, Gobinda and Sudatta Chowdhury, with their extensive expertise, cover an array of topics that introduce readers to the tools and processes for using AI to access information in conventional and novel ways. Users, the search process and critical thinking are addressed in everyday, scholarly and research contexts. They pragmatically share lessons learned, examples and scenarios before pondering whether AI introduces a paradigm shift in teaching, research and professional practices. It should be a fascinating read for educators and everyone working with information, and stimulate much-needed research.'
Professor Ina Fourie, Department of Information Science (iSchool), University of Pretoria, South Africa

'*AI and Information Access: Benefits, Challenges and Lessons* offers timely and insightful perspectives for information practitioners, researchers and students. Gobinda and Sudatta Chowdhury's latest book discusses how generative AI is transforming information seeking, retrieval, and use in different contexts, covering critical topics such as searching, prompt engineering and AI literacy, as well as the assessment and integrity of search results. Importantly, the book provides a balanced perspective of the opportunities afforded by generative AI and the challenges associated with its use. For those who wish to harness generative AI, this book is a must-have resource.'
Professor Dion Goh and Professor Chei Sian Lee, Wee Kim Wee School of Communication and Information, Nanyang Technological University, Singapore

'In an age of threatened democracies and rampant misinformation, this book makes for essential reading. It explores how AI – especially generative tools – can be harnessed critically to empower individuals, protect truth, and promote equitable access to information. As technology transforms how we search, learn, and decide, this timely work offers vital guidance for using AI responsibly in building an informed, just, and democratic society for all.'
Professor Koraljka Golub, Head of the iInstitute, Linnaeus University, Sweden

'As we enter and accelerate through the age of AI, it is imperative that information science professionals keep up with the critical applications and impact of AI on education and research. Information professionals who are directly involved in supporting libraries, memory institutions, R&D centers, and institutions of higher education need to understand how Generative AI is influencing their core activities now and how such activities may benefit by using Generative AI appropriately. The book offers timely, highly readable, and relevant content for information professionals to grasp the foundational Generative AI concepts and applications for information seeking and research tasks.'
Professor Javed Mostafa, Dean, Faculty of Information, University of Toronto, Canada

'Gobinda and Sudatta Chowdhury's new book *AI and Information Access: Benefits, Challenges and Lessons* explores the most pressing challenges for the 2020s, namely, how to harness the power of artificial intelligence. The work discusses AI in everyday life, but also examines its role in scholarly and research contexts, as well as considering its impact on information seeking behaviours and approaches, its potential influence on the information profession more generally, and the tools and technologies around its use and exploitation. This volume is a thoughtful contribution on a crucial topic for information science.'
Professor Peter Reid, School of Law and Social Sciences, Robert Gordon University, Aberdeen

'Everyone doing academic research today should read *AI and Information Access: Benefits, Challenges and Lessons* by Gobinda and Sudatta Chowdhury. It discusses how large language models (LLM) have changed the ways we search for information. The authors provide an introduction to contemporary artificial intelligence systems and include examples based on several research scenarios, including health and wellbeing, personal interest and environment and climate change. This book will help librarians, scholars and students.'
Professor Michael Seadle, Humboldt Universität zu Berlin, Germany, and former executive director, iSchools.org

'As AI is reshaping the contours of information science, this book reveals the transformative power of GenAI through a systematic and comprehensive examination of GenAI's benefits and challenges, supported by practical examples and rigorous analysis. This book is valuable for students, academics, and professionals, because it offers a forward-looking perspective on the future landscape of information science.'
Lihong Zhou, PhD, Professor, Associate Dean, School of Information Management (iSchool), Wuhan University, China

AI and Information Access

Every purchase of a Facet book helps to fund CILIP's advocacy, awareness and accreditation programmes for information professionals.

AI and Information Access

Benefits, Challenges and Lessons

G. G. Chowdhury and
Sudatta Chowdhury

facet
publishing

Published by Facet Publishing
www.facetpublishing.co.uk

Facet Publishing is wholly owned by CILIP:
the Library and Information Association.

British Library Cataloguing in Publication Data
A catalogue record for this book is available from the British Library.

ISBN 978-1-78330-772-2 (paperback)
ISBN 978-1-78330-773-9 (hardback)
ISBN 978-1-78330-774-6 (PDF)
ISBN 978-1-78330-775-3 (EPUB)

First published 2025

FSC
www.fsc.org
MIX
Paper | Supporting responsible forestry
FSC® C013604

The manufacturer's authorised representative in the EU for product safety is Logos Europe, 9 rue Nicolas Poussin, 17000 La Rochelle, France (contact@logoseurope.eu, www.logoseurope.eu).

Typeset from authors' files in 10/13pt Palatino and OpenSans by Flagholme Publishing Services.
Printed and bound by CPI Group (UK) Ltd, Croydon, CR0 4YY.

To our parents –

Uma and Ananda

Anjali and Amar

Contents

Figures and Tables

Figures

Tables

About the Authors

Dr Gobinda Chowdhury is a Professor of Information Science in the Department of Computer & Information Sciences, University of Strathclyde, Glasgow, UK. His research focuses on information access and digital libraries. His recent research focuses on: (1) information systems and services for addressing the global challenges such as the UN Sustainable Development Goals (SDGs); and (2) the role of AI in information access in different use and user contexts. Professor Chowdhury was the European and global Chair of the iSchools. He has written or edited 18 books, and over 160 research papers. Professor Chowdhury can be contacted by e-mail at: gobinda.chowdhury@strath.ac.uk.

Dr Sudatta Chowdhury is a Research Associate in the Department of Computer & Information Sciences, University of Strathclyde, Glasgow, UK. Previously she worked as an academic in Singapore and Australia. Her research focuses on information users, digital libraries and information services. Her recent research includes: (1) information systems and services for addressing the global challenges such as the UN Sustainable Development Goals (SDGs); and (2) the impact of AI on information users. She has co-authored seven books and made invited contributions to three book chapters. She has published over 50 research papers. Dr Sudatta Chowdhury can be contacted by e-mail at: sudatta.chowdhury@strath.ac.uk.

Introduction

The arrival of ChatGPT, a chatbot and virtual assistant developed by OpenAI, in November 2022 (https://openai.com/index/chatgpt/), has brought a new wave of transformative technologies that have a profound impact on all areas of life and activities involving data, information and knowledge. ChatGPT has the Generative Pre-trained Transformer (GPT) architecture as the foundation and is pre-trained on a broad spectrum of generalizeised, unlabelled and sometimes unvalidated data. These LLM (large language model)-based tools have the ability to create human-like content such as images, music, charts, tables and, programme codes, and answer questions in a conversational manner.

Typical information search processes assume an interaction cycle consisting of query specification, receipt and examination of retrieval results, and then either stopping or reformulating the query and repeating the process until a relevant result set is found. Conventional search systems used in libraries, database services and search engines are based on indices that map lexical tokens or semantic embeddings to document identifiers, and these indices are designed for retrieving relevant documents; whereas Gen AI-based chatbots support the integration of these documents into a holistic answer that are presented to the user in response to search queries or prompts.

So, what would be the impact of the Generative (or Gen) AI (Gen AI) tools for access to information? By undertaking an evidence-based approach and some typical use cases, and analysing the output generated by some chosen Gen AI tools for access to specific information in everyday life, research and scholarly contexts, this book discusses the implications of these technologies for the end-users, as well as the education and professional practices in library and information sciences.

The book is designed for students, academics, researchers and professionals in library science, information science, computer science, and cognate disciplines that deal with the design, delivery and management of information systems and services. It takes a practical approach to demonstrate and critically analyse the benefits offered by the emerging Gen AI tools for information access, as well as the potential challenges and questions associated with the use of these tools.

The book comprises nine chapters. Chapter 1 provides a general introduction to Gen AI and briefly discusses how the Gen AI tools can be used for access to information. By providing some typical examples of information access through conventional library search services and scholarly databases, it discusses some fundamental differences between the Gen AI tools and conventional approaches to information access used in libraries, database search services and search engines. In the light of these discussions, the chapter mentions the key questions that are addressed in the book.

Chapter 2 sets the background for the rest of the topics, issues and challenges discussed in the book. It provides an introduction to information access by briefly touching upon the indexing and information searches processes. By drawing examples of some information searches in typical library services, scholarly databases, and search engines, the chapter discusses the various stages that a user has to go through to find information required in specific search contexts.

Several models and theories have been proposed over the past few decades that aim to describe how people seek and interact with various information sources, and the different stages of information search processes that people go through. These theories and models – that have informed the design of various information search systems, database services and search engines over the past few decades – demonstrate that people begin their information searches often with a vague notion of exactly what to search for and where, and the searches become more focused as they progress through different search sessions. Some of the well-known models and theories of information seeking and retrieval in the context of scholarly and everyday life information seeking are discussed in Chapter 3. The basic concepts of these models and theories are revisited later in the book to discuss how far these models and theories are applicable for information seeking using the Gen AI tools.

Chapters 4, 5 and 6 present the results of some case studies on information seeking for everyday life, and research and scholarly information contexts, using some chosen Gen AI tools. Chapter 4 shows the examples of some search sessions with five Gen AI tools – such as Claude, Copilot, Gemini, Perplexity AI and GPT-4o – based on three scenarios of everyday life information seeking: one on health and wellbeing; one on personal interest on an emerging topic, such as Generative AI itself; and another on a topic of common interest to life and society, such as environment and climate change. Query formulation or search prompts, the format and content of the corresponding output, as well as the reliability and reputation of the cited sources, are discussed. These experiments and the corresponding findings are discussed later in this book in the context of the benefits and challenges of Gen AI for everyday life information seeking.

Chapter 5 presents the examples of the search output generated by seven Gen AI tools – Claude, Consensus, Copilot, Gemini, GPT-4o, Perplexity AI and Scholar GPT – based on two scenarios of scholarly information seeking, both for writing undergraduate coursework on a contemporary topic. Results generated by the chosen seven Gen AI tools are critically analysed to highlight the nature of the content, citations and the overall presentation of the output.

Chapter 6 presents the examples of the search output generated by the seven Gen AI tools based on two scenarios of research information seeking: one for preparing for an MA/MSc dissertation on an emerging topic such as Generative AI; and another for preparing for a PhD study on a contemporary topic such as environment and climate change issues. Query formulation or search prompts, the corresponding output, and their suitability in terms of the produced search results or content, and the reliability and reputation of the sources are discussed and critically analysed based on the specific search tasks and user contexts. These findings are discussed later in the book in the context of the benefits and challenges of Gen AI for research information seeking.

Chapter 7 discusses the results of the experiments reported in Chapters 4, 5 and 6. It discusses the typical steps that a user needs to go through to find information on a topic from library search services and scholarly databases. Drawing on the examples of searches presented in Chapters 4 to 6, it shows that Gen AI tools do not require the user to prepare a formal search query, select the target database(s) to search, find and decide on the relevance of the retrieved search output, and finally read and gather the required information from the retrieved items. Chapter 7 argues that most of these stages of information searches are not required for seeking information through the Gen AI tools; and, therefore, these tools have an obvious appeal to the users. However, the chapter points out some of the challenges and pitfalls associated with the use of Gen AI tools for access to information. The chapter also lists some guidelines produced by various libraries to support their users on the use of Gen AI tools.

By providing some simple examples of the search results produced by libraries and scholarly database services that a typical student, scholar or researcher might use to find relevant information on a topic, Chapter 8 shows how the user can control the search sessions, and use various features of the chosen search services, to get the best possible sets of results. By taking a closer look at the search query or prompt, and the corresponding output generated by each chosen tool, the chapter discusses how the user should be prepared to assess the quality and reliability of the sources used to produce the search output, which by nature is new content generated by the tool based on the data and information from one or more retrieved items. The chapter further discusses some techniques – such as prompt engineering and RAG (Retrieval Augmented Generation) – for improving the outcome of the Gen AI tools in specific domains. Chapter 8 also discusses the potential legal and ethical issues associated with the search output generated by the chosen Gen AI tools, as well as the information and AI skills that users need to acquire in order to be able to use these tools effectively to find data and information for everyday life and/or research and scholarly activities.

Technology should amplify the best of us, but always on our terms, democratically decided and publicly debated with benefits widely distributed (Suleyman and Bhaskar, 2023, 61). Generative AI tools will have a profound impact on each of us, and especially in information- and data-intensive activities. Based on the discussions in the book, Chapter 9 addresses an obvious question: how the users, as well as the existing libraries and information services, should be prepared to adopt or adapt the Gen AI tools for accessing information. It also discusses the potential implications of the increasing use of the Gen AI tools for information access in everyday life, work, education, research and scholarly contexts. These, which have so far been user-driven, and libraries and database services have developed tools and training programmes to empower the user in searching and finding the most relevant information. Implications of this paradigm shift in information access and use for information science education and research in different areas, such as information seeking and retrieval, user education and training, as well as the privacy, security, copyright and other issues, are also discussed in Chapter 9.

Given its non-technical and evidenced-based approach to discuss the pros and cons of the use of Gen AI for access to everyday life, research and scholarly information, it is hoped that the book will have a global audience. The book will inform people involved in the knowledge and information sector about the benefits and challenges posed by the emerging Gen AI tools for information access, and how these tools can be adapted to meet the information needs and contexts of different user groups; and also what set of skills would the users need to be able to make optimum use of these tools. It is expected that the book will encourage information services management and professional staff to engage in new discussions and activities in order to adapt their services in the rapidly changing world of Gen AI, and to provide their users the best experience in accessing and using information and data relevant to their specific needs and contexts. It is also expected that the book will encourage information science academics and researchers to engage in discussions on how the information science curricula and research agenda around information retrieval, information access, information seeking, information search process, information behaviour and cognate areas, need to be adapted and/or modified in the context of the widespread use of the Gen AI tools for access to information.

We would like to acknowledge the inspiration and support we received from our sons, Avirup and Anubhav, all through the process of writing this book. We would like to extend our sincere thanks to the Facet Publishing team, especially Andrew James, Director of Content and Publishing and Michelle Lau, Production Manager; also our copy-editor Stephen York and proofreader Emma Stuart for their support throughout the production process.

G. G. Chowdhury and Sudatta Chowdhury
January 2025

CHAPTER 1

Generative AI and Access to Information

Introduction

In today's world, people access information for almost everything – from learning and living to work, entertainment, social and engagement activities. Historically, libraries have been a unique place for collecting, managing and preserving recorded information. People would need to go to the library physically to find and read the items – books, journals, manuscripts, etc. – to get the required information. With the advent of computers and their use in managing information, things began to change rapidly from the 1960s onwards, when, alongside the physical collections of information resources held in the libraries, people could also access digital collections – located within the library buildings or through remote databases for accessing digital information. The next wave came with the advent of the internet and web in the early 1980s and 1990s, respectively, that allowed people to access an unprecedented volume and variety of information — through libraries, repositories, databases and search engines. The internet, web and later on social media technologies and tools brought a paradigm shift in the creation and distribution of content – enabling individuals, communities and institutions to create and distribute content which previously was very much controlled and managed through the formal publication processes, infrastructure and policies.

All through this period, libraries and information services also evolved, adopting and adapting to the capacity and capabilities offered by the emerging technologies. Although new services empowered by robust and powerful search engines emerged, and their popularity and use covered every aspect of life and society, library and information services retained their unique position in society, because 'for ILS [Information and Library Science] professionals, human interest is not an add-on or afterthought but rather the reason we do the work at all – it is fundamentally baked into information generation, management, and use' (Marchionini, 2024). As always, library and information services retained their unique position by:

- being a trusted agency for managing, delivering and preserving human knowledge in recorded forms
- ensuring information quality, integrity and trust through robust collection development policies and practices
- providing equitable access to relevant information on demand, and sometimes in anticipation
- playing a key role in the design, delivery and evaluation of information services and taking a human-centric approach to understand and build systems and services to meet user needs and contexts
- educating, enabling and empowering people through information literacy, digital literacy and data literacy.

Alongside this, the information and library science communities around the world have collaborated with the computer science, engineering and allied research communities to develop and test new models of information retrieval systems, and laid the foundations for model and system assessments, including the creation of metrics beyond traditional recall-precision (Marchionini, 2024).

Generative AI

AI (artificial intelligence) and machine learning have been used for quite some time in many areas in our life and society, ranging from manufacturing to aviation, healthcare, finance, education, research and entertainment to shopping and sports and games. 'AI really isn't "emerging" anymore. It's in products, services and devices you use every day,' remarks Mustafa Suleyman, co-founder of DeepMind and of Inflection AI, one of the world's leading AI companies (Suleyman and Bhaskar, 2023, 61). AI and machine learning technologies have been used in many areas in information access, ranging from automatic classification, query expansion, query processing, filtering and ranking of results to making recommendations. Similarly, natural language processing has also remained an area of research application in information retrieval for several decades. However, the combination of AI, deep learning technologies and large language models (LLMs) have given rise to a transformative technology and tools that are trained on an unimaginably large volume and variety of content and have the power to comprehend and generate human language text and other types of content.

GPTs (Generative Pre-trained Transformers)

While the internet, web and social media technologies appearing over the past four decades brought a paradigm shift in information creation, distribution, access and sharing, the arrival of ChatGPT, a chatbot and virtual assistant developed by OpenAI, in November 2022 (https://openai.com/index/chatgpt), has brought another new wave of transformative technologies that have a profound impact on all areas of life and activities involving data, information and knowledge. ChatGPT is a Gen AI that has the Generative Pre-trained Transformer (GPT) architecture as the foundation and is pre-trained on a broad spectrum of generalised and unlabelled data.

So, what is Gen AI?

Many definitions exist, but essentially, this is a new and transformative technology that can generate new content and data, and the following definitions attest to this:

- 'Generative AI works by using machine learning models – very large models that are pre-trained on vast amounts of data' (AWS, 2024a).
- 'Generative AI can be thought of as a machine-learning model that is trained to create new data, rather than making a prediction about a specific dataset' (Zewe, 2023).
- 'A generative AI system is one that learns to generate more objects that look like the data it was trained on' (Zewe, 2023).
- 'At a high level, generative [AI] models encode a simplified representation of their training data and draw from it to create a new work that's similar, but not identical, to the original data' (IBM, 2025b).

From the users' point of view, Gen AI is a type of AI that can create new content in the form of conversations, stories, images, videos and music, and it works by using very large models that are pre-trained on vast amounts of data (AWS, 2024a). Gen AI works by using large language models (LLMs), which are very large deep learning models pre-trained on vast amounts of data (AWS, 2024b). For example, OpenAI's GPT-3 was trained on 'a dataset comprising the entire internet, as well as 19 billion web texts and 67 billion books. This created a corpus of about 500 billion words for the model to work with' (Houston and Corrado, 2023). The variety and capacity of Gen AI also increased rapidly; for example, 'while previous language models pulled from vectors of between 1.5 and 17 billion parameters, GPT-3 pulls from 175 billion' (Houston and Corrado, 2023). Over the past two years, the progress in capacity of these models is increasing rapidly in a magnitude that is beyond imagination. As of October 2024, GPT-4o ('o' for 'omni') is the OpenAI's most advanced GPT model (OpenAI Platform, 2024).

Gen AI tools are capable of generating content – text, image, audio, video, summary, presentations and so on – based on natural language interactions or prompts – and hence these tools have potential applications in every sector: industry, government, academic and general public (Chui, Roberts and Yee, 2022; Hirvonen et al., 2024; Martineau, 2023; Stryker and Scapicchio, 2024). Since the arrival of ChatGPT in November 2022, many similar chatbots or tools from the ChatGPT family, such as Consensus, Scholar GPT, and other tools like Claude, Perplexity AI, and Scholar AI appeared in the marketplace. These tools can be used for a range of applications, such as text summarisation, content generation, and recommendations in specific areas, such as for travel, specific business applications, programming and coding. These tools have the ability to create human-like text and content – images, music, charts, tables, programme codes – and answer questions in a conversational manner.

Gen AI tools like ChatGPT and similar industry-specific applications have also been embedded in various information search tools of conventional search engines, e.g. the Copilot for Microsoft's Bing and Gemini for the Google search engine. These, and other similar Gen AI tools such as Claude, Consensus, Perplexity AI, GPT-4o, Scholar AI and Scholar GPT, now offer a new experience of information access: people can ask questions in a natural language format, and get the answers in the form of natural language text in summary form, often under specific categories and headings, points or suggestions supported by the relevant data and information. Some of these tools, and their use in information access, are discussed later in this book.

Gen AI for access to information

Gen AI are transformative technologies that have a revolutionary impact on information-driven tasks due to their capacity to emulate knowledge production activities which were previously the exclusive domain of people (Butler et al., 2023). A UK government report suggests that these technologies can facilitate access to information, education and training (UK Parliament, 2023). The UK Russell Group Universities' *Principles on the Use of Generative AI Tools in Education* recommend that university students and staff should be prepared to use the AI tools effectively and appropriately (Russell Group, n.d.). The *Times Higher Education* (2023) reports that it is vital for librarians to work proactively with tech firms to address the limitations and biases of tools like ChatGPT. Research shows that more and more people are now switching from search engines to Gen AI for information seeking (Zhou and Li, 2024).

So, what would be the impact of these tools on information users; on the library and information services sector; and more importantly on the information science education, research and professional practices? These areas have long focused on user interactions with information systems and services through various stages of query formulation to conducting searches, identifying and reading the retrieved documents that are relevant, and then preparing notes and summaries, comparing, and so on, depending on the specific needs and contexts. This book aims to address some of these questions, based on the findings of controlled experiments with some Gen AI tools, and analysis of the relevant research papers, reports and similar documents.

Gen AI tools used in this book

In this book a selected number of Gen AI tools have been used to build some case studies to demonstrate how these can be used for access to information, what output each chosen tool generates and their suitability for the specific user quest and context. Some of these are independently developed tools, some are the Gen AI-driven versions of the previously used search engines, and some belong to the OpenAI group of tools available (OpenAI, 2024c). Brief information on each of these tools is provided below. It is worth mentioning here that these are not the only Gen AI tools currently available, and the book does not intend to compare them. These tools are taken as examples to show how such tools are used for access to information and identify some associated challenges. In fact, new Gen AI tools, and improved versions of the existing tools, have been appearing regularly over the past two years, and this trend is likely to continue.

The following Gen AI tools have been used in this book for examples and case studies:

1. **Claude** is a large language model (LLM) built by Anthropic; Claude 3.5 Sonnet was released in June 2024 (Anthropic, 2024a).
2. **Consensus GPT** is a large language model (LLM) that can 'search references, get simple explanations, write articles backed by academic papers' (https://chatgpt.com/gpts).
3. **Copilot** is an AI-powered digital assistant that combines the power of large language models (LLMs) with users' data in the Microsoft Graph and the Microsoft 365 apps to turn users' words into 'the most powerful productivity tool on the planet' (Microsoft, 2023).
4. **Gemini** that has the 'ability to extract insights from hundreds of thousands of documents through reading, filtering and understanding information' (Google, 2023).
5. **GPT-4o** ('o' for 'omni') from OpenAI is 'a step towards much more natural human-computer interaction – it accepts as input any combination of text, audio, image, and video and generates any

combination of text, audio, and image outputs' (https://openai.com/index/hello-gpt-4o).
6 **Perplexity AI** is for information discovery, answering questions, summarising content, exploring new topics, etc. (www.perplexity.ai/hub/getting-started).
7 **Scholar AI** is a tool that 'simplifies academic, scientific, and legal research by providing instant answers, insights, and analysis from papers, patents, and more – all powered by cutting-edge AI' (https://scholarai.io).
8 **Scholar GPT** is a tool designed to 'enhance research with 200M+ resources and built-in critical reading skills. Access Google Scholar, PubMed, JSTOR, Arxiv, and more, effortlessly' (https://chatgpt.com/gpts).
9 **Semantic Scholar** provides free AI-driven search and discovery of open resources for the global research community (www.semanticscholar.org/about).

Information search process

Typical information search processes assume an interaction cycle consisting of query specification, receipt and examination of retrieval results, and then either stopping or reformulating the query and repeating the process until a relevant result set is found. Over the past few decades, several theories and models have emerged which show that the information-seeking process consists of a series of interconnected but diverse searches on one problem-based theme; and search results for a goal tend to trigger new goals, resulting in a search in new directions, but the context of the problem and the previous searches are carried from one stage of search to the next (Hearst, 1999). A generalised model of information seeking proposes that people's information practices draw on their stocks of knowledge that form the habitual starting point of: (1) information seeking – identifying, preferring and accessing information sources; (2) information use – judging the value of information, filtering information and wielding information into action; and (3) information sharing – giving and receiving information (Savolainen and Thompson, 2022). Basic features of the conventional information search processes are discussed in Chapter 3, and also in other chapters, especially in Chapters 7–9.

Gen AI v. conventional tools for information access

Conventional search systems are based on indices that map lexical tokens or semantic embeddings to document identifiers and these indices are designed for retrieving responsive documents; whereas LLM-based search systems support integrating these documents into a holistic answer that are presented to the user in response to search queries or prompts (Najork, 2023). The appearance of ChatGPT in November 2022 triggered a rapid growth in Gen AI tools for access to information. Some search engines have begun to use these technologies as part of their existing search services, while other specific tools like GPT-4o, Scholar GPT, and Scholar AI have appeared to offer new services for providing access to information and generating content and data.

Figures 1.1 and 1.2 on pages 8 to 11 provide snapshots of some of the search results generated by five Gen AI tools – Claude, Consensus, Copilot, Gemini and GPT-4o, in response to two questions or prompts that were created based on two search scenarios.

- **Scenario 1**: An undergraduate student is required to write an essay on the issues and challenges facing older people in their use of internet for accessing digital government services in the UK, with supporting data and research papers, relevant reports, etc. The search task should produce some basic information on the topic; various issues and challenges; some comparable data; and some research papers and reports supporting it.
- **Question 1**: What major challenges do older people in the UK face for using digital government services?
- **Scenario 2**: An undergraduate student is required to write an essay on how digital skills improve people's work, employment and income, with supporting data and research papers, relevant reports, etc. The search task should produce some basic information on the topic of digital access, digital inclusion, digital skills and work and employment; some comparable data between UK and Europe; and some research papers and reports supporting the data and discussions.
- **Question 1**: Can you suggest some research papers that compare the impact of digital skills on the work and employment opportunities of people in the UK and Europe?

Tool	Result
Claude	Older people in the UK often face several challenges when it comes to using digital government services. Here are some of the major challenges: 1. Digital literacy and skills gap: Many older adults lack the necessary digital skills and knowledge to navigate online platforms and services effectively. This can make it difficult for them to access and use digital government services. ... 6. Limited support and training: Inadequate access to training programs, technical support, or guidance on using digital services can exacerbate the challenges faced by older adults. To address these challenges, it is crucial for government agencies to prioritize digital inclusion initiatives, provide accessible and user-friendly digital services, offer targeted training and support programs, and ensure that alternative non-digital options remain available for those who cannot or prefer not to use digital channels.
Consensus	Older people in the UK face several challenges when using digital government services, which can hinder their ability to fully engage with these platforms. These challenges include: ### 1. **Digital Literacy and Skills** - **Limited Digital Skills**: Many older adults have limited experience with digital technologies, making it difficult for them to navigate online services. This includes a lack of familiarity with basic tasks such as using a mouse, navigating websites, and understanding online forms. - **Fear of Technology**: Some older individuals may feel intimidated by technology, leading to a lack of confidence in using digital services. This "technophobia" can result in avoidance of online platforms altogether. ..... ### 7. **Cultural and Attitudinal Barriers** - **Resistance to Change**: Some older adults may be resistant to change, preferring traditional methods of accessing government services (e.g., face-to-face or phone interactions) over digital alternatives...... ### Conclusion Older people in the UK face a range of challenges when using digital government services, from limited digital literacy and access to technology to concerns about security and privacy. Addressing these barriers .. digital services.
Copilot	**Older people in the UK** face several challenges when it comes to using digital government services. Let's delve into some of these difficulties: **1 Digital Exclusion**: Although many older individuals fully embrace the digital world, **digital exclusion** increases with age and disability. Approximately **2.7 million people aged 65 and above** in the UK do not use the internet at all, equivalent to around **one in five** of this age group[1]. Some older adults may only use the internet in limited ways, which doesn't necessarily mean they have the confidence and skills to safely apply for support online. ...... **6 Equality Considerations**: Digital exclusion disproportionately affects older adults. Age UK urges councils to consider **equality considerations** in the design of policies and service delivery. Ensuring that everyone can choose to access and use public services offline (by phone, letter, or face-to-face) would end discrimination against those who are not digitally savvy[1]. In summary, while digitalization offers convenience, it's essential to ensure that older people are not left behind. Councils need to strike a balance by providing accessible digital services while also offering robust offline alternatives for those who need them[21].

Figure 1.1 *Snippets of sample results for Scenario 1 Question 1*

Tool	Result
Gemini	Older people in the UK face several challenges when using digital government services: • **Digital Literacy and Skills Gap**: Many older adults lack the basic digital skills needed to navigate government websites, complete online forms, or use digital authentication methods. • **Accessibility Issues**: Government websites may not be designed with accessibility in mind, meaning they might have complex interfaces, small fonts, or insufficient colour contrast, all of which can make them difficult for people with visual impairments or dexterity issues to use. • **Confidence and Fear of Technology**: Some older people may be apprehensive about using technology due to unfamiliarity or fear of making mistakes online, especially when it comes to sensitive information like financial details. • **Lack of Access to Technology**: Not all older adults have access to a computer or reliable internet connection, which is essential for using online government services. These challenges can lead to social exclusion and hinder older people's ability to access essential government services.
GPT-4o	Older people in the UK face several major challenges when using digital government services. These challenges can be broadly categorized into technological, educational, and accessibility issues, as well as broader socio-economic factors. Here are some key challenges: **Digital Literacy and Skills**: **Lack of Digital Skills**: Many older adults have not had the same exposure to digital technology as younger generations. This results in a lack of basic digital skills needed to navigate online services effectively. **Economic Factor**s: **Financial Constraints**: Older adults, especially those on fixed incomes, may find it difficult to afford the necessary technology and internet services. **Retirement and Fixed Income**: Limited income post-retirement can restrict their ability to invest in digital tools and services. Addressing these challenges requires a multifaceted approach that includes improving digital literacy through education and training programs, designing user-friendly and accessible digital services, government services.

Figure 1.1 *Continued*

Tool	Result
Claude	Here are some relevant research papers that support the challenges faced by older adults in the UK when using digital government services: 1. "Digital Exclusion in the UK" by the Age UK charity (2021): - This report highlights the digital divide affecting older adults in the UK, with 51% of those aged 75+ not using the internet. - It cites lack of skills, access, and motivation as key barriers to digital inclusion. ... 5. "Digital Inclusion in Later Life: Cohort Changes and the Prospects for Digital Learning" by the Centre for Ageing Better (2018): - This study examined the digital skills and engagement of different age cohorts in the UK. .... These research papers provide evidence-based insights into the digital divide affecting older adults in the UK, the barriers they face in using digital government services, and recommendations for promoting digital ... accessibility.

Figure 1.2 *Snippets of sample results for Scenario 2 Question 1*

Tool	Result
Consensus	Here are some research papers that explore the challenges faced by older people in the UK when using digital government services: 1. **Digital Circles of Support: Meeting the Information Needs of Older People** - **Authors**: M. Godfrey, O. Johnson - **Abstract**: This paper discusses the information needs of older people and how , ... to digital services. - [Link to Paper](https://consensus.app/papers/digital-circles-support-meeting-information-needs-people-godfrey/d2ca0606a78e5331b48918e4d48e89fd/?utm_source=chatgpt) ...... 5. **The Role of Age and Digital Competence on the Use of Online Health and Social Care Services** - **Authors**: T. Heponiemi, A. Kaihlanen, A. Kouvonen, L. Leemann, S. Taipale, K. Gluschkoff .... - [Link to Paper](https://consensus.app/papers/role-competence-online-health-care-services-heponiemi/b86f5967968d5701b441791d9b3d22db/?utm_source=chatgpt) These papers provide valuable insights into the various challenges that older adults in the UK face and...systems.
Copilot	Certainly! Here are some research papers and reports that can support your essay on the challenges older people in the UK face when using digital government services: **1 Age UK Report**: This report discusses the struggles of older people in accessing local public services in an increasingly digital world. **2** .... **4 Digital Inclusion and the Elderly: The Case of Online Banking**: This paper surveys a group of elderly users to identify issues that prevent them from engaging with digital technology, focusing on the challenges faced by the older generation in the digital world[4]. These resources should provide a solid foundation for your essay, offering both qualitative and quantitative insights into the topic. Good luck with your writing! Learn more 1 ageuk.org.uk 2 bmcpublichealth.biomedcentral.com 3 ageuk.org.uk 4 lrec-conf.org
Gemini	Absolutely, your essay on the challenges older people face with digital government services will benefit from these research papers: • **"Older people's access to digitalised services" (ARC GM):** This briefing note by the Applied Research Collaboration Greater Manchester provides a concise overview of the digital divide and how it impacts ..., and low digital literacy [PDF document on ARC Greater Manchester website]. ".... • **"Towards understanding E-Government with older people and designing an inclusive platform with them" (ResearchGate):** This research focuses on designing user-friendly e-government platforms specifically for older adults. It emphasizes the importance of involving .... encounter [ResearchGate website]. Here are some additional resources you might find helpful: • **Age UK:** Age UK is a leading charity in the UK that advocates for older people. Their website has a wealth of information on digital inclusion and the challenges older adults ... services online [Age UK website].

Figure 1.2 *Continued*

Tool	Result
	The Centre for Ageing Better: This organization works to improve the lives of older people in the UK. Their website might have reports or articles related to digital inclusion [Centre for Ageing Better website]. Remember to check the publication dates of the research papers to ensure you're using the most ... available.
GPT-4o	Searched 5 sites When writing your essay on the challenges older people in the UK face when using digital government services, you can reference several research papers and reports that detail these issues extensively. Here are some key ..: **1 Digital Literacy and Skills**: • Many older adults lack the necessary digital skills and confidence to use online services. According to a scoping review in BMC Public Health, intrinsic ....challenges (BioMed Central). • systems are critical for helping older adults use digital services. Initiatives like Age UK's Digital Champion Programme .. training..... technology (BioMed Central) (Oxford Academic). **7 Social Influences and Encouragement**: • Social support and encouragement play a significant role in older adults' adoption of digital technologies. Studies have shown that when older adults have access to supportive networks, they are more likely to engage with and use digital services (BioMed Central). By citing these sources, you can provide a comprehensive overview of the multifaceted challenges older adults face in accessing digital government services in the UK. This approach will help underscore the importance of targeted interventions and support systems to bridge the digital divide.

Figure 1.2 *Continued*

It may be noted that these figures only provide a glimpse of the variety of results that the chosen Gen AI tools can produce. These results are not exhaustive nor sufficient for the given queries, but a quick look at these gives a sense of the capabilities of these tools. Unlike the library and scholarly database services, search engines and similar tools that the university students are familiar with, the Gen AI tools do not generate a list of documents that contain the search terms used in the query. Instead, they search across a range of information sources, gather data and information from multiple sources on the search topic, infuse them and generate new content in the form of answers or responses that can be read easily. Some tools also provide citations or links to the relevant sources. Thus, the Gen AI tools transform the way people have learnt and got used to searching for information using conventional information access tools like library and scholarly database services, search engines and a multitude of digital libraries.

Implications for information education, research and professional practices

As discussed before, the appearance of ChatGPT in November 2022 triggered a rapid growth in the Gen AI tools for providing access to information using conversational tools that allow people to present a natural language query or prompt to the tool, which then undertakes the necessary searches, fuses data and information from multiple retrieved items and presents the results in natural language summary forms. Ryen White, Partner Research Director at Microsoft Research, argues that technology is catching up fast with the long-held vision where information interactions will involve personal search assistants with advanced capabilities, including natural language input, rich sensing, user/task/world models and reactive and proactive experiences (White, 2016; 2024). However, while AI and LLM-based tools are being used in information search, there are concerns for authoritativeness, timeliness and contextualisation of search, especially in academic and research contexts (Hersh, 2024; White, 2024).

Libraries and database search services have, for several decades, served as an intermediary between users and information sources. These services require people to use appropriate search terms to formulate queries using a structured search interface in order to retrieve documents that match the search terms. Although libraries and databases evolved over time, and they offer various useful features and support for searching, filtering and ranking of search results, the onus is still on the users to find the appropriate search terms, select one or more databases, formulate the query and conduct the search and finally go through the retrieved documents to find the required data and information. The key burdens on the user in such a conventional information access scenario are: (1) decomposing the search goals into queries; (2) choosing the right words and phrases, conducting the searches and retrieving the relevant items which requires skills for choosing the right search engines or databases and conducting successful searches; and (3) reading, analysing and synthesising content and data from one or more retrieved documents. All these tasks require a significant amount of time and skills. These are discussed in more detail later in the book.

As shown in the examples in Figures 1.1 and 1.2, all these burdens can be removed by the LLM-driven search tools. These search tools take a conversational approach where users can enter a question in the form of a request or command in a natural language; the tool selects and searches multiple sources or databases; fuses information from multiple documents; and presents the results addressing the question directly in an easy-to-read summary format, often with the supporting data and relevant references; and all these happen almost instantaneously. New opportunities for information seeking emerge as AI systems enable multimodal search, information retrieval in human-like interactions (Hirvonen et al., 2024). This clearly shows a paradigm shift in information access, but it raises some obvious questions and discourse relating to how the library and information services sector should gear up to educate and empower people to enable them to use these tools for access to information in every part of their lives – education, work, research, everyday life and living. Some key questions that such discourse needs to address in the context of access to information, that forms the foundations of today's life and society, are:

1. Will the widespread use of these tools for information access: (a) change people's information access and use behaviour; (b) widen or reduce the gaps in people's affordance to knowledge and information in different contexts; (c) reduce or restrict people's ability to find, analyse and interpret the best data and information to suit their specific needs and contexts; (d) create an environment of machine-generated content and summary and thus negatively impact people's capacity for being analytic and critical; and (e) have implications for privacy, security, cultural and other related concerns for individuals and society at large, and if so, how can these be addressed?
2. How can these tools be trained to select the most reliable, peer-reviewed and trustworthy sources, and fuse and summarise data and information that are most relevant to a user's needs and context?
3. What new skills do people need to acquire in order to be able to make optimum use of these tools to access information and data required for specific education and research activities?
4. What role should libraries and educational institutions play to impart this new set of skills to the students, academics, researchers, and public at large?
5. How may libraries and database search services adapt these tools to improve access to information and data?
6. How would the use of these tools, for information access, generate new knowledge to inform information science education and research around information seeking and retrieval, information literacy and information systems and services as a whole?

This book aims to address these, and some similar, questions. By undertaking a series of case studies based on the interactions with a number of Gen AI tools, based on a series of scenarios of information-intensive activities in education, research and everyday life and living, this book will first raise some evidence-based questions around user interactions with these tools, and the efficacy of these tools in terms of providing the answers and responses that are relevant and suitable for the specific user needs and contexts. Based on these, the book will discuss whether and how the conventional models of information search process, and information seeking and retrieval, are applicable to explain the user interactions with the Gen AI tools for information access. Based on the critical analysis of the answers and responses produced by different search tools in relation to specific search tasks and user contexts, the book will also discuss: (1) what set of knowledge and skills do the users need to acquire in order to be able to make optimum use of these tools, and what implications this will have on the existing models of information seeking behaviour, information literacy and information skills, if any; and (2) how these findings can inform the developers of these tools in improving their products to suit the needs for information access in different contexts. Implications for these for the library and information sector, and database services and other stakeholders, are also discussed.

CHAPTER 2

Information Access: Tools and Processes

Information and data

The term information has different connotations: 'Information-as-process' i.e., the act of informing or the process of being informed; 'Information-as-knowledge' which is intangible but can be regarded as the result of being informed; and 'Information-as-thing' where the term information is used attributively for objects, such as data and documents (Buckland, 1991). So, in order to achieve the intangible, 'Information-as-knowledge', one needs tangibles – documents or data – to communicate, i.e., 'Information-as-thing'. Abundant number of definitions of, and debates around, documents, information and data exist (see for example, Buckland, 2012; Borgman, 2012; 2015). However, the boundary between document and data is becoming increasingly blurry. For example, data can be defined as text, sound, still images, moving images, models, games and simulations, as well as:

> data and databases that generally require the assistance of computational machinery and software in order be useful, such as various types of laboratory data including spectrographic, genomic sequencing, and electron microscopy data; observational data, such as remote sensing, geospatial, and socioeconomic data, numerical data and other forms of data either generated or compiled by humans or machines
>
> (Borgman, Wallis and Mayernik, 2012, 488)

In a recent paper, Petras argues that 'information science is its own discipline, has been so for more than a century and has its own disciplinary identity while operating in an interdisciplinary problem space', and the 'discipline justifies its existence, because of its value to society and its separate status in the scholarly universe' (Petras, 2024). The overall aim of the discipline of information science is to connect people with information, or more precisely 'Information-as-thing', i.e., documents and data, using the appropriate tools and technologies, to ensure that everyone gets the right information at the right time in the right form for all kinds of activities, ranging from education and research to lifelong learning, entertainment, healthcare, agriculture, business, politics and decision making.

Education, research and professional practices in the field of information science have focused on developing a variety of technologies, tools and standards for organising information and data so that they can be accessed easily and meaningfully. Three major drivers that have significantly influenced research, development and professional practices in the field of information science are:

1 the information and communication technologies (ICT)
2 the behaviour, culture and practices of people, communities, institutions and societies
3 international and national government policies and regulations.

Libraries, archives and museums have organised and managed physical information resources – manuscripts, books, journals, maps, records, artefacts and so on – for centuries; and the researchers and professionals in these fields have developed several techniques, tools and standards for managing and providing access to information. However, a new era in information management in general, and information access in particular, began with the introduction of computers in handling information in the late 1950s; and since then several software applications, models and tools have been developed in order to facilitate the organisation and management of digital information objects – such as full texts of journal and conference papers, books, maps, images, audio and video content – so that they can be accessed through basic search keys – such as authors, titles and subject keywords/subject headings – or through elements of content, such as keywords from full text, sample audio or video clips as search keys, and so on. The volume, variety and complexities of various types of content, as well as the tools, technologies and models, increased quite significantly during this period; and these brought significant changes in the nature of education and research in the discipline of information science.

A major wave of change appeared about three decades ago with the advent of the internet and web technologies, whereby the creation and distribution of digital content and data became easier. These new technologies empowered institutions and individuals to publish content and data online without having to go through a formal publication channel and/or peer review processes. A variety of new businesses and technologies in the form of search engines and online data/information services appeared that made online information easily accessible for people. The search engine services are driven by a new business model which not only makes them free at the point of use, but ensures that people can access information anytime from anywhere without having a formal registration or account with the service provider. Several digital libraries and online repositories began to appear from the 1990s that brought new challenges as well as benefits for information access. Web and mobile technologies have become pervasive over the past three decades and these subsequently have brought new platforms for the creation and sharing of user-generated content online through novel digital services like YouTube, Facebook (now Meta) and Twitter (now X).

Internet and web technologies also gave rise to the open access (OA) movement, encouraging academics, scholars and other content creators to make their output freely available to the wider audience. Although it began the journey in the early 90s, the open access movement took a bit of time to get its momentum and became more widespread from the beginning of the new millennium. Various policies of national governments, international agencies and funding bodies over the past few years have brought a major shift in the way information and data is accessed and shared in the OA mode. The ethos behind this is that access to data and information should not be limited to a select few or only a cross-section of society; rather it should, in principle, be open to all.

Information retrieval

The term information retrieval was coined in 1950 by Mooers (1950), who defined information retrieval as follows: 'The problem of directing a user to stored information, some of which may be unknown to him, is the problem of "information retrieval".' Mooers further adds that 'In information retrieval, the addressee or receiver rather than the sender is the active party' (572).

Information retrieval as an area of study gained popularity in the research community from 1961 onwards, especially with the writings of Fairthorne (1961). Information retrieval is defined as the 'process of finding stored information on a computer' (Cambridge Dictionary, 2017); and the information retrieval system is defined as 'a system for recovering specific information from stored data' (Collins English Dictionary, 2017).

Information retrieval is concerned with 'finding materials (usually documents) of an unstructured nature (usually text) that satisfies an information need from within large collections (usually stored on computers)' (Manning, Raghavan and Schütze, 2009). It began with scientific publications and library records but evolved to develop theories and models for providing access to all forms of content – text, images, audio and video (Sparck Jones and Willett, 1997). For several decades, the field was of interest and useful primarily for research and scholarly communities and for information-intensive businesses, such as medicine and law, but with the advent and proliferation of the internet, web and social media, information retrieval became an area of study and application for everyday access to information.

An information retrieval system, variously termed as online database or search engine, allows people to communicate with an information system or a service in order to find information – text, graphic images, sound recordings or video – that meets their specific needs. Although historically information retrieval systems were designed to help people find information from bibliographic and textual databases, in today's world we use information retrieval systems in almost every stage of our daily life: for example, for retrieving a message or e-mail received or sent on a specific date, to or from a specific person, institution; finding something or someone on the web; searching for a book in an online library catalogue or in a digital library; searching a document, an image, a song; or finding a video using a web search engine, on YouTube.

As an academic field of study, information retrieval is concerned with all the activities related to the collection, processing, indexing of, and access to, information resources, or more specifically documents, of all forms and formats. An information retrieval system allows users to communicate with an information system or a service in order to find information, most commonly documents containing text, graphic images, sound recordings or video that meet their specific needs (Chowdhury, G. G., 2010). Thus, the overarching aim of an information retrieval system is to enable users to find relevant information from an indexed collection of documents. In fact, most conventional information retrieval systems are, truly speaking, document retrieval systems, since they are designed to retrieve documents relevant to a user query.

In the context of research and scholarly information, most information retrieval systems are text retrieval systems, which allow users to search one or more databases based on search words or phrases and retrieve records, most commonly documents – books, reports, articles, web pages – that match the search words, with bibliographic details including a summary or abstract, or sometimes full-text and other metadata, such as author, title, journal or conference name, publishers.

Progress in information retrieval may be summarised through the following stages (Agosti, 2008; Chowdhury, G. G., 2010; Chu, 2010; Cool and Belkin, 2011; Lewandowski, Haider and Sundin, 2024):

1 **Stage 1** (from early years to mid-70s): The focus was on document and text retrieval using small test collections and the application areas

included catalogues, bibliographic and full-text documents. The focus was more on designing retrieval systems than on the users and usability. A large number of remote online databases appeared during this period, providing search and retrieval of abstracts, and some full-text documents, of scholarly information resources, such as journal and conference papers.

2 **Stage 2** (mid-70s to mid-80s): The focus was still on systems rather than users, but the retrieval systems became more sophisticated, and more advanced systems were built for managing both unstructured text in databases and structured library management operations. Online public access catalogues (OPACs) and more online databases appeared during this period, facilitating remote access to information, but the systems were largely centralised and the focus was still on text.
3 **Stage 3** (mid-80s to mid-90s): During this period the attention started to move from the collection of documents towards the user and the retrieval model, with the focus on the invention of models that could better support user–system interactions. Various alternative retrieval models, especially natural language processing and knowledge-based retrieval models, as well as hypertext and network-based models, appeared during this period. There was also a major shift in research from systems to users and interactions, giving rise to various information-seeking and retrieval (IS&R) models. This was also the early phase of digital library research, where the focus was on developing robust information retrieval models and systems capable of processing and retrieving large quantities of digital information of different kinds – text as well as multimedia. Free internet search engines began to appear that were several times more powerful than the conventional retrieval systems used in text databases and a new era in IR began.
4 **Stage 4** (mid-90s to early 2010s): This phase saw several major changes in information retrieval in that many new and powerful search engines such as Google, online question-answering systems such as Ask (Ask.com), visual search engines such as Kartoo and Vivisimo, meta-search engines such as Mamma and several multimedia search engines appeared that were based on many old and newly developed information retrieval techniques and models. Large-scale research and evaluation of information retrieval became possible and a common platform for sharing of expertise in information retrieval at the international level was formed in the name of TREC (Text Retrieval Conference). Multilingual and multimedia information-retrieval research became more powerful, and during this time the scope of digital library research was extended from building systems to user interactions,

evaluation and impact studies. Several large-scale digital libraries were created and information access, usability and impact studies became the focus of digital library research. A new open access movement began that gave birth to several open-access digital libraries and repositories, and open-access journals.

5 **Stage 5** (the past few years): Information access in the web and large-scale digital libraries and distributed information systems became more challenging and diverse due to the emergence of Web 2.0, semantic web and social networking technologies. New approaches for creation and organisation/tagging of information appeared through social media such as Youtube and Facebook (now Meta). Twitter (now X) became common; side-by-side search engines, like Google became more powerful and sophisticated; and special search engine services, such as Google Books and Google Scholar and Microsoft Academic, appeared, offering better and more robust interactive information-retrieval services. Open access, eScholarship, eScience, digital humanities and digital culture became new areas of research within digital libraries, posing new challenges for access to a large volume of digital information – free as well as fee-based, created by and available from a multitude of sources in a variety of forms and formats, languages, etc. User-centred design and usability became major areas of research within information access. Of late, the scope of information science research is being extended to both research data and research output, bringing more challenges as well as opportunities for information access, information and data analytics, visualisation and so on.

With the advent of Generative AI, or Gen AI, and more specifically with the appearance of ChatGPT in November 2022, information retrieval has reached a new era. As discussed in this book, these new technologies have brought a paradigm shift in access to information.

Information access

Information access is defined as the ability to identify, retrieve and use information effectively (Encyclopedia.com, 2019). People access information in a number of ways through different systems and services. In the past, information search services were limited to scholarly or business information for which people had to access one or more scholarly or business databases. Examples of these databases that are currently available and commonly used include: ACM Digital Library, Compendex, ERIC, Humanities Index, IEL, LexisNexis, LISA, Scopus and Web of Science. Some of these databases are designed for specific disciplines, while others, like Scopus and Web of Science, cover multiple disciplines. However, they all are designed to provide access to different types of information resources – journal and conference papers, books, reports, legal documents and others, and their interface and search features are designed to meet the requirements of specific types of users. Most of these services offer closed access, meaning that the users need to have a contractual agreement or right to search and access information through them.

However, as discussed above, with the advent of the internet and web, many general-purpose search services, popularly known as search engines, appeared, which are designed to be used by anyone for any kind of information. These services are free at the point of use, and they may or may not provide access to the full content of the retrieved items. Examples of the most used search engines include Google, Bing, Yahoo, and Baidu. Many open-access digital libraries and repositories also appeared over the past two decades that can be searched for free and often the retrieved information can also be accessed for free. Examples of such OA digital libraries include Europeana, American Memory, NDLTD and Internet Archive.

While the various databases, search engines, digital libraries and repositories differ in terms of their content and coverage, search interfaces and retrieval features and so on, the general process of information access can be divided into the following stages:

1. It begins with an 'information need' of a 'user'.
2. The 'information need' is expressed in one or more terms or phrases to form a 'search query'.
3. The 'search query' is entered into the 'search interface' of a 'search service' or 'search engine'; often the search terms are combined with one or more search operators such as Boolean operators (AND, OR, NOT); parentheses are used to create nested queries; special operators are used to created truncated search words.
4. The 'search interface' interacts with one or more 'indexes' of one or more search services.
5. The interface receives the 'search results' from the search services.
6. The interface 'filters' the search results.
7. The interface 'presents' the search results.
8. The user 'selects' one or more search results or filters the results, using the specific options provided to get a preferred set of results.
9. The user 'accesses' the 'content' of the selected search results.
10. The user reads the 'content' online and/or downloads/prints for future use.

The process is not always linear and is often iterative – the user may repeat some or all the steps until satisfactory search results are obtained, or decide to abandon the search process. However, any information search process is triggered by an 'information need' of a 'user'. The concept of 'user' and 'information need' have been used in quotations here to emphasise that these are important concepts, and each plays a key role in the process of information access. An information user can be an individual with specific characteristics or attributes: an expert or a novice in the subject matter of the search, a child, an adult, a student, an academic, a researcher, a businessperson, a politician, and so forth. Obviously, the specific characteristics of a given user, and the specific search context, can play a major role in the overall process of information access. Similarly, the 'information need' of the user may be significantly influenced by the specific context in which they are looking for information.

The 'information need' of a user may range from simple fact finding – such as the name or address of a person or an institution – to answering a specific question, such as how a mathematical or a statistical formula works; or a research question looking for literature to review the progress of research in a specific area or a topic. One of the key challenges is that often users don't know what the actual question is, let alone representing the information need through a specific query to begin a search. One of the key shortcomings of the entire process of information access is that it depends on how precisely the user can identify their information need and how precisely they can convert it into a search query that can be handled by a chosen search service. The problem is often exacerbated by the fact that users are expected to choose the right words to specify their information need when they may not know what they are looking for in the first instance.

Once an 'information user' has an 'information need' and they have formulated a 'search query' to represent their need, it must be entered into the 'search interface' of a 'search service'. The choice of a search service may depend on a number of factors, such as the discipline and domain of search and the user's familiarity with one or more search services; the terms of reference for access and use, such as free services or paid services that may need an account and a login process; or the time and convenience of the user. In many cases a given user may or may not know which 'information service' would be the most appropriate for their information need at a given instance. However, choice of the right search service is very important for the success of a search process and hence many libraries provide a list of databases or search services in specific subjects or disciplines. Each search service or database may have a specific search interface that controls how a user can enter their search query and interact with the chosen search service, and hence familiarity with the interface may be helpful for the user. General-purpose search services, and especially search engines like Google and Bing, do not expect any prior knowledge or expertise, and users are expected to enter their search query almost in any form – with just one or more keywords, a specific question, and even with some misspelt words.

Once the user enters the query, the search interface then interacts with one or more indexes to search for the information, and if a match is found in the index, then the results are brought back to the search interface. In a very simplistic way, this activity may be regarded as the way we look for terms in a book index where terms are arranged in a particular order. In an online index the specific location (URL or web address) of the item where the search term appears is mentioned, as opposed to page numbers as in the case of a book index. This is noted and brought back by the search interface along with a brief description of the index entry that matches the user query. This is of course a very simplistic view; in reality creation of the index, matching of search terms and retrieval of results are controlled by several complex retrieval models and algorithms.

Once the results are brought back, the interface may filter and/or sort the results, based on some pre-defined criteria or based on the knowledge about the user and their preferences. Increasingly, search engines like Google, or services like Amazon, are using a lot of user information and intelligence, gathered through data mining and data analytics of logs (user footprints on the service), to filter the retrieved results in order to improve the effectiveness of the search interactions. Similarly, the retrieved data may be presented in accordance with some user-defined criteria, such as by date of publication, or by relevance judged by the closeness of a match between the query and the retrieved results. In some cases, the presentation of results may be determined by some form of intelligence gathered through the current or other similar users' previous search activities.

Figure 2.1 on the next page shows an example of the typical search results produced by a typical university library search service on a search topic (in this case 'Generative AI'). A closer look at the search results in Figure 2.1 reveals that in addition to retrieving some documents that match the search terms, the search service also provides additional information including the total number of items that matched the search terms, the types of items or documents found (shown in the margin) and so on.

Figure 2.2 presents the results from a database search service LISA (*Library and Information Science Abstracts*) on the same topic ('Generative AI'); and Figure 2.3 shows the results from a search on Google Scholar on the same topic.

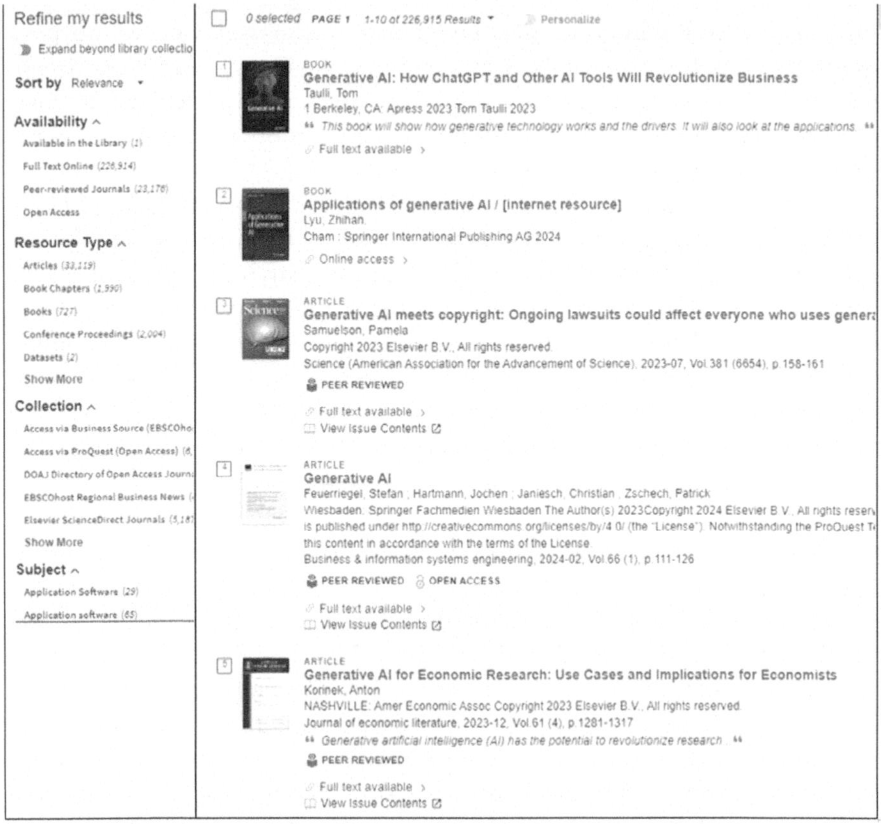

Figure 2.1 *Search results from a typical university library service on the search topic 'Generative AI'*

Figure 2.2 *Examples of search results from LISA on the search topic 'Generative AI'*

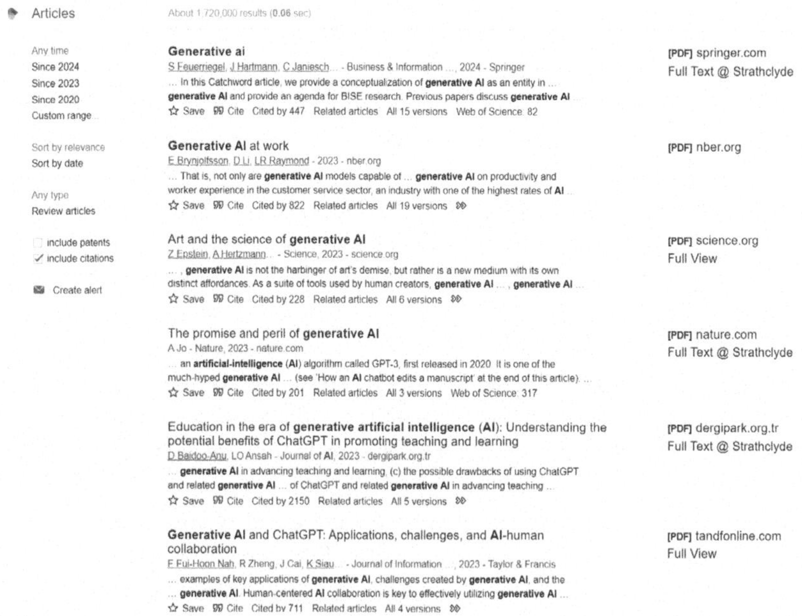

Figure 2.3 *Examples of search results from Google Scholar on the search topic 'Generative AI'*

Once the search results are presented, the user may select one or more retrieved results by reading the brief information that is presented, or may go for more information by clicking on the link and thus going to the online location of the retrieved information resource; and finally the user may read the item online, print or download and save one or more items for future use.

While these typically represent an information access process, specific activities that go on at each stage, and the overall search results and the user experience, depend on many factors and features of the chosen search services or databases.

Indexing

Conventional information retrieval systems are based on indexing, a process through which the candidate search terms and phrases are extracted from the documents in a collection, processed and arranged in index files which are searched with the user query terms and phrases, and the matched items are retrieved. A back-of-the-book index may be regarded as a simple example where candidate search terms are selected and arranged in a way – alphabetically in this case – that a user looking for a term can search and find it and can go straight to the page where the sought term occurs in the book. All attempts at automatic indexing depend in some way or other on the original document texts, or document surrogates. The words occurring in each document are listed as strings or vectors, and certain statistical measurements are made, such as word frequency calculation, total collection frequency or frequency distribution across the documents of the collection.

In an information retrieval environment the search terms from a user's query are matched as strings or vectors (mathematical representation) against the index file created from the contents – words and phrases in the documents in one or more collections – in order to retrieve those items that match. However, simply selecting every term occurring in a document to create the search index is not necessarily the best solution, because not every term occurring in a document can be a candidate term for the index in order to produce result sets that can be ranked based on the documents that best match with the user queries. One way of achieving better search results would be to apply some sort of weighting to the index terms. This suggests that while determining the importance of a given index term one must consider some other characteristics of the terms within a given document as well as the entire collection.

Karen Sparck Jones (1972) is the proponent of the idea of preparing indexes based on *inverse document frequency* (*idf*): if the document frequency (df_i) is defined as the number of documents in a collection of N documents in which a term T occurs, then the inverse function of the document frequency of the term can be taken as an indication of the term value as a document discriminator. The inverse document frequency factor (*idf*) can be calculated as $\log N/df_i$.

Using this the weight of an index term can be calculated through the following formula (Salton and Yang, 1973):

$$W_{ij} = tf_{ij} \times \log N/df_i$$

where W_{ij} is the weight of a term T_j in a document D_i, tf_{ij} is the term frequency for term T_j in document D_i and df_i is the number of documents in a collection of N documents in which term T_j occurs.

Using the *tf.idf* formula, the steps for preparing an index include:

1 identification of all the words occurring in all the documents in a given collection
2 deletion of function words by consulting a stop-word list
3 preparation of word stems by suffix stripping method, which helps reduce the number of words by producing a common stripped form for the words that have the same root (e.g. COMPUT for COMPUTING, COMPUTER, COMPUTATION, COMPUTATIONAL)
4 computation of the value of W_{ij} for each term T_j in each document D_i.

However, this calculation of similarity coefficients involves a rather simple approach, and researchers have noted some of its inherent weaknesses; subsequently a number of other approaches to the indexing and retrieval have been reported in the literature (see for example, Baeza-Yates and Ribeiro-Neto, 1999; Chowdhury, G. G., 2010; Croft, 1986; Grossman and Frieder, 2004; Manning, Raghavan and Schütze, 2009).

Information users

As stated earlier, the overarching aim of an information retrieval system is to facilitate access to information, and therefore users should be at the centre of any design and implementation of such systems. The type and characteristics of users may be defined by the organisation they work for, by the nature of their work or profession, or by age, gender, or other social groups, and so on. Similarly, for a specific information system or service users may be classified as (Chowdhury, G. G., 2010):

- *actual users,* that is, those who are using the information system or service at a given time
- *potential users,* that is, those who are not yet served by the information system or service
- *expected users,* that is, those who not only have the privilege of using the information system or service, but also have the intention of doing so
- *beneficiary users,* that is, those who have derived some benefit from the information system or service.

Users can also be characterised by the environment or context, for example (Chowdhury, G. G., 2010):

- users in an educational and research context, such as students, researchers, academics
- users in a job or business context where they may be classified by the nature of their activity, such as management, research, development, production, services; or by activities in a branch and/or specialist field, such as, the Civil Service, agriculture, industry; or by level of education and responsibility, such as professionals, technicians, workers
- users in society, in the context of everyday life and living, such as health, entertainment, shopping, travel, and a variety of day-to-day personal, family and social activities.

Given this diversity and these contexts, the needs and behaviour of different categories of users have remained a major area of research within the discipline of information science, giving rise to thousands of research papers, books, reports and commentaries. A comprehensive review of research on information users vis-à-vis different models, appear in Given, Case and Wilson (2023). Some of the issues around users, information behaviour and information practices are discussed in the context of the key theme of this book in Chapters 3 to 8.

Summary

Access to information has remained a key area of research and professional practices for decades, and it has rapidly evolved over the past seventy years due to the introduction of computers in processing and accessing information, and more significantly with the appearance of the internet and web. Users' behaviour, information seeking and information practices also changed over these years. While the tools and technologies evolved, the means of, and ease of, accessing information also changed rapidly, enabling people to access information remotely in different forms and formats, using a variety of devices. However, the fundamental approaches to accessing information have remained the same, whereby a user has to articulate their information needs choosing appropriate terms or phrases, select a specific database or service, interact with the interface of the chosen service using the chosen search terms or phrases, select the retrieved documents based on their relevance to the specific use context, read and analyse the selected documents, and assimilate the information to meet the specific needs. Chapter 3 discusses some key research and models for accessing information in different contexts.

CHAPTER 3

Information Seeking

Introduction

Access to information can be direct, for example, by putting a question to a fellow human being, or going straight to a web page; but it can also be indirect, whereby known or unknown items are searched using an automated system like a library or a database search service, or a search engine. Both kind of access – direct and algorithmic (Shah and Bender, 2024) – are influenced by a range of human, contextual and societal factors. How people look and ask for information, how people interact with a search system and how people access and use information have remained some key areas of research in information science.

Human information behaviour is an area that encompasses all kinds of studies in general information behaviour, information-seeking and retrieval behaviour and information use behaviour. Wilson (2000) defines information behaviour as the totality of human behaviour in relation to sources and channels of information, including both active and passive information seeking and information use. According to Case and Given (2016), information behaviour is:

- an overarching term that includes intentional and planned behaviours (such as active seeking) as well as unintentional or serendipitous actions (such as glimpsing or encountering information)
- purposive behaviours that do not involve seeking, such as rejecting or avoiding information, and the thoughts and emotions that accompany all of these.

(Case and Given, 2016, 370)

Human information behaviour is intertwined with 'a person's culture, history, and situation and shaped by geography, gender, and numerous other contextual elements' (Given, Case and Wilson, 2023, 3), and it encompasses, and is shaped or influenced by 'contextual elements like situation, time, affect, culture, and geography' (Case and Given, 2016, 370). Shah and Bender (2024) provide a conceptual view of the different layers or areas of research, and their interrelations for access to information (Figure 3.1).

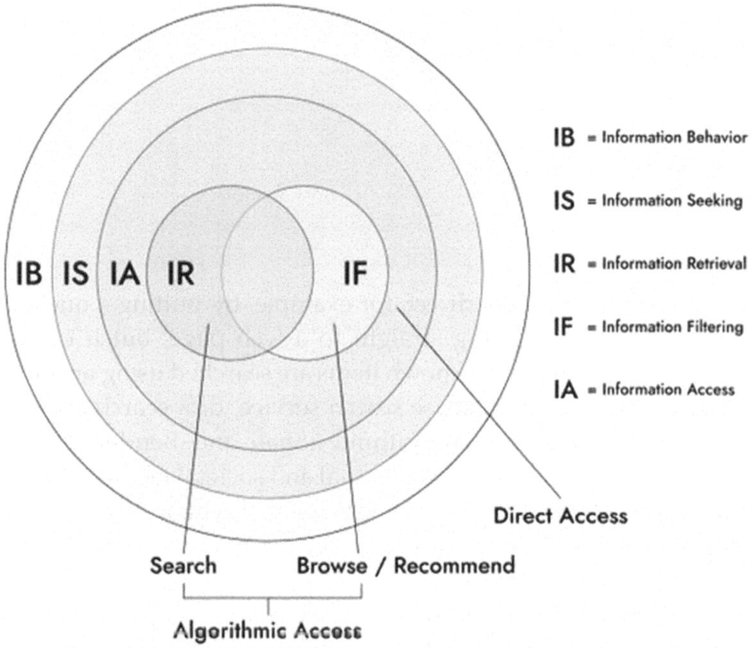

Figure 3.1 *Different layers of research that impact on people's access to information* (Shah and Bender, 2024)

Given this diversity of scope and coverage, researchers in information behaviour 'document, describe, explain, critique, and unravel the complexities of people's engagement with information' (Given, Case and Wilson, 2023, 2). Consequently, information behaviour and related fields, such as information seeking, information practice, and information seeking and retrieval, have remained the most actively researched areas in information science, producing several thousand research papers, and scores of doctoral theses, masters dissertations, books, reports, commentaries, and so on. The basic aim of research in these areas has been to understand the different behavioural and interaction characteristics of people in specific contexts that can improve the design, management and delivery of information services in the most effective and efficient ways. The first study of users in the context of information needs and behaviour appeared in the Royal Society Scientific Information Conference held in 1948 (Wilson, 2006). Research in information behaviour over the past few decades has produced numerous conceptual models and theories in attempts to describing how people seek information, make sense of information, use information and share information in different contexts. While providing a summary of research in the field, Bawden and Robinson (2012) comment that information behaviour is determined primarily by domain, such as occupation, academic subject, but it is also affected by personality differences.

A number of factors influence users' information seeking on the web, such as cognitive styles, search skills, search experience and information overload (Chowdhury and Chowdhury, 2011). The internet, web and social media technologies have now created a somewhat integrated world where access to information has become more holistic, with more available choices, but this also sometimes inundates people with information, causing what is known as 'information overload', or provide information that may have been directed to the users with specific business or other vested interests, and therefore may not be the most appropriate and quality information. In the context of information overload, Blake and Pratt (2006) comment that 'as the quantity of information at our fingertips continues to exceed human-processing capacity, the importance of information systems that integrate findings will continue to increase'. All of these can cause uncertainty, leading to the stress and anxiety of the users. Too much information, or information overload, 'may provoke the information fatigue syndrome that has been poorly considered to date, leading to severe consequences in both work and home contexts' (Graf and Antoni, 2022). A better understanding of the various information channels, people's information-seeking activities and information-seeking problems that cause uncertainty, should contribute to the design of improved information systems and services that can reduce the negative impact of uncertainty (Chowdhury, S., 2010). Research (Chowdhury, Gibb and Landoni, 2014) further suggests that new and/or improved designs should address and incorporate measures to reduce the negative impacts of uncertainty, and provision should be made to help users reap the benefits of the improved technologies for access to information.

Zhou and Li (2024) suggest that 'low information-task fit and information overload' influence users to find an alternative way to seek information. Over the past two years, Generative AI has changed the way people seek and obtain information, and this has implications for information behaviour and information search processes, which are discussed below.

Information searches

Information search can broadly be divided into two broad categories: *lookup search* and *exploratory search* (Marchionini, 2006). A *lookup search* is where the user knows the precise search goals (Athukorala et al., 2016); and an *exploratory search* is thought to centre around the acquisition of new knowledge and considered to be challenging for the user (Athukorala et al., 2016; White and Roth, 2009). Typical exploratory search processes, especially for information-intensive activities in academic, scholarly and research contexts and health and legal contexts, assume an interaction cycle consisting of query specification, receipt and examination of retrieval results, and then either stopping or reformulating the query and repeating the process until a relevant result set is found. Research shows that search results for a goal tend to trigger new goals, resulting in a search in new directions, but the context of the problem and the previous searches are carried from one stage of search to the next (Hearst, 1999). A generalised model of information seeking proposes that people's information practices draw on their stocks of knowledge that form the habitual starting point of: (1) information seeking – identifying, preferring and accessing information source; (2) information use – judging the value of information, filtering information and wielding information into action; and (3) information sharing – giving and receiving information (Savolainen and Thompson, 2022).

Information search tasks can be classified using many factors that include the search goal, the objective and perceived complexity and difficulty of the task, and the knowledge of the user (Athukorala et al., 2016). Task difficulty and task complexity are two important factors that influence user behaviour, and they are subjective because they are both assessed by the task doer with respect to their familiarity and degree of uncertainty within the task requirements (Athukorala et al, 2016; Bell and Ruthven, 2004; Byström, 2002; Vakkari, 2003). Providing a summary of research papers that investigate the effect of search goal, difficulty, complexity, and user knowledge on information search behaviour, Athukorala et al. (2016) argue that in 'exploratory tasks users spend considerable time reading a found page to determine its relevance', and this is particularly important when the search goal is less precise. They further argue that 'task completion time, number of query formulations, click interactions, and reading time are useful metrics of information search behaviors' (Athukorala et al., 2016).

Information search process

Information seeking and information search processes have remained some key areas of research in information science for over five decades. Kuhlthau's Information Search Process (ISP) model presents a holistic view of information seeking in six stages: task initiation, selection, exploration, focus formulation, collection and presentation (Kuhlthau, 1988, 1991, 1993, 1999a, 1999b, 2018; Kuhlthau, Heinstrom and Todd, 2008). According to Kuhlthau's model, thoughts that begin as uncertain, vague, and ambiguous become clearer, more focused and specific as the search process progresses; feelings of anxiety and doubt become greater confidence and certainty; and through their actions people seek information relevant to the general topic in early stages of the search process and pertinent to the focused topic towards the end.

Ellis's model shows six stages that a user goes through in an information search process: starting, chaining, browsing, differentiating, monitoring and extracting (Ellis, 1989). Meho and Tibbo extended this model in 2003, by adding four more stages: accessing, networking, verifying, and information managing (Meho and Tibbo, 2003).

The 'Berrypicking' model of Bates proposes that during an information search process, the user's information need does not remain static; instead, an evolving search occurs as the user goes through an information search process (Bates, 1989). Research also shows that the formulation of a focus or a personal perspective of the topic is a pivotal point in the search process, and 'the main value of the search resided in the accumulated learning and acquisition of information that occurred during the search process, rather than in the final results set' (Hearst, 1999).

Everyday life information seeking

The models discussed in the previous section help us understand how people seek and behave in the context of accessing information in specific contexts, especially in education and research. However, people also seek information to meet the heterogeneous nature of their everyday life information needs – health, education, job and other everyday life activities. Savolainen developed a model in the context of people's Everyday Life Information Seeking (ELIS) practices in the mid-1990s (Savolainen, 1995), describing the concept of way of life as 'order of things', where 'things' stand for various activities taking place in the daily life including job and daily chores and hobbies, and 'order' refers to preferences given to the activities. Individuals engage themselves in a certain order of things and keeping that order if they find it meaningful (Savolainen, 1995). Savolainen further describes the concept of mastery of life as 'keeping things in order'; and argued that the model was developed for 'the need to elaborate the role of social and cultural factors that affects people's way of preferring and using information sources in everyday settings' (Savolainen, 2006).

Savolainen's model suggests that 'way of life' and 'mastery of life' are intertwined. Values and attitudes, and material (such as money), social (such as contact networks), cultural and cognitive capital, and current situation of life (such as health) affect both 'way of life' and 'mastery of life'. Therefore, information seeking is an important component of mastery of life that aims 'to eliminate a continual dissonance between perceptions of 'how things are at this moment' and 'how they should be' ' (Savolainen, 2006). It is important to note that neither of them determines how a person looks for information in individual situations, but the ELIS model provides 'a holistic framework for social and psychological factors affecting people's source preferences in everyday contexts' (Savolainen, 2006).

Savolainen and Kari (2004) emphasise that further research is needed to get a more elaborate picture of the ways in which people perceive their information environments and how they select sources and channels in their everyday-life information seeking. This is particularly important when people are overwhelmed with the choices of information channels, and they do not have adequate knowledge of some essential attributes of the information channels, such as quality, reliability or trustworthiness. A more recent model 'offers a more nuanced picture of the connections between information seeking, use, creating, and sharing. In this regard, the conceptualization of the expressing mode is particularly important because it enables a balanced view of the fundamental factors constitutive of information practices' (Savolainen and Thomson, 2022).

Information access and critical thinking

People with critical thinking skills may or may not use these skills in everyday situations. However, these skills are very important in relation to information seeking and information access. They provide the ability to think critically and aid the decision-making process. In recent years the importance of critical thinking for online information, and particularly the dissemination of misinformation and disinformation during the COVID-19 pandemic, became very clear.

Research shows how the critical thinking skills impact on different fields (Halpern and Dunn, 2021; Prasetyo, Dedi and Ngadiran, 2024). Tunjungsari and Takwin (2021) suggest that critical thinking skills are the prerequisite abilities, while critical thinking practices are actually real activities. Some researchers (Tunjungsari and Takwin, 2021) argue that: (1) critical thinking practice needs to be distinguished from critical thinking skills; (2) detecting the conflict stage between critical thinking and skills becomes a determining factor; and (3) understanding the relationship between skills, dispositions, and critical thinking stages is crucial.

From information literacy to AI literacy

Research shows that in order to be able to successfully access, use and share information, people require an important set of skills, known as information literacy or information skills, that enables people to discover, access and make optimum use of data and information required in the context of everyday living – learning, work, healthy living, citizenship, and so on. Information literacy (CILIP, 2018):

- incorporates a set of skills and abilities which everyone needs to undertake information-related tasks; for instance, how to discover, access, interpret, analyse, manage, create, communicate, store and share information
- incorporates the skills of critical thinking and awareness, and an understanding of both the ethical and the political issues associated with using information
- provides to people the competencies, attributes and confidence needed to make the best use of information and to interpret it judiciously
- helps people to understand the ethical and legal issues associated with the use of information, including privacy, data protection, freedom of information, open access/open data and intellectual property.

UNESCO promotes the concept of media and information literacy (MIL), defined as a set of competencies that help people to get the maximum benefits and reduce the harm in the new information, digital and communication landscapes and enable people to effectively and critically engage with information, different forms and diverse types of content and the use of digital technologies (UNESCO, 2021b). Despite education and training programmes being offered by institutions worldwide, significant gaps still exist amongst various countries in terms of people's media and information literacy. Studies show that although about 60% of the global population, and 70% of youth, are using the internet, wide-scale and sustainable MIL training for all is still missing (UNESCO, 2023).

Information literacy and MIL have now been extended to cover another kind of literacy, called AI literacy, that:

- provides 'the basic ability to become an independent citizen in the AI era' (Yi, 2021)
- provides 'the ability to properly identify, use, and evaluate AI-related products under the premise of ethical standards' (Wang, Rau and Yuan, 2022)

- 'is based on competencies and purpose targeted by existing literacy education' (Yi, 2021); and
- 'includes three components: AI concepts, using AI concepts for evaluation, and using AI concepts for understanding the real world through problem solving' (Kong, Cheung and Zhang, 2021).

AI literacy is discussed further in Chapter 9.

Exploratory search and Gen AI

Gen AI 'creates new content in response to prompts, offering transformative potential across multiple sectors, such as education, entertainment, healthcare and scientific research' (Lorenz, Perset and Berryhill, 2023). The OECD (2023) notes that 'AI can benefit jobs by creating demand for new tasks and complementary skills, resulting in new jobs for which human labour has a comparative advantage'. Some researchers note that 'when people search for information about a new topic within large document collections, they implicitly construct a mental model of the unfamiliar information space to represent what they currently know and guide their exploration into the unknown' (Guo et al., 2023). Exploratory search has developed into an important research area 'concentrating on supporting searches that may be driven by ill-defined and complex information problems, need explorative search strategies or have intellectual growth as the primary goal' (Liu et al., 2024). Guo et al. (2023) point out that complex search tasks require 'not only finding relevant documents but also synthesizing important concepts and the relationships that connect those concepts both within and across documents.'

Research shows that exploratory information search behaviour varies by users' needs and tasks in hand, and context of the information need (Vuong and Ruotsalo, 2024). Hence, 'exploratory search should focus on measuring and designing tools that engage users with directed situated navigation support for improving whole-session performance' (Ruotsalo, Jacucci and Kaski, 2020). These issues are discussed in more detail in Chapters 5, 6 and 8.

Summary

Research in information science related to users, such as human information behaviour, information seeking and information practices, and related areas, such as information literacy and media and information literacy, have helped the information services sector develop better understanding of how people access and use information using different systems and services. The concept of a designated user community is very important here, as all the activities related to search, retrieval and use of information should be designed to meet the information tasks and needs of a designated user community (Chowdhury and Foo, 2012a). Furthermore, information access and information behaviour are greatly influenced by social factors, such as the digital divide, and digital and information skills (Chowdhury and Chowdhury, 2011) and the fast-changing nature of society triggered by the rapidly changing culture caused by the web and mobile technologies and social networking technologies (Chowdhury, 2012). These emerging technologies bring tremendous opportunities but not without challenges for the users and community (Chowdhury, 2012). Various factors, such as target users and their requirements, content, retrieval features, interface, visualisation and others play a role in determining the success of information access and use (Chowdhury and Foo, 2012b).

Recent emergence of the Gen AI technologies offers new ways of finding information: users can ask specific questions or prompt these Gen AI tools for information, and the tool instantly produces summarised information based on the question or prompt. However, researchers argue that it is important to learn how these tools can be effectively used to access information, and how users' information skills can be improved enabling them to assess the authenticity and relevance of the retrieved information. Some researchers argue that Gen AI is likely to be ubiquitous (Mollick, 2023), while others argue that:

- 'AI search answers are the fast food of your information diet – convenient and tasty, but no substitute for good nutrition' (Shah, 2024)
- 'Information access is not merely an application to be solved by the so-called 'AI' techniques du jour. Rather, it is a key human activity, with impacts on both individuals and society' (Shah and Bender, 2024)
- It is imperative to study 'AI's possible impacts in libraries and the broader academic community' (Houston and Corrado, 2023).

Furthermore, the complexity of the ethical, legal and social issues that the Gen AI technologies touch upon calls for collaborative research to better understand and prepare the world for making optimum use of Gen AI for access to information in every sphere of life (Mills, 2023). Discussions in the rest of this book aim to address the human and contextual issues of information access by highlighting the key potentials as well as challenges associated with the use of Gen AI for information access for everyday life as well as for academic and research context.

The remaining chapters of this book discuss how the Gen AI tools can be used for accessing information in different contexts, what kind of results these tools produce, how these tools can be used more effectively, what the users need to learn in making the most effective and efficient use of the Gen AI tools for accessing information, and some implications of these for the education, research and professional practices in information science.

CHAPTER 4

Gen AI for Everyday Life Information

Introduction

People look for a variety of information related to everyday life. Everyday life information seeking (ELIS) is an area of study in information science that refers to the acquisition of informational elements which people employ to orient themselves in daily life or to solve problems that are not directly connected with the performance of professional tasks or full-time study (Savolainen,1995, 2010). Savolainen (2010) traces the origin of ELIS research dating back to the early 1970s, when researchers began to investigate ordinary people's information needs and seeking for 'life information' (Bates, 1974).

In 1995 Savolainen proposed a model for ELIS where he argued that 'information seeking is an integral component of mastery of life, which aims at the elimination of continual dissonance between perceptions of "how things are at this moment" and "how they should be"' (Savolainen, 1995, 272). Savolainen's ELIS model has since been a landmark work that has been studied by several researchers in information science for the past two decades (González-Teruel and Pérez-Pulido, 2020).

In 2008 Savolainen proposed a model of everyday information practices (EIP) (Savolainen, 2008) which was further expanded recently (Savolainen and Thompson, 2022). The EIP model proposes that 'the ways in which people seek, use, and share information be viewed as meaningful in relation to features of their life world, as well as to their values, goals, and interests around ongoing projects, and be understood as affected by the context (or situation) in which these projects sit' (Savolainen and Thompson, 2022, 516). It suggests that 'information seeking, use, and sharing are modes of everyday information practices accomplished in the daily life world', and it includes 'both the totality of one's experiences (the individually perceived life world) and shared social, cultural, and economic factors' as well as specific contextual or situational factors like 'the relative significance of an everyday project and the time available for information use' (516).

The emergence of the internet, web and social media has significantly influenced people's information seeking and information practices. A number of researchers studied how people use the internet and web for everyday life information seeking and information practices (Case, 2010; Hektor, 2001; Savolainen, 1998, 1999, 2010; Savolainen and Kari, 2006a, 2006b). The emergence of the new generation of search tools that are built on the new Gen AI technologies has opened new opportunities for people to find everyday life information. This chapter discusses the results of a series of searches using five selected Gen AI tools for finding information based on some specific user needs and contexts in everyday life.

The discussions in this chapter are based on the outcomes of three case studies involving interactions with five Gen AI tools – for specific search tasks, based on three different scenarios of everyday life information needs – for finding out:

- What kind of search results are generated by these tools and how appropriate these are for the specific user needs and contexts?
- What are the lessons learnt that can inform how users should be prepared to improve their interactions with the Gen AI tools for access to everyday life information?

It should be noted that this is not a comparison of the chosen Gen AI tools *per se*. By investigating what some emerging Gen AI tools return in response to specific questions and prompts, this chapter aims to add new knowledge and trigger further research on how the interactions with these tools, and the corresponding search results, could be improved to meet specific user needs and contexts for research and scholarly activities. These discussions are expected to contribute to further studies and debates around the education, research and professional practices in different areas of information science and cognate disciplines; those are discussed in more details in Chapters 7–9.

The search context

Five Gen AI-driven search tools – Claude, Copilot, Gemini, GPT-4o and Perplexity AI – are chosen for this study. As discussed in Chapter 1, all these tools are very new and have appeared since 2024. These tools are used to find information related to health, AI itself and climate change. The search scenarios and the search questions and prompts are shown in Table 4.1 opposite.

Table 4.1 *Search scenarios and questions/prompts*

Persona	Search scenario	Search questions/prompts
A middle-aged woman with a condition of type 2 diabetes; educated and working; does not have a medical background	1 Looking for information on type 2 diabetes and how to tackle the health condition for a person with type 2 diabetes; wants to know about diet, exercise and various guidelines for health and wellbeing of people with type 2 diabetes	1 What are the symptoms of type 2 diabetes? 2 What kind of food should I avoid (qualifier: as a type 2 diabetic . . .)? 3 Can my type 2 diabetes be passed on to my children? 4 What are the recommended guidelines for managing type 2 diabetes?
A middle-aged person, educated, working, but does not have a science or technology background	2 Wants to know about Gen AI, and how it can be used for finding some general information around everyday life	1 What is meant by Gen AI? 2 How can it be used in everyday life, e.g. for finding information about health and wellbeing? 3 Can Gen AI be used to learn foreign languages? 4 How can I use Gen AI for booking my holidays?
A retired person; high-school educated, does not have a science or technology background	3 Wants to know about climate change issues to make informed decisions in everyday life, and also for taking part in discussions and debates around the environment and climate challenges	1 What are the key climate change issues? 2 As an individual, how can I contribute to the climate change issues? 3 What is meant by carbon footprint? 4 How is it measured?

Search results

Scenario 1: Looking for information on type 2 diabetes

Figures 4.1 to 4.5 on pages 42 to 50 show samples of the results of the searches generated by the chosen Gen AI tools, in response to the four questions for Scenario 1 shown in Table 4.1. (Note: underlining in all of the figures represents a hyperlink in the output.) Overall, the results show that all the chosen search tools produce output in a simple and easy-to-read format; and often the key points are presented under specific headings followed by a summary or a conclusion. Content of the results, and presentation style, vary depending on the question asked and the Gen AI tool used. Some outputs include bullet points or numbers, and some use bold fonts, underlines or asterisks for highlighting the key points. Some tools also ask for prompts for further information, or in some cases provide recommended sources for more information.

Search Tool	Result
Claude	The common symptoms of type 2 diabetes include: 1. Increased thirst 2. Frequent urination ... 9. Numbness or tingling in hands or feet It's important to note that some people with type 2 diabetes may not experience noticeable .... Would you like more information on any specific aspect of type 2 diabetes?
Copilot	Type 2 diabetes often develops gradually, and its symptoms can be mild at first. Here are some common symptoms to watch out for: 1. **Frequent urination**: Needing to urinate more often, especially at night. 2. **Increased thirst**: Feeling very thirsty all the time. 3. .... 4. **Tingling or numbness**: In the hands or feet, which can be a sign of nerve damage[1,2,3]. If you or someone you know is experiencing these symptoms, it's important to see a ... Is there anything else you'd like to know about type 2 diabetes or any other health-related topic?
Gemini	**Symptoms of Type 2 Diabetes** While some people with type 2 diabetes may experience no symptoms at all, others may notice the following: • **Frequent urination:** This is often accompanied by increased thirst. • ..... • **Darkened skin, usually in the armpits and neck:** This condition is called acanthosis nigricans. **It's important to note that these symptoms can be subtle and may not be ...** Would you like to know more about type 2 diabetes or its treatment?
GPT-4o	Type 2 diabetes is a chronic condition that affects the way your body metabolizes glucose (sugar). The symptoms of type 2 diabetes can develop slowly over time... 1. **Increased Thirst (Polydipsia):** Feeling very thirsty even after drinking water is a common sign. .... 10. **Irritability and Mood Changes:** Blood sugar fluctuations can affect mood and lead to irritability or other emotional changes. If you or someone else is experiencing these symptoms, it's important to see a healthcare provider for evaluation and possible testing for diabetes. Early detection 2...
Perplexity AI	Type 2 diabetes often develops gradually, and many people may not notice symptoms in the early stages. However, there are several common signs and symptoms to be aware of: ## Key Symptoms **Increased thirst and frequent urination**: When blood sugar levels are high, the kidneys work harder to filter and absorb the excess glucose. This leads to more frequent urination, which can cause dehydration and increased thirst[1][2]. ...

Figure 4.1 *Examples of search results for Scenario 1, Question 1: What are the symptoms of type 2 diabetes?*

Search Tool	Result
	## Additional Signs **Blurred vision**: High blood sugar can cause the lens in your eye to swell, leading to blurry vision[1][3]. ..... It's important to note that some people with type 2 diabetes may not experience any symptoms initially. If you notice any of these signs or are concerned about your risk, it's best to consult with a healthcare provider for proper evaluation and testing[4]. Citations: [1] https://www.webmd.com/diabetes/type-2-diabetes-symptoms ... [8] https://www.nhs.uk/conditions/type-2-diabetes/

Figure 4.1 *Continued*

Examples of some results produced by the chosen search tools in response to Scenario 1, Question 1 are shown in Figure 4.1. As shown in Figure 4.1 and Table 4.2, all the chosen tools answer the question on the symptoms of type 2 diabetes in an easy-to-read summary form using headings, number and/or bullet points, and a summary with some specific advice, and all these are very useful for a general user. However, a closer look at the results (Figure 4.1) also shows some differences. Results shown in Figure 4.1 also show that only two of the five chosen search tools, i.e. Copilot and Perplexity AI, provide citations for the information provided in the responses; and the number of citations provided by Perplexity AI is higher than that of Copilot. Overall, the results produced by GPT-4o and Perplexity AI are more detailed, compared to the three other tools.

Table 4.2 *Summary of results for Scenario 1, Question 1*

Tool	Comments on the output
Claude	Mentions nine symptoms of type 2 diabetes, with advice to consult a healthcare professional for advice; no sources are cited
Copilot	Mentions eight symptoms, each under a specific heading, and some details. Three NHS sources are cited, with advice to consult a healthcare professional for further advice
Gemini	Mentions eight symptoms, each under a specific heading, and brief details, with advice to consult a healthcare professional for further advice; no sources are cited
GPT-4o	Mentions 10 symptoms, each under a specific heading, and brief explanations, with advice to consult a healthcare professional for further advice; no sources are cited
Perplexity AI	Mentions four key and five additional symptoms, each under a specific heading and further details, and supported by citations; provides advice to consult a healthcare professional in the end. Provides eight citations of relevant sources like the NHS, Diabetes UK, etc.

Snippets of the results generated by the chosen tools in response to Scenario 1, Question 2 are presented in Figure 4.2, and a summary is presented in Table 4.3. Overall, the outputs generated by GPT-4o and Perplexity AI are more detailed compared to the three other tools. Only two of the five chosen search tools, Copilot and Perplexity AI, provide citations for the information provided in the responses; and the number of citations provided by Perplexity AI is higher than that of Copilot. Overall, the outputs generated by GPT-4o and Perplexity AI are more detailed, compared to the three other tools. The outputs from GPT-4o also recommends some alternative diet.

Search Tool	Result
Claude	If you're concerned about type 2 diabetes or managing the condition, you should generally limit or avoid: 1. Sugary foods and drinks: Sodas, candies, desserts, etc. ... 10. Fruit juices: Even 100% fruit juices can be high in sugar Instead, focus on whole grains, lean proteins, vegetables, fruits in moderation, and healthy fats. A dietitian can provide personalized advice based on your specific needs and .... Would you like information on foods that are beneficial for managing blood sugar levels?
Copilot	If you have type 2 diabetes, it's important to be mindful of your diet to help manage your blood sugar levels. Here are some foods you should try to avoid or limit: 1. **Sugary Foods and Drinks**: This includes sweets, candies, cookies, cakes, and sugar-sweetened beverages like soda and sweet tea[1]. ... 6. **Salty Foods**: Processed snacks, canned soups, and fast food, which can contribute to high blood pressure[2]. Instead, focus on a balanced diet that includes plenty of vegetables, whole grains, ... Is there anything else you'd like to know about managing type 2 diabetes ...?
Gemini	**Foods to Avoid with Type 2 Diabetes** While you can still enjoy a variety of foods with type 2 diabetes, it's important to be mindful of certain types. Here are some foods to limit or avoid: **Sugary Foods and Drinks:** • **Added sugars:** These can spike your blood sugar quickly. .... **Unhealthy Fats:** • **Saturated fats:** Found in red meat, full-fat dairy, and tropical oils. ... **Excessive Amounts of:** • **Starchy vegetables:** Potatoes, corn, peas, and beans (in large quantities)..... **Remember:** It's about moderation. You can still enjoy these foods occasionally, but ... **For more specific advice or to create a personalized meal plan, consult with ...**

Figure 4.2 *Examples of search results for Scenario 1, Question 2: What kind of food should I avoid?*

Search Tool	Result
GPT-4o	If you have type 2 diabetes or are trying to manage your blood sugar ... cautious with: ### 1. **Sugary Foods and Drinks** **Sugary beverages:** Soda, fruit juices, energy drinks, and sweetened teas are high ... ### 8. **High-Glycemic-Index Foods** - **Potatoes:** Especially when fried or in forms like chips and fries, ... ### Better Choices: - **Whole grains** (like oats, quinoa, and whole-wheat products).... - **Lean proteins** (such as fish, chicken, turkey, and plant-based proteins like beans and lentils) Balancing your diet with these healthier options and monitoring portion sizes can help...
Perplexity AI	When managing type 2 diabetes, it's important to be mindful of your food choices. ... of: ## Foods to Limit or Avoid **High-sugar foods and drinks**: - Sugar-sweetened beverages like soda, sweet tea, and sports drinks .... **Trans fats**: - Foods containing partially hydrogenated oils .... ## Better Choices Instead of these foods, focus on: - Non-starchy vegetables .... Remember, it's not about completely eliminating foods but rather making healthier ... Citations: [1] https://www.medicalnewstoday.com/articles/317355 .... [8] https://www.diabetes.org.uk/guide-to-diabetes/enjoy-food/eating-with-diabetes/i-have-type-2-diabetes

Figure 4.2 *Continued*

Table 4.3 *Summary of results for Scenario 1, Question 2*

Tool	Output and comments
Claude	Provides 10 suggestions, followed by advice on the kind of food to choose, and consultation with a dietitian; no citations
Copilot	Provides six suggestions, each under a specific heading and some text, and citations, followed by advice on the kind of food to choose, and consultation with a dietitian
Gemini	Provides eight suggestions, each under a specific heading and some text, followed by advice on the kind of food to choose, and consultation with a dietitian; no citations
GPT-4o	Provides eight suggestions, followed by five suggestions on the kind of food to choose, each under a specific heading and some text; and finally advice on consultation with a dietitian; no citations
Perplexity AI	Provides six suggestions, each with three subheadings and text, followed by five suggestions on the kind of food to choose; provides advice to consult with a dietitian; provides eight citations, including NHS, Diabetes.org.uk, etc.

Results of the searches presented in Figure 4.3 (Scenario 1, Question 3) show that only two of the five chosen search tools, Copilot and Perplexity AI, include citations for the information provided in the responses; and the number of citations provided by Perplexity AI is higher than that of Copilot. As summarised in Table 4.4, the outputs generated by GPT-4o and Perplexity AI are more detailed, compared to the three other tools.

Search Tool	Result
Claude	Type 2 diabetes has a genetic component, which means your children may have an . Here a.... Here some key points: 1. Genetic predisposition: Having a parent or sibling with type 2 diabetes increases a person's risk........... 7. Education: Teaching children about healthy habits early can help reduce their risk. It's important to remember that while genetics play a role, lifestyle factors have a substantial impact on whether someone develops type 2 diabetes. Encouraging healthy... Would you like more information on preventive measures or how to discuss this with your children?
Copilot	Yes, type 2 diabetes can be passed on to your children, but it's not guaranteed. Both genetics and lifestyle factors play a role in the development ...Here are some key points: **1.Genetic Predisposition**: If you have type 2 diabetes, your children are .. it. Having a close relative with diabetes can increase their risk by two to six times[1]. **3.Preventive Measures**: Encouraging healthy eating, regular exercise, ... type 2 diabetes[2]. It's important to focus on creating a healthy environment for your children to help ... Is there anything else you'd like to know about managing diabetes or any other health-related topic?
Gemini	**Yes, type 2 diabetes can be passed on to your children.** However, it's important to understand that genetics is just one factor. Other lifestyle choices, such as diet and ... If you have type 2 diabetes, your children are at a higher risk of developing it ... By making healthy lifestyle choices and encouraging your children to do the same, you can reduce their risk of developing type 2 diabetes. Would you like to know more about preventing type 2 diabetes in children?
GPT-4o	Type 2 diabetes has a genetic component, meaning that it can be passed on to your .... ### **Genetic Risk** - **Family History:** If you have type 2 diabetes, your children have a higher risk ... ### **Lifestyle and Environmental Factors** - **Diet and Exercise:** While genetics play a role, lifestyle factors like diet, ... - **Obesity:** Being overweight or obese is a major risk factor for type 2 diabetes, ... - **Socioeconomic Factors:** Access to healthy foods, opportunities for physical ...

Figure 4.3 *Examples of search results for Scenario 1, Question 3: Can my type 2 diabetes be passed on to my children?*

Search Tool	Result
	### **Prevention and Management** Even if there is a genetic predisposition, it's possible to delay or prevent the onset ... - **Healthy Diet:** Encouraging a balanced diet rich in whole grains, fruits, vegetables, lean proteins, and healthy fats can help manage weight and reduce the risk..... ### **Conclusion** While type 2 diabetes can run in families due to genetic factors, it is not inevitable...
Perplexity AI	While type 2 diabetes is not directly inherited in the same way as some genetic disorders, there is a significant hereditary component that can increase your children's risk of ... ## Genetic Influence Type 2 diabetes has a stronger genetic link compared to type 1 diabetes [5]. If you ... ## Risk Factors Several factors contribute to your children's likelihood of developing type 2 diabetes: **Family history**: Having a parent or sibling with type 2 diabetes increases the risk[1]... ## Inheritance Pattern Type 2 diabetes does not follow a clear inheritance pattern. However: ## Prevention While genetic risk can't be changed, lifestyle factors play a crucial role in the ..... Remember, having a genetic predisposition doesn't guarantee that your children will ... Citations: [1] https://www.healthline.com/health/type-2-diabetes/genetics ..... [8] https://www.mayoclinic.org/diseases-conditions/type-2-diabetes/symptoms-causes/syc-20351193

Figure 4.3 *Continued*

Table 4.4 *Summary of results for Scenario 1, Question 3*

Tool	Output and comments
Claude	The question is answered in easy-to-read summary form under seven headings, followed by a summary: no citations
Copilot	The question is answered in easy-to-read summary form under three headings, each with some text and citations; followed by a summary
Gemini	The question is answered in some short descriptive text form; no citations
GPT-4o	The question is answered under three broad headings, each with 2–3 subheadings, with easy-read summary text; followed by another heading with 3 suggestions on what needs to be done to avoid the risk; and a conclusion
Perplexity AI	The question is answered under five broad headings, each with 2–3 subheadings, with easy-read summary text; and a conclusion, and 8 citations

Results of the searches presented in Figure 4.4 (Scenario 1, Question 4), and summarised in Table 4.5, show that only two of the five chosen search tools, Copilot and Perplexity AI, provide citations for the information provided in the responses; and the number of citations provided by Perplexity AI is higher than that of Copilot. Overall, the outputs generated by all the tools are quite detailed, compared to the three other questions representing scenario 1. Outputs from Copilot and Perplexity AI include citations of documents from NICE and NHS in the UK, with hyperlinks, but results from Claude, Gemini and GPT-4o did not provide any citations. Hence, just to be sure, Question 4 for Scenario 1 was modified to prompt for the NHS (National Health Service) guidelines. Results presented in Figure 4.5 show that the NHS recommended guidelines are mentioned in the results generated by all three tools, and all the guidelines are quite detailed, but they do not include any citations.

Search Tool	Result
Claude	The recommended guidelines for managing type 2 diabetes typically include: 1. Blood glucose monitoring: - Regular self-monitoring of blood glucose levels ...... 12. Alcohol consumption: - Limiting alcohol intake and only drinking with food These guidelines should be personalized based on individual needs and health status. Would you like more detailed information on any specific aspect of diabetes ... ?
Copilot	Managing type 2 diabetes involves a combination of lifestyle changes, medication, and regular monitoring. Here are some key guidelines: 1. Healthy Eating: Focus on a balanced diet rich in vegetables, whole grains, lean proteins, and healthy fats. Limit sugary foods, refined carbs, and high-fat meats[1]. 2. ... 3. Education and Support: Engage in diabetes self-management education programs to learn more about managing your condition and making informed decisions[3]. These guidelines are designed to help you maintain a healthy lifestyle and prevent .... Is there anything else you'd like to know about managing type 2 diabetes or any ...?
Gemini	Recommended Guidelines for Managing Type 2 Diabetes Managing type 2 diabetes involves a combination of lifestyle changes, ... key guidelines: Lifestyle Changes: • Healthy Diet: Focus on whole, unprocessed foods, fruits, vegetables, lean proteins, and whole grains......... Medication: • Oral Medications: These can help lower blood sugar levels. Types include ...

Figure 4.4 *Snippets of search results for Scenario 1, Question 4: What are the recommended guidelines for managing type 2 diabetes?*

Search Tool	Result
	Regular Monitoring: • Blood Sugar Monitoring: Regularly check your blood sugar levels to • .... It's crucial to work closely with your healthcare provider to develop a personalized .... Would you like more information on a specific aspect of managing type 2 diabetes, ...?
GPT-4o	Result Managing type 2 diabetes effectively involves a combination of lifestyle changes, ... Here are the recommended guidelines for managing type 2 diabetes: ### 1. **Healthy Eating** - **Balanced Diet:** Focus on a diet rich in vegetables, fruits, whole grains, lean proteins, and healthy fats. Incorporate foods with a low glycemic index (GI) to .... ### 10. **Managing Other Health Conditions** - **Comorbidity Management:** If you have other health conditions such as high blood pressure, high cholesterol, or kidney disease, managing these effectively is important to reduce the risk of complications. Following these guidelines can help you manage type 2 diabetes effectively ... needs.
Perplexity AI	Based on the search results, here are the key guidelines for managing type 2 diabetes: ## Patient-Centered Approach - Provide individualized care and treatment goals based on patient preferences, needs, and circumstances[1][3] .... ## Ongoing Care - Regularly assess and address cardiovascular risk factors[2] ...... The guidelines emphasize a patient-centered approach, lifestyle management .... Citations: [1] https://www.nice.org.uk/guidance/ng28 .... [8] https://www.mayoclinic.org/diseases-conditions/type-2-diabetes/symptoms-causes/syc-20351193

Figure 4.4 *Continued*

Reply from Claude:
The NHS (National Health Service) in the UK provides specific guidelines for managing type 2 diabetes. Here are the key recommendations:
1. Blood glucose targets:
   - Before meals: 4 to 7 mmol/L
   - 2 hours after meals: less than 8.5 mmol/L
2. HbA1c target:
   - 48 mmol/mol (6.5%) or below

.....

10. Self-monitoring:
    - Regular blood glucose monitoring as advised by healthcare team

These guidelines are general and may be adjusted based on individual circumstances. The NHS emphasizes ...
Would you like more information on any specific aspect of these guidelines

Figure 4.5 *Examples of search results for modified Question 4*

Reply from Gemini
The NHS (National Health Service) in the UK has specific guidelines for managing type 2 diabetes. These guidelines are based on the ... with type 2 ..Here are some key recommendations from the NHS:
Lifestyle Changes:
• Healthy Diet: Follow a healthy diet that includes plenty of fruits, vegetables, whole grains, lean ...
• Smoking Cessation: If you smoke, quitting can significantly improve your health and reduce ...
......
Additional Recommendations:
• Self-Management Education: Attend diabetes education programs to learn more about .....
It's important to note that these are general guidelines, and your individual treatment plan may vary.....
Would you like more information on a specific aspect of managing type 2 diabetes, such as ...?

Reply from GPT-4o
The NHS (National Health Service) in the UK provides specific guidelines for managing type 2 diabetes. These recommendations emphasize the importance of lifestyle ... Here's an overview of the NHS guidelines:
1. **Healthy Eating**
- **Balanced Diet:** The NHS advises eating a healthy, balanced diet that includes plenty of vegetables...
.....
11. **Personalized Care**
- **Individualized Care Plans:** The NHS promotes a personalized care approach, where care ...
Following these NHS guidelines can help manage type 2 diabetes effectively, reduce the risk of ....

Figure 4.5 *Continued*

Table 4.5 *Summary of results for Scenario 1, Question 4*

Tool	**Results and comments**
Claude	Responses provide 12 guidelines, each under a specific heading, and 2–4 subheadings, with easy-to-read text, followed by a summary; no citations
Copilot	Responses provide seven guidelines, each under a specific heading, with easy-to-read text and citations, followed by a summary
Gemini	Responses provide 11 guidelines, under three broad headings, each with 2–5 bullet points, and easy-to-read text, followed by a summary; no citations
GPT-4o	Responses provide a number of guidelines, under 10 broad headings, each with 2–4 subheadings with easy-to-read text, followed by a summary; no citations
Perplexity AI	Responses provide a number of guidelines, under five broad headings, each with 3–4 subheadings with easy-to-read text and citation, followed by a summary; total eight citations

Figures 4.6 and 4.7 provide examples of two search results from Google on two simple queries. These examples are provided here to show the typical results that one would receive from a Google search, which is usually the first step people normally would take to find information on a topic. The results also show that even when a specific source is not mentioned, as in the question shown in Figure 4.5, the search engine provides results from the relevant and trustworthy sources like 'Diabetes UK', and 'NHS'. These examples show how a general user would search and find information.

Type 2 diabetes treatments

1. Eating well and moving more.
2. Weight loss.
3. Metformin (usually taken as a tablet)
4. Insulin along with other medication that helps lower blood sugar levels.
5. Other types of diabetes medicine that is injected or taken as tablets.
6. Weight loss surgery.
7. Support with your emotional health.

Diabetes.org.uk
Type 2 diabetes treatments

NHS

https://www.nhs.uk › Health A to Z › Type 2 diabetes

A healthy diet and keeping active **will** help you **manage** your blood sugar level. It'**ll** also help you **control** your weight and gener**ally** feel better.

Figure 4.6 *Examples of top two results from a Google search on 'How to manage type 2 diabetes?'*

Staying healthy if you have type 2 diabetes

- eat a wide range of foods – including fruit, vegetables and some starchy foods like pasta, potatoes and rice.
- keep sugar, fat and salt to a minimum.
- avoid missing meals if you take medicines that can cause hypos.

Food and keeping active - Type 2 diabetes - NHS

Type 2 diabetes in adults: management | Guidance - NICE

nice.org.uk
https://www.nice.org.uk › guidance

This **guideline** covers care and **management** for adults (aged 18 and over) with **type 2 diabetes**. It focuses on patient education, dietary advice, **managing** ...

Figure 4.7 *Examples of Google search results on 'NHS guidelines for managing type 2 diabetes'*

Scenario 2: Using Gen AI for everyday life questions

Figures 4.8 to 4.11 show the snippets of results for Scenario 2, Questions 1–4. Results of the searches presented in Figure 4.8 (Scenario 2, Question 1), and summarised in Table 4.6, show that only two of the five chosen search tools, Copilot and Perplexity AI, provide citations for the information provided in the responses; and the number of citations provided by Perplexity AI is higher than that of Copilot. Overall, the outputs generated by Claude, GPT-4o and Perplexity AI are more detailed, compared to the three other tools.

Search Tool	Results
Claude	Gen AI, short for Generative Artificial Intelligence, refers to a category of AI systems that can create new content, ideas, or data based on .... Here's a brief overview: 1. Definition: AI systems capable of generating new, original content such as text, images, ... 7. Ethical considerations: Raises questions about authorship, potential misuse, and ... Gen AI represents a significant advancement in AI capabilities, enabling machines .... Would you like more information on any specific aspect of Gen AI?
Copilot	Generative AI, often abbreviated as Gen AI, is a type of artificial intelligence that can create original content in response to user prompts. This content can include text, images, videos, audio, and even software code[1,2]. Here's a bit more detail: 1. **Content Creation**: Gen AI can generate new content by learning patterns and structures from large datasets. For example, it can write stories, create artwork, compose music, or generate realistic images based on text descriptions[1,2]. .... 3.**Applications**: Gen AI is used in various fields, including entertainment, ..., and software ... Tools like ChatGPT and DALL-E are popular examples of generative AI applications[2]. .... Generative AI has revolutionized how we interact with technology, making it possible ... Is there a specific aspect of Gen AI you're curious about?
Gemini	**Gen AI** is short for **Generative Artificial Intelligence**. It's a type of AI that can create ... Here are some examples of what Gen AI can do: • **Write creative content:** It can generate poems, stories, scripts, and even code. • .... • **Design products:** It can help design products by generating new ideas and .... Basically, Gen AI is a powerful tool that can be used to create new and innovative content.

Figure 4.8 *Examples of search results for Scenario 2, Question 1: What is meant by Gen AI?*

Search Tool	Results
GPT-4o	"Gen AI," short for "Generative AI," refers to a class of artificial intelligence models ... ### Key Features of Generative AI: - **Content Creation:** Gen AI models can produce various types of content. ... ### Examples of Generative AI Models: - **GPT (Generative Pre-trained Transformer):** A type of model that generates human-.. - **Ethical Considerations:** The ability of Gen AI to create realistic content also raises concerns, particularly regarding misinformation, copyright issues, ... (e.g., deepfakes). Generative AI represents a significant advancement in the field of artificial .. industries.
Perplexity AI	Generative AI, often abbreviated as Gen AI, refers to artificial intelligence systems .. Here are the key points to understand about Gen AI: ## Core Concept Generative AI uses machine learning models, particularly deep learning algorithms.... ## How It Works Generative AI typically operates in three phases: 1. Training on large datasets Generative AI represents a significant advancement in artificial intelligence, ... Citations: [1] https://www.mckinsey.com/featured-insights/mckinsey-explainers/what-is-generative-ai .. [8] https://medlineplus.gov/genetics/condition/type-2-diabetes/

Figure 4.8 *Continued*

Table 4.6 *Summary of results for Scenario 2, Question 1*

Tool	Results and comments
Claude	Responses provide seven points, each under a specific heading, two with subheadings, with easy-to-read text, followed by a summary; no citations
Copilot	Responses provide three points, each under a specific heading, with easy-to-read text and citations, followed by a summary
Gemini	Responses provide four points, with easy-to-read text, followed by a summary; no citations
GPT-4o	Responses provide some detailed points under four broad headings, each with three to four subheadings with easy-to-read text, followed by a summary; no citations
Perplexity AI	Responses provide some detailed points under broad headings, each with three to six subheadings with easy-to-read text and citation, followed by a summary; total eight citations

Results of the searches presented in Figure 4.9 (Scenario 2, Question 2), and summarised in Table 4.7 on the next page, show that only one of the five chosen search tools, Perplexity AI, provides citations for the information provided in the responses. Overall, the outputs generated by Claude, GPT-4o and Perplexity AI are more detailed.

Tool	Result
Claude	Gen AI can be applied in various ways to help with health and wellbeing information: 1. Personalized health information: - Answering specific health queries .. 10. Research assistance: - Summarizing recent health studies - Compiling information from multiple sources Important note: While Gen AI can be a useful tool for health information, it should not …… Would you like more details on any specific application of Gen AI in health and wellbeing?
Copilot	Generative AI can be incredibly useful in everyday life, especially for finding information about health and wellbeing. Here are some practical ways you can use it: **1.Personalized Health Advice**: AI can provide tailored health tips based on your specific needs and conditions. For example, it can suggest dietary changes, exercise routines, and lifestyle … **6.Educational Content**: AI can generate articles, summaries, and explanations on … information. These applications can make managing your health more convenient and accessible.. Is there a specific health or wellbeing topic you're interested in exploring further?
Gemini	**Gen AI can be a valuable tool in everyday life, especially when it comes to finding information about health and wellbeing.** Here are a few ways it can be used: **1. Personalized Health Information:** • **Symptom Checker:** Gen AI can be used to create symptom checkers that can help you assess potential health issues based on your symptoms. • .. **4. Medical Education:** • **Virtual Patients:** Gen AI can create virtual patients for medical students to practice on, providing a realistic learning experience. • .. It's important to note that while Gen AI can be a helpful tool, it should not replace professional medical advice. Always consult with a healthcare provider for any health concerns.
GPT-4o	Generative AI can be incredibly useful in everyday life, particularly when it comes to finding information about health and wellbeing. Here are some ways it can be applied: ### 1. **Personalized Health Advice** - **Symptom Checking:** Generative AI can be integrated into symptom checker apps, where .. .. ### 8. **Disease Management Support** - **Chronic Disease Monitoring:** For those managing chronic conditions like diabetes or … In these ways, generative AI can make health and wellbeing information more accessible, personalized, and actionable, helping individuals take control of their health in their everyday lives.

Figure 4.9 *Examples of search results for Scenario 2, Question 2: How can it be used in everyday life, e.g. for finding information about health & wellbeing?*

Tool	Result
Perplexity AI	Generative AI has several potential applications for finding information about health and wellbeing in everyday life: ## Information Access and Summarization - **Quick health information**: Gen AI can provide concise, easy-to-understand summaries of health conditions, symptoms, and treatments when you have questions. .. ## Medication Information - **Drug interaction checks**: You can ask about potential interactions between medications you're taking. ... While Gen AI can be a valuable tool for health information, it's crucial to remember that it .... Citations: [1] https://www.alpha-sense.com/blog/trends/generative-ai-healthcare/ .. [8] https://blog.google/technology/health/google-generative-ai-healthcare/

Figure 4.9 *Continued*

Table 4.7 *Summary of results for Scenario 2, Question 2*

Tool	Results and comments
Claude	Responses are provided under 10 headings, two with subheadings, with easy-to-read text, followed by a summary; no citations
Copilot	Responses are provided under six headings, with easy-to-read text and citations, followed by a summary; no citations
Gemini	Responses are provided under five headings, each with two to three bullet points, with easy-to-read text, followed by a summary; no citations
GPT-4o	Responses are provided under eight headings, each with two bullet points, with easy-to-read text, followed by a summary; no citations
Perplexity AI	Responses are provided under five headings, each with two to three bullet points, with easy-to-read text, followed by a summary; total eight citations

Results of the searches presented in Figure 4.10 (Scenario 2, Question 3), and summarised in Table 4.8, show that only two of the five chosen search tools, Copilot and Perplexity AI, provide citations for the information provided in the responses; and the number of citations provided by Perplexity AI is higher than that of Copilot. Overall, the outputs generated by Claude, GPT-4o and Perplexity AI are more detailed, compared to the two other tools.

Search Tool	Result
Claude	Yes, Gen AI can be a powerful tool for learning foreign languages. Here are some ways it can be used: 1. Conversational practice: - Simulating dialogues in the target language - Providing instant feedback on grammar and vocabulary usage .... 12. Accent and dialect exposure: - Generating examples of different accents or regional variations While Gen AI can be a valuable language learning tool, it's important to combine it ... Would you like more information on any specific aspect of using Gen AI for ...?
Copilot	Yes, generative AI can be a fantastic tool for learning foreign languages! Here are some ways it can help: **1.Real-Time Translation and Pronunciation**: AI tools can provide instant translations and correct your pronunciation. This is great for practicing speaking and understanding the language in real-time[1]. .... 5.**Language Games and Exercises**: AI-powered apps can create interactive games and exercises that make learning fun and effective[1]. These tools can make language learning more accessible and enjoyable. Have you tried any AI tools for language learning yet, or is there a specific language you're interested in?
Gemini	**Absolutely!** Gen AI can be a powerful tool for learning foreign languages. Here are some ways it can be used: • **Personalized Language Tutor:** Gen AI can create personalized language lessons based on your learning style and pace. • ... • **Language Immersion:** AI-powered language learning apps can create immersive environments where you can practice using the language in real-world scenarios. By leveraging Gen AI, you can make language learning more efficient, engaging, and ....
GPT-4o	Yes, Generative AI can be a powerful tool for learning foreign languages. It offers a range of .... Here's how Gen AI can be used for language learning: ### 1. **Conversational Practice** - **AI-Powered Chatbots:** Generative AI can simulate real-life conversations in the target language, allowing learners to practice speaking and writing. .. ### 10. **Engagement and Motivation** - **Gamification:** AI can generate language learning games and challenges that ... ### Conclusion Generative AI can significantly enhance the language learning experience by providing .. a range of possibilities that make learning a new language more accessible and effective.
Perplexity AI	Yes, generative AI (Gen AI) can be a powerful tool for learning foreign languages. Here are some key ways Gen AI can be used to support language learning: ## Conversation Practice - Gen AI chatbots like ChatGPT can engage in conversational exchanges in the .. ## Cultural Context

Figure 4.10 *Examples of search results for Scenario 2, Question 3: Can Gen AI be used to learn foreign languages?*

Search Tool	Result
	- Gen AI can offer insights into cultural aspects related to the language, enhancing learners' understanding of idiomatic expressions and cultural references. While Gen AI offers these benefits, it's important to note that it should be used .. Citations: [1] https://www.sciencedirect.com/science/article/pii/S2666557324000156 .. [8] https://www.candlinandmynard.com/gen_ai.html

Figure 4.10 *Continued*

Table 4.8 *Summary of results for Scenario 2, Question 3*

Tool	Results and comments
Claude	Responses are provided under 12 headings, each with two subheadings, with easy-to-read text, followed by a summary; no citations
Copilot	Responses are provided under five headings, with easy-to-read text with citations, followed by a summary
Gemini	Responses are provided under four headings, with easy-to-read text, followed by a summary; no citations
GPT-4o	Responses are provided under 10 headings, each with two bullet points, with easy-to-read text, followed by a summary; no citations
Perplexity AI	Responses are provided under eight headings, each with two bullet points, with easy-to-read text, followed by a summary; total eight citations

Results of the searches presented in Figure 4.11 (Scenario 2, Question 4), and Table 4.9, show that only one of the five chosen search tools, Perplexity AI, provides citations for the information provided in the responses. Overall, the results are more detailed, compared to the other questions for Scenario 2.

Search Tool	Result
Claude	Gen AI can be a useful tool for planning and booking holidays. Here's how you can use it: 1. Destination research: - Generating lists of destinations based on your preferences - Providing information on climate, attractions, and local culture .... 12. Virtual tours: - Generating descriptions of attractions or destinations for preview Remember, while Gen AI can provide valuable assistance, it's important to verify critical information (like visa requirements or booking details) through official sources... Would you like more details on any specific aspect of using Gen AI for holiday planning?

Figure 4.11 *Examples of search results for Scenario 2, Question 4: How can I use Gen AI for booking my holidays?*

Search Tool	Result
Copilot	Generative AI can be a great asset for planning and booking your holidays. Here are some ways you can use it: 1.Destination Recommendations: AI can suggest travel destinations based on your preferences, such as climate, activities, budget, and travel dates. ..... 6.Budget Management: AI can help you keep track of your travel expenses and suggest ways to save money during your trip. Would you like help with any specific part of your holiday planning?
Gemini	Gen AI can be a helpful tool for planning your holidays. Here are some ways you can use it: 1. Personalized Recommendations: • Travel Recommendations: Based on your preferences (e.g., budget, interests, travel style), Gen AI can suggest suitable destinations, accommodations, and activities. • Customizable Itineraries: It can help you create personalized itineraries that align with your interests and time constraints......................... 5. Virtual Tours: • Explore Destinations: Before you book, you can use Gen AI to explore virtual tours of potential destinations, giving you a better sense of what to expect. Remember: While Gen AI can be a valuable tool, it's always a good idea to verify information through official sources or consult with a travel agent for expert advice.
GPT-4o	Using Generative AI for booking holidays can streamline the process, making it more personalized, efficient, and enjoyable. Here's how you can leverage Gen AI to plan and book your holidays: ### 1. **Personalized Travel Recommendations** - **Destination Suggestions:** Generative AI can suggest travel destinations based on ... ### 10. **Post-Trip Feedback and Reviews** - **Review Writing:** AI can help you draft reviews for hotels, restaurants, or attractions you visited during your trip, based on your experiences and ratings. - **Memory Books:** AI can help you create a digital memory book or photo album, organizing your travel photos and adding captions, maps, and notes from your trip. ### Summary Generative AI can be an invaluable tool throughout the entire holiday planning and ... AI can help you organize every detail, leaving you more time to enjoy the journey.
Perplexity AI	Generative AI can significantly enhance the process of booking holidays by providing personalized and efficient planning tools. Here are some ways you can use Gen AI for holiday bookings: ## AI Trip Planners - **Booking.com's AI Trip Planner**: This tool allows travelers to ask ...... .or adventure trips[1][5]. ## Personalized Recommendations - **Real-Time Refinement**: As you interact with the AI, you can refine your preferences ... [1][5]. ## Streamlined Booking Process ..... ## Enhanced Customer Experience

Figure 4.11 *Continued*

Search Tool	Result
	By leveraging these capabilities, Gen AI can transform the way you plan ... and enjoyable. Citations: [1] https://news.booking.com/bookingcom-launches-new-ai-trip-planner-to-enhance-travel-planning-experience/ ... [8] https://www.wolterskluwer.com/en/expert-insights/the-future-of-generative-ai-in-healthcare-is-driven-by-consumer-trust

Figure 4.11 *Continued*

Table 4.9 *Summary of results for Scenario 2, Question 4*

Tool	Results and comments
Claude	Responses are provided under 12 headings, each with one to two subheadings, with easy-to-read text, followed by a summary, and a follow-up question; no citations
Copilot	Responses are provided under six headings, with easy-to-read text, followed by a summary and a follow-up question; no citations
Gemini	Responses are provided under five headings, each with one to two bullet points, easy-to-read text, followed by a summary; no citations
GPT-4o	Responses are provided under 10 headings, each with two bullet points, with easy-to-read text, followed by a summary; no citations
Perplexity AI	Responses are provided under eight headings, each with two bullet points, with easy-to-read text, followed by a summary; total eight citations

Scenario 3: Using Gen AI to investigate climate change

Results of the searches presented in Figure 4.12 (Scenario 3, Question 1), and Table 4.10, show that all the responses are quite detailed, but only two of the five chosen search tools, Copilot and Perplexity AI, provide citations for the information provided in the responses; and the number of citations provided by Perplexity AI is higher than those of Copilot. Overall, the outputs from Claude, GPT-4o and Perplexity AI are more detailed.

Search Tool	Result
Claude	The key climate change issues include: 1. Rising global temperatures: - Increasing average temperatures worldwide - More frequent and intense heatwaves ... 12. Feedback loops: - Self-reinforcing cycles that could accelerate warming (e.g., melting permafrost releasing methane)

Figure 4.12 *Examples of search results from Scenario 3, Question 1: What are the key climate change issues?*

Search Tool	Result
	These issues are interconnected and have wide-ranging impacts on the .... Would you like more information on any specific aspect of climate change?
Copilot	Climate change presents several critical challenges that impact our planet and society. Here are some of the key issues: 1.**Extreme Weather Events**: Increasingly frequent and severe weather events, such as hurricanes, floods, droughts, and heatwaves, are a direct consequence of climate change[1]. .... 6.**Food and Water Security**: Changes in climate patterns affect agricultural productivity and water availability, posing risks to food and water security[4]. Addressing these issues requires global cooperation and urgent action to reduce ... Is there a specific aspect of climate change you're particularly interested in?
Gemini	**Key Climate Change Issues** Climate change is a pressing global issue with far-reaching consequences. Here are some of the key areas of concern: **1. Global Warming:** • **Rising Temperatures:** The average global temperature has been steadily increasing due to the accumulation of greenhouse gases in the atmosphere. • ... **7. Health Impacts:** • **Heat-Related Illnesses:** Increased heat waves can lead to heat-related illnesses and deaths. .... These are just a few of the key climate change issues facing the ... ..sustainable future.
GPT-4o	Climate change is one of the most pressing global challenges today, affecting every aspect of life on Earth. The key issues related to climate change include: ### 1. **Global Warming** - **Rising Temperatures:** The Earth's average temperature is increasing due to the accumulation of greenhouse gases (GHGs) like carbon dioxide (CO2), methane (CH4), and .... ### 12. **Policy and Governance Challenges** - **International Cooperation:** Addressing climate change requires coordinated global action, which can be challenging due to differing national interests, economic priorities, and levels of development. .... ### Conclusion These climate change issues are interconnected, with each exacerbating the others. Addressing them requires urgent action at local, national, and global.. climate change.
Perplexity AI	Based on the search results, some of the key climate change issues include: 1. Rising global temperatures: The Earth has warmed by over 1°C since pre-industrial times, with 2015-2020 being the hottest years on record. Further warming is expected to have severe impacts. .... 10. Disproportionate impacts: Developing countries and vulnerable populations are likely to be hit hardest despite contributing least to emissions.

Figure 4.12 *Continued*

Search Tool	Result
	The key drivers are human activities like burning fossil fuels, deforestation, and ..... Citations: [1] https://www.who.int/news-room/fact-sheets/detail/climate-change-and-health ... [8] https://implementationscience.biomedcentral.com/articles/10.1186/s13012-024-01357-9

Figure 4.12 *Continued*

Table 4.10 *Summary of results for Scenario 3, Question 1*

Tool	Results and comments
Claude	Responses are provided under 12 headings, each with one to two subheadings, with easy-to-read text, followed by a summary; no citations
Copilot	Responses are provided under six headings, with easy-to-read text and citations, followed by a summary
Gemini	Responses are provided under seven headings, each with one to three bullet points, easy-to-read text, followed by a summary; no citations
GPT-4o	Responses are provided under 12 headings, each with two bullet points, with easy-to-read text, followed by a summary; no citations
Perplexity AI	Responses are provided under 10 headings, with easy-to-read text, followed by a summary; total eight citations

Results of the searches presented in Figure 4.13 (Scenario 3, Question 2), and Table 4.11, show that all the responses are quite detailed, but only two of the five chosen search tools, Copilot and Perplexity AI, provide citations for the information provided in the responses; and the number of citations provided by Perplexity AI is higher than that of Copilot. Overall, the outputs generated by Claude, GPT-4o and Perplexity AI are more detailed.

Search Tool	Result
Claude	As an individual, there are many ways you can contribute to addressing climate change issues: 1. Reduce energy consumption: - Use energy-efficient appliances - Turn off lights and electronics when not in use - Improve home insulation ... 12. Support climate-focused organizations: - Volunteer or donate to environmental groups Remember, while individual actions are important, collective efforts and ... Would you like more details on any of these suggestions?

Figure 4.13 *Examples of search results for Scenario 3, Question 2: As an individual, how can I contribute to the climate change issues?*

Search Tool	Result
Copilot	There are many ways you can contribute to addressing climate change as an individual. Here are some impactful actions you can take: **1.Reduce Energy Consumption**: Use energy-efficient appliances, switch to LED bulbs, and unplug devices when not in use. Consider using renewable energy sources like solar panels[1]. ... **7.Educate and Advocate**: Spread awareness about climate change and encourage others to take action. Participate in community initiatives and support environmental organizations[2]. Every small action adds up and can make a significant difference. By making ... change. Is there a specific area where you'd like more detailed advice or tips?
Gemini	**Here are some ways you can contribute to addressing climate change:** **Reduce Your Carbon Footprint:** • **Energy Efficiency:** Use energy-efficient appliances and light bulbs, and reduce energy consumption by turning off lights and electronics when not in use. .... **Support Sustainable Practices:** • **Choose Sustainable Products:** Buy products made from sustainable materials and support companies with environmentally friendly practices. .... **Advocate for Change:** • **Vote for Climate-Conscious Leaders:** Support politicians who prioritize addressing climate change. ..... **Make Lifestyle Changes:** • **Reduce Meat Consumption:** Eating less meat can significantly reduce your carbon footprint.... By taking these steps, you can contribute to a more sustainable future and help mitigate the impacts of climate change.
GPT-4o	As an individual, you can make meaningful contributions to addressing ... Here's how: ### 1. **Reduce Your Carbon Footprint:** - **Transportation:** Opt for public transportation, biking, walking, or carpooling. If possible, switch to an electric vehicle or use hybrid options. .... ### 6. **Personal Lifestyle Adjustments:** - **Minimalism:** Adopt a minimalist lifestyle by consuming less and focusing on experiences rather than material goods. - **Water Use:** Conserve water by fixing leaks, using water-efficient fixtures, and reducing overall consumption. By integrating these actions into your life, you can make a significant impact on ...
Perplexity AI	As an individual, there are several meaningful ways you can contribute to addressing climate change issues: 1. Reduce your carbon footprint: - Use energy-efficient appliances and lighting - .... 7. Consider your financial impact: - Invest in environmentally responsible companies/funds .... While individual actions may seem small, they can create a ripple effect by .. effectively.

Figure 4.13 *Continued*

Search Tool	Result
	Citations: [1] https://crowdsourcingsustainability.org/climate-change-can-one-person-really-make-a-difference/ ..... [8] https://www.who.int/health-topics/climate-change

Figure 4.13 *Continued*

Table 4.11 *Summary of results for Scenario 3, Question 2*

Tool	Results and comments
Claude	Responses are provided under 12 headings, each with two to three subheadings, with easy-to-read text, followed by a summary; no citations
Copilot	Responses are provided under seven headings, with easy-to-read text and citations, followed by a summary and a follow-up question
Gemini	Responses are provided under four headings, each with three bullet points, easy-to-read text, followed by a summary; no citations
GPT-4o	Responses are provided under six headings, each with two to four bullet points, with easy-to-read text, followed by a summary; no citations
Perplexity AI	Responses are provided under seven headings, with two to five subheadings, easy-to-read text, followed by a summary; total eight citations

Results of the searches presented in Figure 4.14 (Scenario 3, Question 3), and Table 4.12, show that only two of the five chosen search tools, viz. Copilot and Perplexity AI, provide citations for the information provided in the responses; and the number of citations provided by Perplexity AI is higher than that of Copilot. Outputs from Claude, GPT-4o and Perplexity AI are more detailed than the two other tools.

Search Tool	Result
Claude	A carbon footprint refers to the total amount of greenhouse gases, primarily carbon dioxide (CO2), emitted directly or indirectly .... Here's a breakdown of the concept: 1. Definition: - The total amount of CO2 and other greenhouse gases emitted due to human activities 2. Measurement: - Usually expressed in tonnes (or kilograms) of CO2 equivalent (CO2e) ... 8. Carbon offsetting: - Investing in projects that reduce or remove CO2 from the atmosphere to compensate for emissions Understanding your carbon footprint is a first step in taking action to reduce your .. Would you like more information on how to calculate or reduce your carbon footprint?

Figure 4.14 *Examples of search results for Scenario 3, Question 3: What is meant by carbon footprint?*

Search Tool	Result
Copilot	A **carbon footprint** refers to the total amount of greenhouse gases, particularly carbon dioxide (CO_2), that are emitted into the atmosphere as a result of the activities of an individual, organization, or community[12]. This includes emissions from ... such as: • **Transportation**: Cars, planes, and other vehicles. .... • ... • **Food Production**: Agriculture and food processing. The carbon footprint is usually measured in units of weight, such as tons of CO_2 equivalent per year[2]. Reducing your carbon footprint can help mitigate ... Would you like to know more about how to reduce your carbon footprint or any other related topic?
Gemini	Carbon footprint refers to the total amount of greenhouse gases, primarily carbon dioxide, produced directly or indirectly by an individual, organization, or country. It's a measure .. by human activities, such as burning fossil fuels for energy, transportation, and .... A high carbon footprint means that an individual or entity is contributing significantly to climate change, while a low carbon footprint indicates a reduced environmental impact. Would you like to know more about how to reduce your carbon footprint?
GPT-4o	A **carbon footprint** refers to the total amount of greenhouse gases (GHGs), particularly carbon dioxide (CO_2), that are emitted directly or indirectly by human ... ### Components of a Carbon Footprint: 1. **Direct Emissions:** - **Transportation:** Emissions from vehicles you use, such as cars, airplanes, or buses. This includes the fuel burned in personal cars, flights, and public transport. - **Home Energy Use:** Emissions from electricity, heating, and cooling in your .. .. 3. **Lifestyle Choices:** - **Diet:** The type of food you consume plays a significant role in your carbon footprint. For example, meat, especially beef, has a higher carbon footprint due to the resources required to raise livestock........... ### Why It Matters: Reducing your carbon footprint helps lower the amount of greenhouse gases released into the atmosphere, which is critical .... make more sustainable choices in your daily life.
Perplexity AI	A carbon footprint refers to the total amount of greenhouse gases, particularly carbon dioxide (CO_2) and methane (CH4), that are emitted directly or indirectly as a result .. ## Key Aspects of Carbon Footprint 1. **Measurement**: The carbon footprint quantifies the emissions associated with various activities, such as transportation, energy use, food consumption, and ... ... 5. **Global Context**: The average carbon footprint varies significantly by country and individual lifestyle. For example, residents of developed countries typically have .... By measuring and analyzing carbon footprints, individuals and organizations ...change.

Figure 4.14 *Continued*

Search Tool	Result
	Citations: [1] https://dictionary.cambridge.org/dictionary/english/carbon-footprint ... [8] https://crowdsourcingsustainability.org/climate-change-can-one-person-really-make-a-difference/

Figure 4.14 *Continued*

Table 4.12 *Summary of results for Scenario 3, Question 3*

Tool	Results and comments
Claude	Responses are provided under eight headings, each with one to three subheadings, with easy-to-read text, followed by a summary; no citations
Copilot	Responses are provided under two headings and four bullet points, with easy-to-read text and citations, followed by a summary and a follow-up question
Gemini	Responses are provided as easy-to-read but brief text; no citations
GPT-4o	Responses are provided under three headings, each with two subheadings, with easy-to-read text, followed by a summary; no citations
Perplexity AI	Responses are provided under five headings, with easy-to-read text, followed by a summary; total eight citations

Results of the searches presented in Figure 4.15 (Scenario 3, Question 4), and Table 4.13, show only two of the five chosen search tools, Copilot and Perplexity AI, provide citations for the information provided in the responses; and the number of citations provided by Perplexity AI is higher than that of Copilot. Output generated by GPT-4o also shows the formula for calculating carbon footprint; and results from Claude, Copilot and Perplexity AI are more detailed than the three other tools.

Search Tool	Result
Claude	Carbon footprint is measured through various methods, typically involving these steps: 1. Data collection: - Gather information on energy use, transportation, consumption habits, etc. ... 10. Limitations: - Accuracy can vary depending on the method and data available - Some indirect emissions can be challenging to quantify accurately For individuals, online calculators provide a good starting point for estimating ... Would you like information on specific calculators or more details on any aspect of ...?

Figure 4.15 *Examples of search results for Scenario 3, Question 4: How is it measured?*

Search Tool	Result
Copilot	A carbon footprint is measured by calculating the total amount of greenhouse gases (GHGs) emitted directly and indirectly by an individual, ... Here's how it's typically done: 1.Identify Emission Sources: Determine all the activities that produce GHGs. This includes direct emissions from burning fossil fuels (e.g., driving a car) and indirect emissions from the production of goods and services (e.g., manufacturing a product) [12]. .... 4.Sum Up Emissions: Add up the emissions from all sources to get the total carbon footprint. This is usually expressed in terms of carbon dioxide equivalent (CO_2e), which accounts for the different global warming potentials of various GHGs [12]. There are many online calculators and tools available that can help you ... Would you like to know more about how to reduce your carbon footprint or any ... topic?
Gemini	Carbon footprint is typically measured in units of carbon dioxide equivalents (CO2e). .. and other greenhouse gases are converted to CO2e based on their global warming .... Here are some of the main factors that contribute to your carbon footprint: • Energy consumption: The use of electricity, natural gas, and other fuels for heating, cooling, lighting, and appliances. • ... • Consumption of goods and services: The production and transportation of goods and services, such as food, clothing, and electronics. By calculating your carbon footprint, you can identify areas where you can make changes to reduce your environmental impact.
GPT-4o	A carbon footprint is measured by calculating the total greenhouse gas emissions (typically in units of carbon dioxide equivalent, or CO_2e) associated with ... several steps: ### 1. **Identify Sources of Emissions:** - **Direct Emissions:** These are emissions from sources directly controlled by the individual or organization, such as burning fossil fuels for heating or transportation. - **Indirect Emissions:** These include emissions from the production and .... ### Example Calculation: Suppose you drive 10,000 kilometers in a year, and your car consumes 8 liters of gasoline per 100 kilometers. Gasoline has an emission factor of about 2.31 kg CO_2 per liter. - **Calculation:** - Fuel used: \(10,000 \, \text{km} \times \frac{8 \, \text{liters}}{100 \, \text{km}} = 800 \, \text{liters} \) - CO_2 emissions: \(800 \, \text{liters} \times 2.31 \, \text{kg CO_2/liter} = 1,848 \, \text{kg CO_2} \) or 1.848 metric tons CO_2e. ... By accurately measuring your carbon footprint, you can identify high-. ... emissions.
Perplexity AI	Carbon footprint is typically measured in terms of carbon dioxide equivalent (CO2e) emissions. Here are the key aspects of how carbon footprints are measured:

Figure 4.15 *Continued*

Search Tool	Result
	1. Scope of emissions: - Scope 1: Direct emissions from owned or controlled sources - Scope 2: Indirect emissions from purchased electricity, steam, heating, and cooling - Scope 3: All other indirect emissions in a company's value chain 8. Verification: - Third-party verification can be used to ensure accuracy and credibility of carbon ... The choice of measurement method often depends on the entity being measured..... Citations: [1] https://www.carbonfootprint.com/docs/carbon_footprint_appraisal_-_methodology_document_v10.pdf ... [8] https://www.nationalgeographic.com/environment/article/what-is-a-carbon-footprint-how-to-measure-yours

Figure 4.15 *Continued*

Table 4.13 *Summary of results for Scenario 3, Question 4*

Tool	Results and comments
Claude	Responses are provided under 10 headings, each with one to three subheadings, with easy-to-read text, followed by a summary; no citations
Copilot	Responses are provided under four headings, with easy-to-read text and citations, followed by a summary and a follow-up question
Gemini	Responses are provided under four bullet points, brief but with easy-to-read text; no citations
GPT-4o	Responses are provided under eight headings, each with one to five subheadings, with easy-to-read text, followed by a summary; no citations
Perplexity AI	Responses are provided under eight headings, each with one to three subheadings and easy-to-read text, followed by a summary; total eight citations

Summary

The sample searches conducted on the 12 questions, based on three scenarios, show that all the chosen Gen AI tools provide some useful and easy-to-read summaries for each question, often under some useful headings or bullet points. However, only Copilot and Perplexity AI, in these examples, provide citations to support the generated content or summary; and in most cases, the results generated by Claude, GPT-4o and Perplexity AI are more detailed than the others.

It may be noted that Perplexity AI always provides more detailed citations. However, where citations are provided by the Gen AI tools, the quality and relevance of the cited items are not always the best for the specific user and search context. Where the outputs produced by the Gen AI tools do not include citations, it becomes difficult to judge the credibility and relevance of the information. There are some other challenges too. For example, as the examples of the search queries or prompts demonstrate, often the user may need to ask different or alternative questions or prompts to get the best search outcomes. More details of prompts, as well as the skills that the users need for using Gen AI tools for everyday life information seeking, are discussed in Chapters 6 and 7.

Everyday life information-seeking behaviour of people is determined by the values, attitudes and interests characteristic of their way of life; the relevance of different information sources and channels is evaluated on the basis of their familiarity and effectiveness in information use situations (Savolainen, 1995). In today's world, people are faced with a need to take care of their own health, for example by choosing a healthy lifestyle, healthy eating and regular exercises, but at the same time the media is filled with lay information on health issues (Chew and Khoo, 2016), and consequently it is often difficult for people to know where to find credible and relevant information. Therefore, users need some skills to assess the reliability of information produced by the Gen AI tools. The same applies to seeking information in other areas, for example on emerging topics of climate change or AI. Examples of the search results here clearly show that the Gen AI tools generate some useful results and summaries for everyday life information, but the users need some skills for formulating the questions or prompts and should also have to learn about the quality and reliability of information sources, but in many cases the sources are not cited. These issues, and their implications for the users, as well as for education, research and professional practices in information science, are discussed in Chapters 6–8.

CHAPTER 5

Gen AI for Scholarly Information

Introduction

This chapter discusses the results of a series of searches using some selected Gen AI tools for finding information based on some specific user needs in the context of scholarly information for teaching and learning in higher education. It is important to note that it is not a comparison of different Gen AI tools *per se*. By investigating what some emerging Gen AI tools return in response to specific questions and commands, and how suitable these responses are for specific user needs in the contexts of coursework in higher education, this chapter aims to add new knowledge and trigger further discussions and debates on how the interactions with these tools, and the corresponding search results, can be improved to meet specific user needs and contexts for education and learning activities.

The search context

The discussions in this chapter are based on the outcomes of two case studies involving interactions with seven Gen AI tools to find answers for four scenario-based search tasks within the specific coursework-related questions of university students. The scenarios are based on the typical search tasks for writing coursework essays for two undergraduate students. In order to mimic the typical interactions with the conversational AI tools, four natural language questions or prompts were created for each scenario. It should be noted that these four questions may not be exhaustive to generate all the information and data required for the search tasks and goals associated with each scenario and the search context. However, they show the variety of search results produced by the Gen AI tools used here. The scenarios, and the associated search tasks, questions and prompts, are shown in Table 5.1 on the next page.

Seven Gen AI-driven search tools, – Claude, Consensus, Copilot, Gemini, GPT-4o, Perplexity AI and Scholar GPT – were chosen for this study. Each of the eight questions or prompts (Table 5.1) was presented to all the chosen tools, and the corresponding results are noted.

Table 5.1 *Scenarios, search context and search questions/interactions*

Scenario and search topic	Search context	Questions/Interactions with the AI tool
1 Older people's use of the internet for digital government services in the UK	An undergraduate student is required to write an essay on the topic to discuss issues and challenges facing older people in their use of the internet for digital government services, with supporting data and research papers and relevant reports. The search task should produce some basic information on the topic; point out various issues and challenges; present some comparable data; and some research papers and reports supporting this.	1 What major challenges do older people in the UK face for using digital government services? 2 I am writing an essay on the above topic; so, can you suggest some research papers supporting this? 3 Can you suggest some more research papers on the digital exclusion of older people in the UK? 4 Can you suggest some research papers that compare the data between UK and Europe on digital exclusion for older people?
2 Relations between digital skills and work and employment of people in the UK and Europe	An undergraduate student is required to write an essay on how digital skills improve people's work, employment and income, with supporting data and research papers and relevant reports. The search task should produce some basic information on the topic of digital access/inclusion, digital skills and work and employment; some comparable data between UK and Europe; and some research papers and reports supporting the data and discussions.	1 How do digital skills improve people's work, employment and income? 2 Can you give me some supporting research literature on this? 3 How does the UK compare to other European countries in terms of digital inclusion? 4 Can you suggest some research papers that compare the impact of digital skills on the work and employment opportunities of people in the UK and Europe?

Search results

The outputs generated by the chosen Gen AI tools are discussed in this section. For some questions, only snippets of the outputs are produced, and for some questions/prompts, where the tool is asked to recommend research literature, the entire set of results/output is presented in tables.

Scenario 1: An undergraduate student looking for information for writing coursework

Figure 5.1 shows the snippets of some results. The overall outputs generated by the chosen tools for Scenario 1, Question 1 vary, e.g.:

- Results from Claude are presented under six headings, each describing a specific challenge. There is a summary highlighting how those challenges can be addressed; no citations are provided.
- Results from Consensus are presented under seven headings each with two bullet points; and there is a conclusion; no citations are provided.
- Results from Copilot are presented under five headings. The search results cite three sources (in response to the question on relevant research papers): Age UK, which is a charity working in this area; an article from BMC Public Health; and a conference paper.
- Results from Gemini are presented under four headings, each describing a specific challenge; no citations are provided.
- Results from GPT-4o are presented under six headings, each followed by two to three subheadings, each discussing specific challenges supported by citations, mainly from the UK government sites, followed by a conclusion discussing how those challenges may be addressed.
- Results from Perplexity AI are summarised under five headings, each supported by citations. Altogether five items are cited, four of which are from the UK government sites.
- Results from Scholar GPT are presented under seven major headings, each with two subheadings. This is followed by five points discussing how the challenges can be addressed, followed by a conclusion; no citations are provided.

Tool	Result
Claude	Older people in the UK often face several challenges when it comes to using digital government services. Here are some of the major challenges: 1. Digital literacy and skills gap: Many older adults lack the necessary digital skills and knowledge to navigate .... 6. Limited support and training: Inadequate access to training programs, ... To address these challenges, it is crucial for government agencies to prioritize digital inclusion ... options remain available for those who cannot .....

Figure 5.1 *Snippets of search results for Scenario 1, Question 1*

Tool	Result
Consensus	Older people in the UK face several challenges when using digital government services, which can hinder their ability to fully engage with these platforms. These challenges include: ### 1. **Digital Literacy and Skills** - **Limited Digital Skills**: Many older adults have limited experience with digital technologies, making it difficult for them to navigate online services. .... ### 7. **Cultural and Attitudinal Barriers** - **Resistance to Change**: Some older adults may be resistant to change, preferring traditional methods of .... ### Conclusion Older people in the UK face a range of challenges when using digital government services, .. training programs to ensure that older adults can fully benefit from digital services.
Copilot	**Older people in the UK** face several challenges when it comes to using digital government services. Let's delve into some of these difficulties: 2 **Digital Exclusion**: Although many older individuals fully embrace the digital world, **digital exclusion** increases with age and disability. Approximately **2.7 million people aged 65 and above** in the UK do not use the internet at all, equivalent to around **one in five** of this age group[1]. .... 3 **Equality Considerations**: Digital exclusion disproportionately affects .... Ensuring that everyone can choose to access and use public services offline (by phone, letter, or face-to-face) would end discrimination against those who are not digitally savvy[1]. In summary, while digitalization offers convenience... left behind. Councils need to strike a balance by providing accessible digital services while also offering robust offline alternatives for those who need them[2][1].
Gemini	Older people in the UK face several challenges when using digital government services: • **Digital Literacy and Skills Gap:** Many older adults lack the basic digital skills needed to navigate government websites, complete... .... • **Lack of Access to Technology:** Not all older adults have access to a computer or reliable internet connection, which is essential for using online government services. These challenges can lead to social exclusion and hinder older people's ability to access essential government services.
GPT-4o	Older people in the UK face several major challenges when using digital government services. These challenges can be broadly categorized into ... .. **Digital Literacy and Skills**: **Lack of Digital Skills**: Many older adults have not had the same exposure to .. .... **Economic Factors**: **Financial Constraints**: Older adults, especially those on fixed incomes, may find it difficult to afford the necessary technology and internet services. Addressing these challenges requires a multifaceted approach that includes ... to assist older adults in navigating digital government services.

Figure 5.1 *Continued*

Tool	Result
Perplexity AI	Older people in the UK often face several challenges when using digital government services: 1. Digital Literacy and Skills Gap: Many older adults lack the necessary digital skills and confidence to navigate .. digital government offerings. [1] .... 5. Preference for Traditional Methods: Some older adults may simply prefer traditional methods of accessing ... [1] To address these challenges, the UK government has recognized the importance of providing ..... services are ... [2] Citations: [1] https://granicus.com/dictionary/digital-government-services/ ...... [5] https://www.gov.uk/government/organisations/government-digital-service
Scholar GPT	Answer Older people in the UK face several major challenges when using digital government services. These challenges can be broadly categorized into the following areas: ### 1. **Digital Literacy and Skills** - **Lack of Digital Skills**: Many older adults may not have the necessary skills to navigate digital ... ### 7. **Support and Assistance** - **Lack of Assistance**: Limited availability of in-person or over-the-phone assistance to help older adults ... ### Addressing These Challenges #### 1. **Digital Literacy Programs** - Implementing comprehensive digital literacy programs specifically tailored for older adults to improve their ..... #### 2. **Accessible Design** - ... ### Conclusion By addressing these challenges through targeted interventions and support systems, older people in the UK can be better equipped to utilize digital government services, leading to greater inclusion and improved access to essential services.

Figure 5.1 *Continued*

Figure 5.2 (Scenario 1 Question 2) on the next page shows that the results vary significantly, e.g.:

- Claude recommends five items, each with a summary of the key points that the item covers with citations. Altogether five items are cited – two of these are research papers, and three are reports/documents from the websites of relevant NGOs/charities like ageuk.org.uk. It concludes with a summary.
- Consensus recommends five items – each with the title, authors and a link to the cited item. There is also a summary.
- Copilot recommends four items, each under a specific heading with brief information about the key content of the item, two of which are scholarly information sources, and two are from a charity like AgeUK.

- Gemini recommends five items under five headings, each with a supported citation. The cited items are mixed: some are scholarly papers, and the others from a charity like AgeUK.
- GPT-4o recommends items under seven headings supported by citations to the relevant items in Biomed Central, Oxford University Press, Frontiers in Computer Science and Gov.UK.
- Perplexity AI provide five headings highlighting five key challenges followed by five points discussing how to address those challenges, each supported by one or more citations. Altogether five items are cited – two of these are research papers, and three are reports/documents from the websites of relevant NGOs/charities like ageuk.org.uk.
- Scholar GPT recommends five example articles and reports, followed by advice on where to find them. The output also provides a strategy for how to find more relevant research papers and reports.

Tool	Result
Claude	Here are some relevant research papers that support the challenges faced by older adults in the UK when using digital government services: 1. 'Digital Exclusion in the UK' by the Age UK charity (2021): - This report highlights the digital divide affecting older adults in the UK, with 51% of those aged 75+ not using the internet. - It cites lack of skills, access, and motivation as key barriers to digital inclusion. 2. 'Digital Skills and Inclusion in Health and Care' by the Good Things Foundation (2021): - This study found that 22% of those aged 65+ in the UK lack basic digital skills, impacting their ability to access online health and government services. - It recommends providing targeted support and training for older adults. 3. 'Exploring Digital Exclusion in the UK' by the Royal Society of Public Health (2020): - This report identified older age, low income, and disability as risk factors for digital exclusion. - It found that digitally excluded individuals face barriers in accessing essential services, including government services. 4. 'Older Adults' Access to Digital Services: A Human Rights Perspective' by the Scottish Human Rights Commission (2019): - This report examines the human rights implications of digital exclusion for older adults in Scotland. - It highlights the need for accessible and inclusive digital services to ensure equal access to public services. 5. 'Digital Inclusion in Later Life: Cohort Changes and the Prospects for Digital Learning' by the Centre for Ageing Better (2018): - This study examined the digital skills and engagement of different age cohorts in the UK. - It found that older cohorts are less likely to engage with digital technologies, posing challenges for accessing digital services.

Figure 5.2 *(Scenario 1 Question 2): I am writing an essay on the above topic; so, can you suggest some research papers supporting this topic?*

Tool	Result
	These research papers provide evidence-based insights into the digital divide affecting older adults in the UK, the barriers they face in using digital government services, and recommendations for promoting digital inclusion and accessibility.
Consensus	Here are some research papers that explore the challenges faced by older people in the UK when using digital government services: 1. **Digital Circles of Support: Meeting the Information Needs of Older People** - **Authors**: M. Godfrey, O. Johnson - **Abstract**: This paper discusses the information needs of older people and how digital support networks can help meet these needs. It emphasizes the importance of social contacts and trust, facilitated by technology-literate mediators, in improving older adults' access to digital services. - [Link to Paper](https://consensus.app/papers/digital-circles-support-meeting-information-needs-people-godfrey/d2ca0606a78e5331b48918e4d48e89fd/?utm_source=chatgpt) 2. **It Could Be Useful, but Not for Me at the Moment: Older People, Internet Access, and E-Public Service Provision** - **Author**: Maria Sourbati - **Abstract**: This study focuses on the barriers older people face in accessing internet-based public services. It highlights the need for user-centered e-service provision that considers the diverse needs and preferences of older adults. - [Link to Paper](https://consensus.app/papers/could-moment-people-access-service-provision-sourbati/9643e5b99dfb56208b3a51fe131d192f/?utm_source=chatgpt) 3. **Older People and Technology: Time to Smarten Up Our Act** - **Authors**: H. Ahmed, Iqraa Haq, Ammar Rahman, E. Tonner, Rami Abbass, Faraz Sharif, S. Asinger, M. Sbai - **Abstract**: This paper discusses the potential benefits of digital healthcare technologies for older people in the UK, emphasizing the need for thoughtful design and support to ensure that older adults can effectively use these technologies. - [Link to Paper](https://consensus.app/papers/people-technology-time-smarten-ahmed/04973232407f5521871bbb2af9f2f3a2/?utm_source=chatgpt) 4. **Towards Digital Inclusion: Engaging Older People in the 'Digital World'** - **Authors**: C. Olphert, L. Damodaran, A. May - **Abstract**: This paper examines the barriers to digital inclusion for older people in the UK, such as cost, skills, and disability. It also explores strategies to improve digital engagement among older adults. - [Link to Paper](https://consensus.app/papers/towards-inclusion-engaging-people-world-olphert/63bb52d8921d55b98c9fd396dcffc459/?utm_source=chatgpt) 5. **The Role of Age and Digital Competence on the Use of Online Health and Social Care Services** - **Authors**: T. Heponiemi, A. Kaihlanen, A. Kouvonen, L. Leemann, S. Taipale, K. Gluschkoff - **Abstract**: This study investigates how age and digital competence affect the use of online health and social care services, highlighting the risk of digital exclusion among older adults.

Figure 5.2 *Continued*

Tool	Result
	- [Link to Paper](https://consensus.app/papers/role-competence-online-health-care-services-heponiemi/b86f5967968d5701b441791d9b3d22db/?utm_source=chatgpt) These papers provide valuable insights into the various challenges that older adults in the UK face when using digital government services, ranging from digital literacy and access issues to the need for user-friendly design and support systems.
Copilot	Certainly! Here are some research papers and reports that can support your essay on the challenges older people in the UK face when using digital government services: 3 **Age UK Report**: This report discusses the struggles of older people in accessing local public services in an increasingly digital world. It highlights the difficulties faced by those who are not 'computer savvy' in applying for a Blue Badge and other local public services[1]. 4 **Barriers and Facilitators to the Use of E-health by Older Adults**: A scoping review published in BMC Public Health that explores how and why older adults engage with e-health services, and the factors that impact this. It identifies barriers such as lack of self-efficacy and knowledge, and facilitators like active engagement in design and delivery of e-health programs[2]. 5 **Digital Inclusion Evidence Review 2018 - Age UK**: This evidence review addresses the gaps in research regarding older people's use of digital technology, including the challenges they face and how digital interfaces can be improved for the older user experience[3]. 6 **Digital Inclusion and the Elderly: The Case of Online Banking**: This paper surveys a group of elderly users to identify issues that prevent them from engaging with digital technology, focusing on the challenges faced by the older generation in the digital world[4]. These resources should provide a solid foundation for your essay, offering both qualitative and quantitative insights into the topic. Good luck with your writing! 📝📚 Learn more 1 ageuk.org.uk 2 bmcpublichealth.biomedcentral.com 3 ageuk.org.uk 4 lrec-conf.org
Gemini	Absolutely, your essay on the challenges older people face with digital government services will benefit from these research papers: • **'Older people's access to digitalised services' (ARC GM):** This briefing note by the Applied Research Collaboration Greater Manchester provides a concise overview of the digital divide and how it impacts older adults' access to government services. It highlights factors like internet access, affordability, and low digital literacy [PDF document on ARC Greater Manchester website]. • **"Tackling the Digital Divide among Elderly in the UK' (LSE):** This paper takes a theoretical approach, analyzing the challenges through the lens of Activity Theory and Installation Theory. It delves into the user journey of older adults and explores solutions to bridge the digital gap [LSE website]. • **"Towards understanding E-Government with older people and designing an inclusive platform with them' (ResearchGate):** This research focuses on designing user-friendly e-government platforms specifically for older adults. It emphasizes the importance of involving them in the design process and highlights common usability barriers they encounter [ResearchGate website].

Figure 5.2 *Continued*

Tool	Result
	Here are some additional resources you might find helpful: • **Age UK:** Age UK is a leading charity in the UK that advocates for older people. Their website has a wealth of information on digital inclusion and the challenges older adults face accessing government services online [Age UK website]. • **The Centre for Ageing Better:** This organization works to improve the lives of older people in the UK. Their website might have reports or articles related to digital inclusion [Centre for Ageing Better website]. Remember to check the publication dates of the research papers to ensure you're using the most current information available.
GPT-4o	Searched 5 sites When writing your essay on the challenges older people in the UK face when using digital government services, you can reference several research papers and reports that detail these issues extensively. Here are some key sources and findings: **2 Digital Literacy and Skills**: Many older adults lack the necessary digital skills and confidence to use online services. According to a scoping review in BMC Public Health, intrinsic barriers such as physical and sensory limitations, lack of motivation, and perceived self-efficacy significantly impact older adults' ability to use digital platforms. Additionally, extrinsic barriers like inexperience with digital technology exacerbate these challenges (BioMed Central). **3 Access to Technology**: A report by Age UK highlights that nearly two million people over 75 in England remain digitally excluded due to lack of access to technology and the internet. This digital divide prevents many older adults from engaging with online government services (BioMed Central). **4 Design and Usability**: The Government Digital Inclusion Strategy emphasizes the need for government digital services to be designed with user capabilities in mind. Simplifying interfaces and ensuring they are accessible to those with limited digital skills is crucial. The strategy outlines actions to integrate digital inclusion into broader government policies and programs (Gov UK). **5 Privacy and Security Concerns**: Concerns about privacy and security are significant deterrents for older adults using digital services. The BMC Public Health review also notes that privacy and trust issues, alongside fears of data misuse, are common among older users (BioMed Central). **6 Physical and Cognitive Limitations**: The physical and cognitive decline associated with aging, such as poor vision, hearing loss, and reduced dexterity, make it difficult for older adults to interact with digital devices. These limitations necessitate more user-friendly designs and support systems (Frontiers). **7 Support and Assistance**: Effective support systems are critical for helping older adults use digital services. Initiatives like Age UK's Digital Champion Programme aim to provide training and support to improve digital skills among older people. This program recruits volunteers to assist older adults in becoming more comfortable with technology (BioMed Central) (Oxford Academic).

Figure 5.2 *Continued*

Tool	Result
	8 Social Influences and Encouragement: Social support and encouragement play a significant role in older adults' adoption of digital technologies. Studies have shown that when older adults have access to supportive networks, they are more likely to engage with and use digital services (BioMed Central). By citing these sources, you can provide a comprehensive overview of the multifaceted challenges older adults face in accessing digital government services in the UK. This approach will help underscore the importance of targeted interventions and support systems to bridge the digital divide.
Perplexity AI	Older adults in the UK often face several challenges when accessing and using digital government services, as highlighted in the provided research papers: 1. Digital Literacy and Skills Gap: Many older adults lack the necessary digital skills and confidence to navigate online platforms effectively. This digital divide can make it difficult for them to access digital government services. [1][2] 2. Accessibility Issues: Some digital government services may not be designed with accessibility in mind, posing challenges for those with disabilities or impairments like vision or hearing loss, limited mobility, or cognitive decline. [1][5] 3. Lack of Access to Technology: A significant portion of older adults, particularly those with lower incomes or living in rural areas, may not have access to reliable internet connections, computers, or other devices required to access digital services. [1][2] 4. Trust and Security Concerns: Older individuals may have concerns about the security and privacy of their personal information when using online services, deterring them from adopting digital government offerings. [1] 5. Preference for Traditional Methods: Some older adults may prefer traditional methods of accessing services, such as in person visits or paper-based forms, due to familiarity or habit. [1][4] To address these challenges, the research papers suggest: - Providing assisted digital support and improving accessibility standards for digital government services. [1][2][3] - Offering alternative channels for accessing services, such as non-digital options. [3][4] - Embedding digital support within other community services and public services. [3] - Measuring success by attainment of non-digital outcomes rather than just digital skills. [3] - Developing more nuanced strategies for engagement and delivery that recognize individual circumstances and perceptions. [3] Overall, the research highlights the need for a more inclusive and accessible approach to digital government services, considering the diverse needs and preferences of older adults. Continued efforts are required to bridge the digital divide and ensure equitable access to essential services. Citations: [1] www.sciencedirect.com/science/article/abs/pii/S0740624X2100085X [2] www.ageuk.org.uk/globalassets/age-uk/documents/reports-and-publications/age_uk_digital_inclusion_evidence_review_2018.pdf [3] https://ageing-better.org.uk/sites/default/files/2018-06/The-digital-age.pdf

Figure 5.2 *Continued*

Tool	**Result**
	[4] www.ageuk.org.uk/latest-press/articles/2023/age-uk-research-finds-many-older-people-are-struggling-to-access-local-public-services-in-an-increasingly-digital-world/ [5] www.researchgate.net/publication/293822696_Towards_understanding_E-Government_with_older_people_and_designing_an_inclusive_platform_with_them
Scholar GPT	Scholar GPT wants to talk to actions.sider.ai **Consented** **Answer** I encountered an issue while trying to retrieve specific research papers. However, I can suggest some steps and sources to find relevant research papers on the challenges older people face in using digital government services in the UK: ### Suggested Sources and Search Strategies 1. **Google Scholar**: - Use search queries like 'challenges older people face using digital government services UK' or 'digital literacy barriers for elderly in UK government services.' 2. **University Libraries**: - Access databases such as JSTOR, PubMed, and IEEE Xplore through your institution's library. Use search terms similar to those suggested for Google Scholar. 3. **Professional Organizations and Conferences**: - Check publications and proceedings from organizations like the British Society of Gerontology or conferences on digital inclusion and public policy. 4. **Government and NGO Reports**: - Look for reports from UK government agencies, non-profits, and research institutions focusing on digital inclusion and aging populations. ### Example Articles and Reports 1. **Digital Exclusion of Older Adults: Insights from a National Survey in the UK** - Focuses on the extent of digital exclusion among older adults and its implications. - Available through journals on social inclusion or gerontology. 2. **Barriers to Online Public Services for Older People in the UK** - Examines specific barriers faced by older adults when accessing online public services. - Available in public policy and administration journals. 3. **The Role of Digital Literacy in the Use of E-Government Services by Older Adults** - Discusses the importance of digital literacy and proposes interventions to improve access. - Available in journals on information systems and digital literacy. 4. **Ageing and the Digital Divide: Insights from UK Data** - Explores the digital divide and its impact on older adults in accessing online services. - Available in journals on social policy and gerontology. 5. **Evaluating the Effectiveness of Digital Inclusion Programs for Older Adults in the UK** - Analyzes the effectiveness of various programs aimed at improving digital inclusion for the elderly. - Available in journals on social work and public health.

Figure 5.2 *Continued*

Tool	Result
	### How to Access These Articles 1. **Google Scholar**: [Google Scholar](https://scholar.google.com) 2. **JSTOR**: [JSTOR](www.jstor.org) 3. **PubMed**: [PubMed](https://pubmed.ncbi.nlm.nih.gov) 4. **IEEE Xplore**: [IEEE Xplore](https://ieeexplore.ieee.org) ### Additional Tips - **Check References**: Once you find a relevant paper, check its references for additional sources. - **Use Citation Tools**: Tools like Zotero or EndNote can help manage and format your references. By following these strategies and utilizing these sources, you should be able to find comprehensive research papers to support your essay on the challenges older people face in using digital government services in the UK. If you need further assistance or specific articles, feel free to ask!

Figure 5.2 *Continued*

In Figure 5.3 opposite, outputs generated for Scenario 1, Question 3 show that:

- Claude recommends five journal articles, each with the title, author and date of publication followed by a summary of the key points or focus of the given study. However, finding the items, with the citation data provided, seemed somewhat difficult.
- Consensus recommends five items, each under a specific heading with brief details of the content and a link to the cited item.
- Gemini recommends three items, each with brief details of the content and a link. It also provides a summary and some guidelines on how to find the relevant items.
- Copilot recommends five items under specific headings. The cited sources are: Ofcom.org.uk; ageuk.org.uk, BMC Geriatrics journal (bmcgeriatr.pubmedcentral.com), Citizensonline.org.uk, and Noisolation.com.
- Perplexity AI recommends five items with a summary and citations: two of these are reports from AgeUK (ageuk.org.uk), one is a report from Ofcom (Ofcom.org.uk), and one refers to a report from a university research institute. Interestingly one citation leads to coursework submitted at a university, and is not a peer-reviewed item.
- GPT-4o recommends five items under five headings. Four of the cited items are from BioMedCentral, and one from the Mental health Foundation.
- Scholar GPT recommends nine items with a brief description of the key points followed by a link to the document.

Tool	Result
Claude	Certainly, here are some additional research papers that focus specifically on the digital exclusion of older people in the UK: 1. 'Digital Exclusion Among the Elderly: A Qualitative Study of Internet Non-Users in the UK' by Tsai et al. (2019), published in the Journal of Consumer Policy. - This qualitative study explores the reasons behind non-use of the internet among older adults in the UK, identifying factors such as lack of interest, skills, and perceived benefits. 2. 'Older People and Digital Disengagement: A Fourth Digital Divide?' by Olphert and Damodaran (2013), published in Gerontology. - The paper examines the phenomenon of digital disengagement among older adults who have access to digital technologies but choose not to use them, highlighting the role of attitudes and motivations. 3. 'Digital Inclusion and Older People: How Those That Help Older Citizens Use Digital Skills Say We Could Do Better' by Righi et al. (2017), published in the Journal of Enabling Technologies. - This study explores the perspectives of professionals and volunteers working with older adults, identifying challenges and strategies for promoting digital inclusion. 4. 'Digital Exclusion in the Context of Silver Surfers: A Literature Review' by Ferri et al. (2020), published in the Journal of Medical Internet Research Aging. - This literature review synthesizes research on the digital exclusion of older adults, highlighting factors such as age, education, and socioeconomic status. 5. 'Exploring Digital Exclusion Among Older Adults in England: From Access to Digital Engagement' by Yates et al. (2022), published in the International Journal of Environmental Research and Public Health. - This study examines the different levels of digital exclusion among older adults in England, ranging from lack of access to lack of digital engagement, and explores the underlying factors. These research papers provide in-depth analyses of the digital exclusion experienced by older adults in the UK, offering insights into the causes, consequences, and potential solutions to this issue.
Consensus	Here are some additional research papers that explore the digital exclusion of older people in the UK: 1. **Older Adults' Perceived Sense of Social Exclusion from the Digital World** - **Authors**: A. Seifert, Matthias Hofer, Jörg Rössel - **Abstract**: This paper examines the social exclusion of older adults from the digital world, analyzing how lower levels of internet use among older people can lead to a perceived sense of social exclusion. - [Link to Paper](https://consensus.app/papers/adults-perceived-exclusion-world-seifert/c94c15b70ed958b3b9b6e335a16cd910/?utm_source=chatgpt) 2. **A Double Burden of Exclusion? Digital and Social Exclusion of Older Adults in Times of COVID-19** - **Authors**: A. Seifert, S. Cotten, Bo Xie - **Abstract**: This paper discusses the dual burden of digital and social exclusion faced by older adults, especially during the COVID-19 pandemic, and provides recommendations to address this issue. - [Link to Paper](https://consensus.app/papers/double-burden-exclusion-digital-social-exclusion-older-seifert/23462e093bca55529a957f646513c3f9/?utm_source=chatgpt)

Figure 5.3 *(Scenario 1, Question 3): Can you suggest some more research papers on the digital exclusion of older people in the UK?*

Tool	Result
	3. **Digital Exclusion Despite Digital Accessibility: Empirical Evidence from an English City** - **Authors**: Sabrina Bunyan, A. Collins - **Abstract**: This study investigates the socio-economic determinants of digital exclusion within Portsmouth, UK, highlighting the factors that contribute to digital exclusion despite access to digital infrastructure. - [Link to Paper](https://consensus.app/papers/digital-exclusion-despite-digital-accessibility-bunyan/088429c013c85258ad95a526f59870bf/?utm_source=chatgpt) 4. **Strategies for Teaching Older People to Use the World Wide Web** - **Authors**: A. Dickinson, R. Eisma, P. Gregor, A. Syme, Scott Milne - **Abstract**: This paper discusses strategies for teaching older adults how to use the internet, with a focus on overcoming barriers to digital inclusion through simplified interfaces and targeted training programs. - [Link to Paper](https://consensus.app/papers/strategies-teaching-people-world-wide-dickinson/d0f558e32c7654578c8ceb503e3b7f9c/?utm_source=chatgpt) 5. **Older People and Digital Disengagement: A Fourth Digital Divide?** - **Authors**: Wendy Olphert, L. Damodaran - **Abstract**: This paper explores the phenomenon of digital disengagement among older adults, which the authors term a 'fourth digital divide,' and examines its implications for social inclusion. - [Link to Paper](https://consensus.app/papers/people-digital-disengagement-fourth-digital-divide-olphert/4a78ba7c16cb5c83bda7d143e3c97eb4/?utm_source=chatgpt) These papers provide valuable insights into the factors contributing to the digital exclusion of older adults in the UK, as well as potential strategies to address these challenges.
Copilot	Certainly! Here are additional research papers and resources that delve into the issue of digital exclusion among older people in the UK: 1 **Digital Exclusion Review by Ofcom**: This report provides an overview of Ofcom's research on digital exclusion among adults in the UK, including the impact of the Covid-19 pandemic and the factors contributing to digital exclusion[1]. 2 **Digital Exclusion and Cognitive Impairment in Older People**: A study published in BMC Geriatrics that investigates the relationship between digital exclusion and cognitive impairment in older adults across 23 countries, including the UK[2]. 3 **Research on Digital Exclusion During the Pandemic**: This research focuses on digitally excluded people aged 50–70 and examines how digital support delivery changed during the pandemic[3]. 4 **Age UK Briefing Paper**: This briefing presents data from the English Longitudinal Study of Ageing (ELSA) Covid-19 Substudy, which looks at the impact of the pandemic on internet use among people aged 52+ in England[4]. 5 **Digital Exclusion Report by No Isolation**: This report reveals how touchscreen technology may be difficult for older people to use due to health barriers, contributing to digital exclusion[5]. These papers and reports should provide a comprehensive view of the challenges faced by older people in the UK regarding digital exclusion and its implications. They will be valuable for your essay to understand the scope and depth of the issue. 📖🔍 Learn more 1 ofcom.org.uk 2 bmcgeriatr.biomedcentral.com 3 citizensonline.org.uk 4 ageuk.org.uk 5 d1h06bsnqv2xsg.cloudfront.net+2 more

Figure 5.3 *Continued*

Tool	Result
Gemini	Sure, here are some additional research papers on the digital exclusion of older people in the UK, focusing on various aspects of the issue: • **'A rapid review of the effectiveness of interventions for addressing digital exclusion in older adults' (Health and Care Research Wales Evidence Centre):** This paper focuses on the effectiveness of various interventions designed to help older adults overcome digital exclusion. It reviews existing research on training programs, technology adaptations, and other support methods [website of Health and Care Research Wales Evidence Centre]. • **'An in-depth study of digital inclusion projects for older people living with, or at risk, of social isolation and loneliness' (The National Lottery Community Fund):** This report explores the link between digital exclusion and social isolation in older adults. It examines different digital inclusion projects and their impact on reducing social isolation [website of The National Lottery Community Fund]. • **'Digital Inclusion and Financial Well-being in Later Life' (University of Strathclyde):** This research paper investigates how digital exclusion can affect older adults' financial well-being. It explores the challenges they face in accessing online banking services and managing finances digitally [University of Strathclyde website]. By incorporating these papers, you can broaden the scope of your essay to address not only access to government services but also the wider social and financial implications of digital exclusion for older people in the UK. Here are some additional tips for finding relevant research papers: • **Use academic databases:** Search for relevant keywords in databases like Google Scholar, JSTOR, or ScienceDirect. • **Check reference lists:** Look at the reference lists of the papers you've already found to see if they cite any other relevant research. • **Search by author:** If you find a researcher whose work interests you, search for their other publications on digital exclusion in older adults.
GPT-4o	Searched 3 sites Here are some additional research papers and reports that explore the digital exclusion of older people in the UK, which you can reference for your essay: 1 **'Digital Exclusion and Cognitive Impairment in Older People'**: This study published in BMC Geriatrics investigates the relationship between digital exclusion and cognitive impairment among older adults. It highlights how lack of internet use can be linked to poorer cognitive functions, emphasizing the need for accessible digital literacy programs for the elderly (BioMed Central). 2 **'Digital Exclusion in Later Life: A Narrative Review'**: This review in Springer discusses how multiple inequalities, including age, exacerbate digital exclusion. It explores various barriers faced by older adults, such as accessibility issues and the complexity of digital interfaces, and suggests that these challenges can widen existing social inequalities (BioMed Central). 3 **Age UK's 'Digital Inclusion Evidence Review 2018'**: This comprehensive report from Age UK provides statistics and analysis on the digital divide among older people in the UK. It identifies key barriers to digital inclusion, such as affordability, lack of skills, and motivational issues, and suggests various interventions to address these problems (BioMed Central).

Figure 5.3 *Continued*

Tool	Result
	4 Mental Health Foundation's Report on Tackling Digital Exclusion: This report examines the impact of the COVID-19 pandemic on digital exclusion among older adults. It discusses the heightened sense of isolation due to lack of digital connectivity and emphasizes the importance of tailored training and support programs to bridge this gap (Mental Health Foundation). **5 'Ensuring Digital Inclusion'**: Published in ScienceDirect, this article discusses the broader societal impacts of digital exclusion among older adults. It covers the role of socio-economic factors and the importance of inclusive policies to ensure that older people are not left behind in the digital age (BioMed Central). These sources provide a comprehensive overview of the various dimensions of digital exclusion faced by older adults in the UK, from cognitive and physical barriers to socio-economic and motivational challenges. They also offer insights into potential solutions and interventions to promote digital inclusion among the elderly.
Perplexity AI	Here are some additional research papers that provide insights into the digital exclusion of older people in the UK: 1. 'Digital Exclusion in the COVID-19 Era: Implications for Older People' by Minocha et al. (2021) [1][2] This paper examines the impact of the COVID-19 pandemic on digital exclusion among older adults, highlighting the challenges they faced in accessing essential services and information online. 2. 'Exploring Digital Exclusion in Older Age' by Olphert and Damodaran (2013) [2][3] This study investigates the factors contributing to digital exclusion among older adults, such as lack of skills, motivation, and access to technology, and suggests strategies to promote digital inclusion. 3. 'Digital Inclusion and Older People: A Review of the Literature' by Friemel (2016) [2][4] This literature review provides a comprehensive overview of the research on digital inclusion and exclusion among older adults, identifying key barriers and potential solutions. 4. 'Digital Exclusion and Implications for Older People's Health and Well-being' by Hunsaker and Hargittai (2018) [4][5] This paper explores the relationship between digital exclusion and the health and well-being of older adults, highlighting the importance of digital literacy and access to online health resources. 5. 'Overcoming Digital Exclusion in Later Life: A Theory of Cognitive Barriers and Support Strategies' by Sayago et al. (2020) [5] This study proposes a theoretical framework for understanding the cognitive barriers faced by older adults in adopting digital technologies and suggests support strategies to facilitate their digital inclusion. These research papers provide valuable insights into the various dimensions of digital exclusion among older adults in the UK, including the underlying factors, consequences, and potential solutions. They can serve as useful references for your essay on this topic. Citations: [1] www.ageuk.org.uk/globalassets/age-uk/documents/reports-and-publications/reports-and-briefings/active-communities/policy-briefing---facts-and-figures-about-digital-inclusion-and-older-people.pdf [2] www.ageuk.org.uk/globalassets/age-uk/documents/reports-and-publications/age_uk_digital_inclusion_evidence_review_2018.pdf

Figure 5.3 *Continued*

Tool	Result
	[3] www.lse.ac.uk/PBS/assets/documents/PEL-coursework/2021-2022/PB403-Psychology-of-Economic-Life-Summative-coursework-2021-2022-Group6.pdf [4] www.ofcom.org.uk/__data/assets/pdf_file/0022/234364/digital-exclusion-review-2022.pdf [5] https://arc-gm.nihr.ac.uk/media/page-images/ARC/Healthy%20Ageing/DI%20Briefing%20Note%2006%20Jan%202022.pdf
Scholar GPT	Here are some recent research papers and articles addressing the digital exclusion of older people in the UK: 1. **'Bridging the Digital Divide in Ethnic Minority Older Adults'** - Focuses on the digital exclusion among ethnic minority older adults in the UK. - Available on Springer. - [Link to article](https://link.springer.com/article/10.1007/s10796-021-10126-8) 2. **'A rapid review of the effectiveness of interventions for addressing digital exclusion in older adults'** - Reviews the effectiveness of various interventions aimed at reducing digital exclusion among older adults. - Available on MedRxiv. - [Link to article](www.medrxiv.org/content/10.1101/2024.03.21.24304670v2) 3. **'Older people's access to digitalised services'** - Discusses issues of digital and technological exclusion for older people in the UK. - Available on ARC GM. - [Link to PDF](https://arc-gm.nihr.ac.uk/media/page-images/ARC/Healthy%20Ageing/DI%20Briefing%20Note%2006%20Jan%202022.pdf) 4. **'BRIDGING THE GAP - EXPLORING ELDERLY CITIZENS'** - Explores digital exclusion among elderly citizens and proposes solutions. - Available on DiVA Portal. - [Link to PDF](www.diva-portal.org/smash/get/diva2:1317500/FULLTEXT01.pdf) 5. **'Low digital skills households and the path to digital inclusion'** - Examines the reality of digital exclusion and outlines pathways to digital inclusion. - Available on AbilityNet. - [Link to article](https://abilitynet.org.uk/free-tech-support-and-info/low-digital-skills-households-and-path-digital-inclusion) 6. **'Digital exclusion amongst older people - ArcGIS StoryMaps'** - Provides an overview of digital exclusion among older people, with research by ONS. - Available on ArcGIS StoryMaps. - [Link to article](https://storymaps.arcgis.com/stories/9f8978f9b6184d28895c8d423219435a) 7. **'Methods and (Lack of) Theory in Digital Inclusion, Digital Divide, and Older Adults'** - Analyzes methodologies and theories employed in digital inclusion research on older adults.

Figure 5.3 *Continued*

Tool	Result
	- Available on ScholarSpace. - [Link to PDF](https://scholarspace.manoa.hawaii.edu/bitstreams/d9c22c45-cba3-4cca-aece-cc8e38170691/download) 8. **'Tackling digital exclusion in older people'** - Discusses the stark reality of digital exclusion in later life and proposes measures to address it. - Available on the Mental Health Foundation website. - [Link to article](www.mentalhealth.org.uk/explore-mental-health/blogs/tackling-digital-exclusion-older-people) 9. **'Older people and the internet - ILCUK'** - Investigates the influence of internet content on digital exclusion among older people. - Available on the International Longevity Centre website. - [Link to article](https://ilcuk.org.uk/older-people-and-the-internet/) These articles provide a comprehensive overview of the challenges and proposed solutions for addressing digital exclusion among older people in the UK. If you need further assistance or specific articles, feel free to ask!

Figure 5.3 *Continued*

Figure 5.4 opposite shows that the outputs generated for Scenario 1, Question 4 vary:

- Five journal articles are cited by Claude, each with the title, author and date of publication; and brief details of the key points or focus of the given study. Full citations of items or links would have made it easier to locate and access the cited items.
- Results from Consensus are presented under five headings, with some details of the content cited item and a link to the source.
- Results from Copilot are presented under three headings, with two sources: bmcgeriatr.Biomedcentral.com and a chapter from a Springer publication. Two additional sources are also recommended for further reading: ageuk.org.uk and Ofcom.org.uk.
- Results from Gemini are presented under five headings, each with brief details of the content and link to the item. The cited items include reputed European and UK sources, including the journal *The Lancet*.
- Results from GPT-4o are presented under four headings with two sources: BioMedcentral.org (three times), and a paper from a journal available at the Oxford University Press.
- Perplexity AI recommends five items with a summary and citation. Two of the recommend citations lead to reports from AgeUK (ageuk.org.uk), one to an Ofcom report. (Ofcom.org.uk), one to a journal paper, and one to a coursework submitted at a university.

- Scholar GPT provides more detailed output under five headings with a brief summary of the key points followed by a link to the document.

Tool	Result
Claude	Sure, here are some research papers that compare digital exclusion among older adults in the UK with other European countries: 1. 'Digital Exclusion in Europe: Evidence from the European Union Statistics on Income and Living Conditions Survey' by Blank and Groselj (2022), published in the Journal of Digital Social Research. - This paper uses data from the EU-SILC survey to examine digital exclusion across European countries, including the UK. - It compares levels of digital exclusion among older adults and identifies factors contributing to the digital divide. 2. 'Comparing Digital Engagement Between the UK and Sweden: A Study of Older Adults' by Olsson et al. (2019), published in the Journal of Enabling Technologies. - This study compares the digital engagement and inclusion of older adults in the UK and Sweden, exploring factors such as access, skills, and attitudes. - It provides insights into the similarities and differences between the two countries. 3. 'Digital Inclusion Across the European Union: A Cross-National Study of Older Adults' Internet Use' by Friemel (2016), published in the European Journal of Communication. - This cross-national study examines internet use and digital inclusion among older adults across 27 European countries, including the UK. - It identifies country-level factors contributing to variations in digital inclusion. 4. 'The Digital Divide Among Older Adults in Europe: Exploring the Role of Socioeconomic and Demographic Factors' by Andreasson et al. (2022), published in the International Journal of Environmental Research and Public Health. - This study analyzes data from the Survey of Health, Ageing and Retirement in Europe (SHARE) to explore digital exclusion among older adults in various European countries, including the UK. - It compares the impact of socioeconomic and demographic factors on digital exclusion across countries. 5. 'Digital Exclusion and Older Adults in the European Union: A Systematic Review' by Veloso et al. (2022), published in the Journal of Aging and Health. - This systematic review synthesizes research on digital exclusion among older adults in European Union countries, including the UK. - It provides a comprehensive overview of the factors contributing to digital exclusion and compares findings across different European contexts. These research papers offer valuable comparative perspectives on digital exclusion among older adults, allowing you to contrast the situation in the UK with other European countries and identify common challenges and potential solutions.
Consensus	Here are some research papers that compare digital exclusion among older people in the UK and Europe: 1. **The Gray Digital Divide in Social Networking Site Use in Europe: Results From a Quantitative Study** - **Authors**: E. Sala, A. Gaia, Gabriele Cerati

Figure 5.4 *(Scenario 1, Question 4): Can you suggest some research papers that compare the data between UK and Europe on digital exclusion for older people?*

Tool	Result
	- **Abstract**: This study examines the gray digital divide in social networking site (SNS) use among older adults across Europe, highlighting intergenerational and cross-country differences in SNS use. The findings underscore the persistence of digital exclusion among older populations and the importance of addressing these disparities across European countries. - [Link to Paper](https://consensus.app/papers/gray-digital-divide-social-networking-site-europe-results-sala/16c0b5f34fa4536d8b61d00ac5e069d4/?utm_source=chatgpt) 2. **Old-Age Digital Exclusion as a Policy Challenge in Estonia and Finland** - **Authors**: A. Leppiman, I. Riivits-Arkonsuo, Anneli Pohjola - **Abstract**: This chapter explores digital exclusion as a policy challenge affecting older adults in Estonia and Finland. It discusses the impact of digital services on older populations and the challenges posed by rapidly evolving digital societies in these countries, offering insights into policy solutions that could be applied more broadly in Europe. - [Link to Paper](https://consensus.app/papers/oldage-digital-exclusion-policy-challenge-estonia-leppiman/29a5981484c65f1987cfe68e389aab74/?utm_source=chatgpt) 3. **Self-Assessed Health Among Older People in Europe and Internet Use** - **Author**: A. Tavares - **Abstract**: This study explores the relationship between self-assessed health and internet use among older people across European countries. The research highlights how eHealth policies impact digital inclusion and the health outcomes of older adults, with a particular focus on cross-country comparisons within Europe. - [Link to Paper](https://consensus.app/papers/selfassessed-health-among-people-europe-internet-tavares/be966603e6f85bc386cf50a9b156ac19/?utm_source=chatgpt) 4. **Digital Exclusion Despite Digital Accessibility: Empirical Evidence from an English City** - **Authors**: Sabrina Bunyan, A. Collins - **Abstract**: This study investigates the socio-economic determinants of digital exclusion in Portsmouth, UK. It provides insights into how digital exclusion persists despite the availability of digital infrastructure, offering a comparison with digital inclusion efforts in other European countries. - [Link to Paper](https://consensus.app/papers/digital-exclusion-despite-digital-accessibility-bunyan/088429c013c85258ad95a526f59870bf/?utm_source=chatgpt) 5. **Telehealth and Digital Developments in Society for Persons 75 Years and Older in European Countries: A Scoping Review** - **Authors**: M. Raja, Jorunn Bjerkan, I. Kymre, K. Galvin, L. Uhrenfeldt - **Abstract**: This scoping review examines the impact of telehealth and digital technologies on older adults in Europe, focusing on barriers to and facilitators of digital inclusion for those aged 75 and older across various European countries. - [Link to Paper](https://consensus.app/papers/telehealth-developments-society-persons-years-older-raja/67bb43f9d80d5fe2a5eeb325bddf9bcc/?utm_source=chatgpt) These papers provide comparative insights into the challenges of digital exclusion among older people in the UK and other European countries, highlighting both common issues and country-specific differences.

Figure 5.4 *Continued*

Tool	Result
Copilot	Absolutely, here are some research papers that compare digital exclusion among older people in the UK with those in Europe: 1 **Digital Exclusion and Cognitive Impairment in Older People**: This study investigates the relationship between digital exclusion and cognitive impairment in older adults across 23 countries, including the UK, using data from five longitudinal studies. It provides comparative insights into how digital exclusion varies by country and its association with cognitive health[1]. 2 **Digital Exclusion: A Review of Ofcom's Research**: This review offers an overview of digital exclusion among adults in the UK, including older citizens. It discusses the impact of the Covid-19 pandemic and compares the UK situation with broader European trends[2]. 3 **Digital Exclusion in Later Life: A Narrative Review**: This narrative review discusses internet usage among older populations in the UK and compares it with trends in the U.S. and Europe, highlighting the increase in internet use among over 75-year-olds[3]. These papers should provide a comparative perspective on digital exclusion among older people in the UK and Europe, which will be valuable for your research. Good luck with your essay! 📚 Learn more 1 bmcgeriatr.biomedcentral.com 2 ofcom.org.uk 3 link.springer.com 4 ageuk.org.uk
Gemini	Here are some research papers that compare data between the UK and Europe on digital exclusion for older people: • **'Digital exclusion and functional dependence in older people: Findings from five longitudinal cohort studies' (The Lancet):** This research utilizes data from several European countries, including the UK, to analyze the association between digital exclusion and functional dependence in older adults. It allows for a comparative perspective on the issue [The Lancet website]. • **'Seniors and the digital world: Participation, inequalities and policy responses across Europe' (European Commission):** This report by the European Commission provides a comprehensive overview of digital participation among older adults in Europe. It includes data on the UK and compares it to other European countries, highlighting key disparities [European Commission website]. • **'Digital Divide in Europe: A Multidimensional Analysis' (Center for Social and Economic Research - CASE):** This paper takes a broader approach, analyzing the digital divide across various European countries. While not exclusively focused on older adults, it can provide valuable insights into the overall digital landscape in Europe compared to the UK [Center for Social and Economic Research website]. In addition to these specific papers, here are some resources that might be helpful for finding comparative data: • **Eurostat:** The statistical office of the European Union provides data on various topics, including information and communication technologies (ICT) access and usage. You can compare data on internet usage or digital skills by age group between the UK and other European countries [Eurostat website]. • **The Digital Agenda for Europe Reports:** The European Commission publishes regular reports on the progress of the Digital Agenda for Europe, which includes information on digital inclusion. These reports often compare data between member states [European Commission website].

Figure 5.4 *Continued*

Tool	Result
	By using these resources, you can effectively compare digital exclusion data for older people between the UK and Europe, enriching your essay with a broader European context.
GPT-4o	Searched 3 sites For your essay on the digital exclusion of older people in the UK and Europe, several research papers provide comparative insights into the challenges faced by older adults in these regions. Here are some key sources and their findings: 1 **'Digital exclusion and cognitive impairment in older people: findings from five longitudinal studies'**: This study, published in BMC Geriatrics, examines digital exclusion among older adults across several countries, including the UK, and its association with cognitive impairment. The research highlights significant variation in digital exclusion rates, with 30.4% in the UK compared to other European countries such as Denmark (23.8%). This paper provides a detailed analysis of how digital exclusion correlates with cognitive health, socio-economic factors, and other demographic variables (BioMed Central). 2 **'Digital exclusion and functional dependence in older people: Findings from a multi-cohort study'**: This study, published in ScienceDirect, compares digital exclusion among older adults in different countries, including the UK and various European nations. It reports that digital exclusion is significantly influenced by functional dependence, with higher rates observed in countries with less supportive digital infrastructure for older adults (BioMed Central). 3 **'Double Burden of Exclusion? Digital and Social Exclusion of Older Adults'**: Published in the Journals of Gerontology, this paper discusses the combined effects of digital and social exclusion on older adults in Europe. The study compares data from several European countries and finds that older adults in the UK face unique challenges due to socio-economic disparities and varying levels of digital literacy and infrastructure (Oxford Academic). 4 **'Ensuring digital inclusion for older people in Europe'**: This article from ScienceDirect explores the broader context of digital inclusion policies across Europe. It emphasizes the need for targeted interventions and inclusive policies to address the diverse needs of older adults, highlighting successful strategies from countries like Denmark and contrasting them with the UK's approach (BioMed Central). These sources provide a comprehensive view of the digital exclusion landscape for older adults in the UK compared to Europe. They highlight the importance of considering cognitive health, functional dependence, and socio-economic factors in developing effective digital inclusion strategies. By integrating these findings, your essay can present a well-rounded analysis of the challenges and potential solutions for digital exclusion among older adults.
Perplexity AI	Here are some research papers that compare digital exclusion among older adults in the UK with other European countries: 1. 'Digital Exclusion in Later Life: A Study on Being Apart, Becoming Ill-Adapted and Wanting to Participate' by Olsson et al. (2019) [1][2] This study compares the digital exclusion experiences of older adults in Sweden, Spain, and the UK, highlighting cross-national differences and similarities in factors like access, skills, and motivations. 2. 'Digital Exclusion in Europe: Evidence from the European Union Statistics on Income and Living Conditions (EU-SILC) Survey' by Friemel (2016) [2][3]

Figure 5.4 *Continued*

Tool	Result
	This paper analyzes data from the EU-SILC survey to examine the prevalence and determinants of digital exclusion among older adults across multiple European countries, including the UK. 3. 'The Digital Divide Among Older Adults in Europe: Exploring the Roles of Individual and Regional Factors' by Berner et al. (2022) [3][4] This research investigates the individual and regional factors influencing digital exclusion among older Europeans, comparing the UK with other nations like Germany, France, and Italy. 4. 'Digital Exclusion and Implications for Older People's Health and Well-being' by Hunsaker and Hargittai (2018) [4][5] While not focused solely on Europe, this paper includes data from the UK and other European countries, examining the relationship between digital exclusion and health outcomes for older adults. 5. 'Overcoming Digital Exclusion in Later Life: A Theory of Cognitive Barriers and Support Strategies' by Sayago et al. (2020) [5] This study proposes a theoretical framework for understanding cognitive barriers to digital inclusion among older adults, drawing on data from the UK, Spain, and other European contexts. These research papers provide valuable comparative insights into the digital exclusion challenges faced by older adults in the UK relative to other European nations. They can serve as useful references for your essay, highlighting similarities, differences, and potential strategies for addressing this issue across different cultural and policy contexts. Citations: [1] www.ageuk.org.uk/globalassets/age-uk/documents/reports-and-publications/age_uk_digital_inclusion_evidence_review_2018.pdf [2] www.ofcom.org.uk/__data/assets/pdf_file/0022/234364/digital-exclusion-review-2022.pdf [3] www.ageuk.org.uk/globalassets/age-uk/documents/reports-and-publications/reports-and-briefings/active-communities/policy-briefing—-facts-and-figures-about-digital-inclusion-and-older-people.pdf [4] www.lse.ac.uk/PBS/assets/documents/PEL-coursework/2021-2022/PB403-Psychology-of-Economic-Life-Summative-coursework-2021-2022-Group6.pdf [5] https://journals.sagepub.com/doi/full/10.1177/00469580221096272
Scholar GPT	Here are some research papers that compare the digital exclusion of older people in the UK with other European countries: 1. **'The Grey Digital Divide and Welfare State Regimes: A Comparative Study of European Countries'** - This study examines the digital divide among older adults across different welfare state regimes in Europe, including the UK. - Available on Emerald Insight. - [Link to article](www.emerald.com/insight/content/doi/10.1108/ITP-11-2020-0803/full/pdf?title=the-grey-digital-divide-and-welfare-state-regimes-a-comparative-study-of-european-countries) 2. **'Older people and the internet - International Longevity Centre'** - This paper discusses the factors causing digital exclusion among older people and includes comparative insights from the UK and other European countries. - Available on the International Longevity Centre website. - [Link to PDF](https://ilcuk.org.uk/wp-content/uploads/2018/10/pdf_pdf_181.pdf)

Figure 5.4 *Continued*

Tool	Result
	3. **'Ensuring Access to Public Services in Digital Societies'** - This publication by the European Union Agency for Fundamental Rights highlights the risk of digital exclusion among older persons across European Union countries, including the UK. - [Link to report](https://fra.europa.eu/en/publication/2023/older-people-digital-rights?page=6) 4. **'Exploring Factors and Moderators of Internet Non-Use in the UK'** - This study identifies the main factors associated with digital exclusion in the UK and provides comparative insights with other European contexts. - Available on ScienceDirect. - [Link to article](www.sciencedirect.com/science/article/pii/S0040162523006200) 5. **'Socio-economic Inequalities in the Breadth of Internet Use Before and During COVID-19: A Comparative Study of Older Adults'** - This cohort study uses data from older adults in England to compare digital inequalities with other European countries. - Available on NCBI. - [Link to article](www.ncbi.nlm.nih.gov/pmc/articles/PMC11081243/) These articles provide a comprehensive overview of the digital exclusion issues faced by older people in the UK and offer comparative insights with other European countries. If you need further assistance with accessing specific articles or more detailed information, feel free to ask!

Figure 5.4 *Continued*

Scenario 2: An undergraduate student is looking for information for coursework

Outputs generated by the Gen AI tools for Scenario 2, Question 1 (Figure 5.5), vary significantly:

- Claude provides seven headings, each with two points, written in an easy-to-understand summary form; no citations are provided.
- Consensus provides more detailed output under six headings, each with one or two subheadings, discussing the specific issues; no citations are provided.
- Copilot presents the output under five broad headings, some with subheadings and bullet points. Text associated with two subheadings have the associated citations, and both cite the same site, goodthingsfoundation.org.
- Gemini presents the output under three broad headings, each with three subheadings, discussing the key issues; no citations are provided.
- GPT-4o presents the output in summary form under six headings, each with two bullet points. Some text has the associated citations, e.g. the text in two sections cite four sites in all: BioMedcentral, Gov.uk, Frontiersin.org and an article in a journal from the Oxford University Press. In addition, there is a brief summary and 10 sources are listed and all of these are OA reports on different sites like the International Labour Organisation, European Commission, OECD, UNICEF, British Council, and others.

- Perplexity AI provides five points, each with a citation and summary of the cited item. However, some of the recommendations may lead to items that are not relevant for the given search and user contexts.
- Results from Scholar GPT mentions seven areas of benefits, each with two brief subsections summarising the specific benefits of digital skills; and also provides a list of three major international sources, followed by a conclusion.

Tool	Result
Claude	Digital skills can improve people's work, employment, and income prospects in several ways: 1. Access to job opportunities: - Many job opportunities, particularly in sectors like technology, finance, and business, require proficient digital skills. ... 7. Cost savings: - Digital skills can help individuals save money by accessing online services, finding better deals, and managing finances more effectively... While digital skills alone may not guarantee employment or higher incomes, they are increasingly becoming a necessary asset in the ... stability
Consensus	Answer Digital skills significantly improve people's work, employment opportunities, and income by enhancing productivity, expanding access to jobs, and enabling career advancement. Here's how: ### 1. **Increased Productivity and Efficiency** - **Automation of Routine Tasks**: Digital skills enable individuals to use software and tools that automate routine tasks, such as .. .... ### 6. **Improved Work-Life Balance** - **Flexibility**: Digital skills enable workers to take advantage of flexible work arrangements, such as remote work or freelancing. This ... ### Conclusion Digital skills are essential in today's job market, as they enhance productivity, expand employment opportunities, enable career ... security
Copilot	Certainly! **Digital skills** play a crucial role in enhancing work, employment, and income for individuals. Let's explore how: **1 Productivity Boost**: Having digital skills allows workers to be more .... For instance, using spreadsheets, project management software, or communication tools can significantly improve productivity in the workplace[1]. .... **1 Holistic Approach to Digital Capability**: • Beyond technical skills, a holistic approach emphasizes confidence, curiosity, adaptability, and problem-solving. • Developing digital skills opens up various aspects of everyday life, contributing to overall well-being ... stability. In summary, digital skills empower individuals in the workforce, enhance employability, and positively impact income. They are essential for navigating the modern job market and improving overall quality of life.

Figure 5.5 *Examples of search results for Scenario 2, Question 1: How do digital skills improve people's work, employment and income?*

Tool	Result
Gemini	Digital skills are increasingly crucial in today's job market, impacting people's work, employment prospects, and ultimately, .. Here's how: **Increased Efficiency and Productivity:** • **Automating Tasks:** Digital skills allow workers to leverage software and technology to automate repetitive tasks, freeing up time for more complex and strategic work. This can significantly improve individual and overall team productivity. **Increased Earning Potential:** • **Higher Salaries:** Studies show that jobs requiring digital skills often come with higher salaries compared to those with no digital component......... **Overall, digital skills empower individuals to work smarter, not harder, increasing their value in the job market and opening doors to better employment opportunities and higher earning potential.**
GPT-4o	Digital skills significantly enhance people's work, employment, and income prospects through several mechanisms. Here are some key ways in which digital skills make a positive impact: **1. Increased Employability** • **Job Market Relevance**: As the job market increasingly relies on technology, possessing digital skills makes individuals more attractive to employers. Many jobs now require proficiency in digital tools and platforms, from basic office software to advanced data analytics **4. Remote Work Opportunities** **6. Social and Economic Inclusion** • **Bridging the Gap**: Digital skills contribute to social and economic inclusion by providing access to online education, financial services, and employment resources. This is particularly beneficial for marginalized communities and individuals in remote areas ...... In summary, digital skills are crucial for enhancing employability, career progression, income potential, and overall economic inclusion. They enable individuals to adapt to the evolving job market, embrace new opportunities, and improve their productivity and innovation capabilities. **Sources**: International Labour Organization .... 12. British Council
Perplexity AI	Based on the provided research papers, gaining digital skills can improve people's work, employment, and income outcomes in several ways: 1. Improved Employment Prospects: - Digital skills enhance individuals' ability to search for and apply for job opportunities online, giving them an edge in the job market. [3] .... 5. Entrepreneurship and Self-Employment: - Digital skills enable individuals to leverage online platforms, digital marketing, and e-commerce to start and grow their own businesses.... [4] However, the research also highlights that the outcomes of digital skills can vary based on the specific dimensions of skills acquired, ... Citations: [1] https://eprints.lse.ac.uk/111598/4/14614448211043189.pdf .... [5] https:// /clok.uclan.ac.uk/47845......................

Figure 5.5 *Continued*

Tool	**Result**
Scholar GPT	Digital skills play a crucial role in improving people's work, employment opportunities, and income levels in various ways. Here are some key aspects: ### 1. **Enhanced Employability** - **Job Market Relevance**: Possessing digital skills makes individuals more attractive to employers, as many modern jobs require some level of digital literacy. ...... ### 7. **Greater Job Security** - **Future-Proofing**: As industries become more digitized, having digital skills ensures that individuals remain relevant and competitive in the .... ### Case Studies and Research Findings 1. **World Economic Forum Report**: - The report highlights that individuals with advanced digital skills can earn significantly more than those without such skills.......... ..... 3. **European Commission Digital Skills Index**: - Findings show that individuals with higher digital skills are more likely to be employed and earn higher incomes..... ### Conclusion Digital skills are essential in today's economy for enhancing employability, productivity, and earning potential. They provide individuals with the tools needed to navigate and succeed in a rapidly evolving digital landscape. Investing in digital literacy and continuous skill development is crucial for personal and professional growth, as well as for maintaining competitiveness in the job market.

Figure 5.5 *Continued*

Results generated by the search tools for Scenario 2, Question 2, shown in Figure 5.6 on the next page, vary:

- Six items are recommended by Claude, each with a summary and data, and some citation data. Together these results provide useful information. However, some of the cited items and data cannot be verified.
- Results from Consensus are presented under 10 broad headings, each with three subheadings discussing the key points; and there is a conclusion, but no citations are provided.
- Results from Copilot are fairly detailed, presented under four broad headings; and each point is supported by a citation. Altogether, three sites have been cited: goodthingsfoundations.org (twice), europa.eu, and a site from Oxford University.
- Gemini recommends four items under four headings, each with a supporting citation. There are also recommendations for further sources like the World Bank and OECD.

- Results from GPT-4o are more comprehensive, presented as five points, each referring to a specific resource: one review paper, three research papers, and a digital skills index from Coursera.
- Five items are recommended by Perplexity AI, each with a summary and citation. Three of the recommended items are research papers, one is a review report, and the other is a blog.
- Results from Scholar GPT include 10 items; each with a one-sentence summary of its content, followed by a link to the source.

Tool	Result
Claude	Certainly, here are some research papers and studies that support the positive impact of digital skills on work, employment, and income: 1. 'Digital Skills for Life and Work' by the European Commission (2017): - This report highlights the importance of digital skills for employment, productivity, and economic growth. - It suggests that individuals with advanced digital skills can earn up to 38% higher wages compared to those with basic or no digital skills. 2. 'The Digital Skills Crisis: Report on Digital Skills in the Workforce' by the British Chambers of Commerce (2021): - This report found that 70% of businesses in the UK reported a digital skills shortage among their employees, hindering productivity and competitiveness. - It emphasizes the need for digital upskilling to improve employment prospects and business performance. 3. 'Digital Skills and the Digital Economy' by the World Bank (2021): - This study examines the relationship between digital skills and labor market outcomes across various countries. - It suggests that higher digital skills are associated with increased employment rates and higher earnings, particularly in technology-intensive sectors. 4. 'The Impact of Digital Skills on Employability and Earning Potential' by the OECD (2019): - This report analyzes data from the Programme for the International Assessment of Adult Competencies (PIAAC) across OECD countries. - It found that individuals with advanced digital problem-solving skills have higher employment rates and earn an average of 29% more than those with limited digital skills. 5. 'Digital Skills and Online Gig Work: Evidence from the Online Labour Market' by the International Labour Organization (2022): - This study examines the role of digital skills in accessing online gig work opportunities, which can provide additional income streams. - It suggests that individuals with stronger digital skills are more likely to participate in online freelancing and earn higher incomes. 6. 'The Digital Skills Gap: Quantifying the Impact on UK Businesses' by the Department for Digital, Culture, Media & Sport (2022): - This UK-based report estimates that closing the digital skills gap could add £14.5 billion to the UK economy and create over 200,000 new jobs. - It highlights the importance of digital skills for business productivity, innovation, and job creation. These research papers and studies provide evidence from various organizations and countries, supporting the positive relationship between digital skills and improved work opportunities, employability, productivity, and income potential.

Figure 5.6 *(Scenario 2, Question 2): Can you give me some supporting research literature on this?*

Tool	Result
Consensus	Answer The **future job market** is rapidly evolving due to advancements in technology, automation, and digital transformation across various industries. To stay competitive and relevant, individuals need to develop a diverse set of **digital skills**. Below are some of the most important digital skills that will be essential for future employment: ## 1. **Digital Literacy** - **Basic Computer Skills:** Proficiency in using computers, operating systems, and common software applications. - **Internet Navigation:** Ability to effectively search for, evaluate, and utilize information from the internet. - **Online Communication:** Skills in using email, instant messaging, and video conferencing tools. ## 2. **Data Analysis and Interpretation** - **Data Literacy:** Understanding how to collect, analyze, and interpret data to make informed decisions. - **Statistical Analysis:** Ability to use statistical methods and tools to interpret complex data sets. - **Data Visualization:** Skills in presenting data through graphs, charts, and other visual formats using tools like Tableau or Power BI. ## 3. **Artificial Intelligence and Machine Learning** - **Understanding AI Concepts:** Basic knowledge of how AI and machine learning work and their applications in various industries. - **Programming Skills:** Proficiency in languages commonly used in AI development such as Python or R. - **Algorithm Design:** Ability to create and understand algorithms that can learn and make predictions or decisions. ## 4. **Cybersecurity** - **Security Awareness:** Understanding common security threats and how to protect against them. - **Risk Management:** Ability to identify and mitigate potential security risks. - **Knowledge of Security Tools:** Familiarity with antivirus software, firewalls, and encryption techniques. ## 5. **Cloud Computing** - **Understanding Cloud Services:** Knowledge of cloud platforms like AWS, Microsoft Azure, and Google Cloud. - **Cloud Architecture:** Ability to design, deploy, and manage applications and services on the cloud. - **Security and Compliance:** Understanding how to maintain security and compliance standards in cloud environments. ## 6. **Programming and Software Development** - **Coding Skills:** Proficiency in one or more programming languages such as Java, JavaScript, Python, or C++. - **Software Development Lifecycle:** Understanding the processes involved in developing software from planning to deployment. - **Agile Methodologies:** Familiarity with agile frameworks like Scrum or Kanban for efficient project management. ## 7. **Digital Marketing** - **Content Creation:** Ability to create engaging digital content across various platforms. - **SEO and SEM:** Understanding how to optimize content for search engines and manage online advertising campaigns. - **Social Media Management:** Skills in leveraging social media platforms for branding and customer engagement.

Figure 5.6 *Continued*

Tool	Result
	## 8. **User Experience (UX) and User Interface (UI) Design** - **Design Principles:** Understanding of layout, color theory, typography, and visual hierarchy. - **Prototyping Tools:** Proficiency in using tools like Sketch, Adobe XD, or Figma to design and test interfaces. - **User Research:** Ability to conduct and apply user research to improve product design and usability. ## 9. **Digital Project Management** - **Planning and Organization:** Skills in setting goals, defining project scopes, and managing resources. - **Use of PM Tools:** Familiarity with project management software like Asana, Trello, or Jira. - **Team Collaboration:** Ability to coordinate and communicate effectively with diverse teams in a digital environment. ## 10. **Adaptability and Continuous Learning** - **Lifelong Learning:** Openness to continually updating skills and knowledge in response to technological advancements. - **Problem-Solving:** Ability to adapt to new challenges and find innovative solutions. - **Critical Thinking:** Evaluating information critically to make reasoned decisions and strategies. ## How to Develop These Skills - **Online Courses and Certifications:** Platforms like Coursera, Udemy, and LinkedIn Learning offer courses on various digital skills. - **Workshops and Bootcamps:** Intensive training programs provide hands-on experience in specific skill areas. - **Practical Experience:** Working on personal projects, internships, or contributing to open-source projects can help build and demonstrate skills. - **Networking:** Engaging with professional communities and attending industry events to learn from others and stay updated on trends. - **Reading and Research:** Keeping up with industry publications, blogs, and journals to stay informed about the latest developments. **Conclusion** Investing time and effort into developing these digital skills will significantly enhance employability and prepare individuals to thrive in the future job market. Embracing continuous learning and staying adaptable to change are key components to success in an increasingly digital and interconnected world.
Copilot	Certainly! Here are some research papers and reports that provide valuable insights into the impact of digital skills on work, employment, and income: 1 **'Improving Digital Skills for Employability'** by Good Things Foundation: • This report explores challenges related to improving employability through digital skills for people facing significant disadvantage. It emphasizes the holistic needs of individuals, the importance of motivation, and the critical role of local support ecosystems. It also highlights the lasting benefits of developing digital skills beyond employment[1]. 2 **'Developing Essential Digital Skills'** (POSTnote Number 643): • This POSTnote provides an overview of digital skills in the UK, their impact on outcomes (including employment), and initiatives to improve digital skills. It discusses the implications of a lack of digital skills for health, employment prospects, and the economy. The note focuses on basic digital skills needed for everyday life[2].

Figure 5.6 *Continued*

Tool	Result
	3 'Changing Demand for Skills in Digital Economies and Societies' (ILO Report): • This report sheds light on changing demand for skills in digital economies and societies, based on a literature review and case studies from low- and middle-income countries. It discusses the impact of digitalization on skills and related policy recommendations[3]. **4 'Fostering Digital Skills in Developing Countries'**: • This report emphasizes the benefits of acquiring digital skills, including increased job security and better employment prospects. It highlights the importance of overcoming internal obstacles to technology adoption and adapting to digital trends[4]. Remember to explore these resources further to gain deeper insights into the impact of digital skills on various aspects of life and work.
Gemini	Certainly! Here's some research literature to support the positive impact of digital skills on work, employment, and income: • **'Improving digital skills for employability' (Good Things Foundation):** This report by the Good Things Foundation analyzes the economic impact of digital skills in the UK. It highlights the correlation between higher digital skills and increased earnings potential, with basic digital skills leading to a 2.8% lifetime earning increase [Good Things Foundation website]. • **'Measuring Relationship between Digital Skills and Employability' (ResearchGate):** This research emphasizes the role of digital skills as a key factor in employability. It explores the link between digital skills and securing higher-status jobs, especially when combined with higher education [ResearchGate website]. • **'The economic impact of Basic Digital Skills and inclusion in the UK' (Good Things Foundation):** This report delves into the broader economic benefits of digital skills. It highlights how digital skills not only improve individual employment prospects but also contribute to increased tax revenue and economic growth [Good Things Foundation website]. • **'Digital Skills To Improve Work Performance' (ResearchGate):** This research explores the direct impact of digital skills on work performance. It finds a positive correlation between digital skills and employee efficiency and productivity [ResearchGate website]. In addition to these specific studies, you can also explore resources from organizations like the World Bank or OECD (Organisation for Economic Co-operation and Development). These organizations often publish reports on the digital skills gap and its impact on labor markets.
GPT-4o	Certainly! Here are some research papers and articles that discuss how digital skills can improve people's work, employment, and income: **1** 'The Impact of Digital Skills on Employment and Income: Evidence from the UK' by Mirko Draca, Ralf Martin, and Tommaso Valletti. This paper explores the relationship between digital skills and employment outcomes, using data from the UK Labour Force Survey. **2** 'Digital Skills and the Future of Work in Africa' by World Bank Group. This report examines the importance of digital skills in driving economic growth and employment opportunities in Africa, with a focus on youth employment. **3** 'Digitalization and Its Impact on Work and Employment: A Literature Review' by Emma Lindberg and Linda Widar. This literature review provides an overview of existing research on the impact of digitalization on work and employment, including discussions on skill requirements and income effects.

Figure 5.6 *Continued*

Tool	Result
	4 'Digital Skills for a Digital World: 2019 Global Skills Index' by Coursera. This report analyzes data from Coursera's Global Skills Index to assess the demand for digital skills in the global job market and their impact on employment and income opportunities. **5** 'The Impact of Digital Skills Training on Women's Livelihoods and Agency: Findings from South Asia' by the International Center for Research on Women (ICRW). This study examines how digital skills training programs can empower women economically by improving their employment prospects and income-generating opportunities. These resources should provide you with valuable insights into the relationship between digital skills and various aspects of work, including employment and income.
Perplexity AI	Here are some relevant research papers that provide supporting literature on the challenges older adults in the UK face in using digital government services: 1. 'Digital Exclusion in Later Life: A Study on Being Apart, Becoming Ill-Adapted and Wanting to Participate' by Olsson et al. (2019) [1][2] This study examines the digital exclusion experiences of older adults in the UK, highlighting factors like lack of access, skills, and motivation as barriers to using digital services. 2. 'Digital Exclusion and Implications for Older People's Health and Well-being' by Hunsaker and Hargittai (2018) [4] While not focused solely on the UK, this paper includes data from the UK and explores the relationship between digital exclusion and health outcomes for older adults, which can impact their ability to access digital government services related to healthcare. 3. 'Overcoming Digital Exclusion in Later Life: A Theory of Cognitive Barriers and Support Strategies' by Sayago et al. (2020) [5] This study proposes a theoretical framework for understanding cognitive barriers to digital inclusion among older adults, drawing on data from the UK and other contexts, which can inform strategies to improve access to digital government services. 4. 'Digital Inclusion Evidence Review 2018' by Age UK [5] This report by Age UK provides a comprehensive review of the research on digital inclusion and exclusion among older adults in the UK, including barriers such as lack of skills, access, and motivation, as well as potential solutions. 5. 'Exploring Digital Exclusion in Older Age' by Olphert and Damodaran (2013) [2][3] This study investigates the factors contributing to digital exclusion among older adults in the UK, such as lack of skills, motivation, and access to technology, which can hinder their use of digital government services. These research papers provide valuable insights into the various challenges faced by older adults in the UK when it comes to using digital services, including government offerings. They highlight barriers related to digital literacy, accessibility, access to technology, trust and security concerns, and preferences for traditional methods, among others. Citations: [1] www.frontiersin.org/journals/psychology/articles/10.3389/fpsyg.2023.1122277/full [2] www.ncbi.nlm.nih.gov/pmc/articles/PMC10341140/ [3] www.tandfonline.com/doi/full/10.1080/02660830.2022.2133268 [4] https://communitytechnetwork.org/blog/new-research-bridging-the-digital-divide-by-addressing-barriers-with-digital-literacy-strategies-for-older-adults/

Figure 5.6 *Continued*

Tool	Result
	[5] www.ageuk.org.uk/globalassets/age-uk/documents/reports-and-publications/age_uk_digital_inclusion_evidence_review_2018.pdf
Scholar GPT	Here are some research papers and articles that explore the impact of digital skills on employment and income: 1. **'Digital Skills Drive Gains for Organisations and Economy'** - This article highlights that workers with advanced digital skills in high-income countries earn significantly more than those without such skills. - [Link to article](https://technologymagazine.com/articles/digital-skills-drive-gains-for-organisations-and-economy) 2. **'Digital Skills and Older Workers' - Urban Institute** - This paper discusses how digital skills positively impact employment and earnings, especially for older workers. - [Link to PDF](www.urban.org/sites/default/files/publication/104771/digital-skills-and-older-workers_1.pdf) 3. **'Changing Demand for Skills in Digital Economies and Societies' - International Labour Organization (ILO)** - Examines how digitalization has influenced skills demand and its implications for work and income in various economies. - [Link to PDF](www.ilo.org/media/378741/download) 4. **'Digitalization and Employment' - International Labour Organization (ILO)** - This publication explores the consequences of digital skills training on employment and economic inclusion. - [Link to PDF](https://webapps.ilo.org/wcmsp5/groups/public/—-ed_emp/documents/publication/wcms_854353.pdf) 5. **'Measuring Relationship between Digital Skills and Employability'** - Investigates the long-term impact of digital skills on employment and earnings, emphasizing their significance in the job market. - [Link to PDF](https://papers.ssrn.com/sol3/Delivery.cfm/SSRN_ID2382939_code2038327.pdf?abstractid=2382939&mirid=1) 6. **'Research on the Impact of Digital Literacy on the Overall Income of Individuals'** - Defines digital literacy and its positive impact on income and employment. - [Link to PDF](https://drpress.org/ojs/index.php/HBEM/article/view/2589/2489) 7. **'How Digital Skills Affect Rural Labor Employment Choices' - MDPI** - Discusses the positive impact of digital skills on employment choices among the rural labor force. - [Link to article](www.mdpi.com/2071-1050/15/7/6050) 8. **'The Economic Impact of Basic Digital Skills and Inclusion in the UK' - Good Things Foundation** - Explores how acquiring digital skills benefits earnings and contributes to national income. - [Link to PDF](www.goodthingsfoundation.org/wp-content/uploads/2021/02/the_economic_impact_of_digital_skills_and_inclusion_in_the_uk_final_v2.pdf) 9. **'How Digital Skills Are Transforming the Global Economy' - Lightcast** - Concludes that jobs requiring more digital skills tend to offer higher salaries. - [Link to article](https://lightcast.io/resources/blog/how-digital-skills-are-transforming-the-global-economy)

Figure 5.6 *Continued*

Tool	Result
	10. **'Digital Skills Gap Index 2021' - Wiley** - Discusses the impact of digital skills on employment opportunities and income potential. - [Link to PDF](https://dsgi.wiley.com/wp-content/uploads/2021/10/DSGI-whitepaper.pdf) These papers provide comprehensive insights into how digital skills influence employment and income, highlighting the importance of digital literacy in the modern economy. If you need further assistance or specific articles, feel free to ask!

Figure 5.6 *Continued*

Results generated by the chosen tools for Scenario 2, Question 3 (Figure 5.7 opposite), vary, e.g.:

- Claude provides six items, each with a summary and data, and some citation data. Together these results provide useful information. However, some of the cited items and data cannot be verified.
- Results from Consensus are quite detailed, presented under four main headings, each with one to three bullet points, supported by citations from reputed sites such as the OECD, Eurostat and European Commission, and charities like GoodThingsFoundation. There is also a section with advice on how to find more data on the topic.
- Copilot presents the output under three headings, two of which present data and comments from the Ofcom report (Ofcom.org.uk), and the third point is a summary of the key points. These summary points are useful and provide some interesting insights on the topic.
- Results from Gemini are somewhat similar to those of Consensus, fairly detailed, presented under four main headings, each with one to three bullet points, and are supported by citations from reputed sites suh as the OECD, Eurostat and European Commission, and charities like GoodThingsFoundation. There is a section with advice on how to find more data on the topic.
- Results from GPT-4o are comprehensive and are presented in a summary form under six points, each of them supported by a specific study, e.g. by the European Commission report (point to the Digital Divide Index), Good Things Foundation and CEBR report, the European Federation of Public Service Unions (EPSU) and Eurofound (eurofound.europa.eu) reports, and the Lloyds Bank report.
- Perplexity AI presents the output under three headings, each with two to three subheadings with relevant data and citations. Altogether five citations are provided: four are relevant reports from reputed organisations, and one is a journal paper.

- Scholar GPT output presents five areas of comparison, each with two subsections – comparing the data for UK and Europe. Three major sources of data are also shown, followed by a conclusion.

Tool	Result
Claude	Certainly, here are some research papers and studies that support the positive impact of digital skills on work, employment, and income: 1. "Digital Skills for Life and Work" by the European Commission (2017): - This report highlights the importance of digital skills for employment, productivity, and economic growth....... .... 6. "The Digital Skills Gap: Quantifying the Impact on UK Businesses" by the Department for Digital, Culture, Media & Sport (2022): - This UK-based report estimates that closing the digital skills gap could add £14.5 billion to the UK economy and create over 200,000 new jobs. - It highlights the importance of digital skills for business productivity, innovation, and job creation. These research papers and studies provide evidence from various organizations and countries, supporting the positive relationship between digital skills and improved work opportunities, employability, productivity, and income potential.
Consensus	The UK's digital inclusion landscape compared to other European countries presents a mixed picture. Here's a breakdown of some key... **Areas where the UK lags behind:** •**Overall Digital Inclusion:** Several European countries outperform the UK in overall digital inclusion. The Digital Agenda..: •**Private Sector Involvement:** The UK has a thriving private sector with a strong focus on digital... [OECD website]. Here are some resources for further comparison: •**Eurostat:** This website provides data on Information and Communication Technologies (ICT) ... [Eurostat website]. •**Digital Agenda for Europe Reports:** These reports by the European Commission ... [European Commission website]. By examining these resources, you can get a more nuanced understanding of the UK's position in digital inclusion compared to other European countries. Remember, the landscape is constantly evolving, so the latest data is crucial for an accurate comparison.
Copilot	Certainly! Let's explore how digital exclusion among older people in the UK compares with other European countries: **1. UK Digital Exclusion**: • According to Ofcom's research, **6% of UK households** did not have access to the internet at home in December 2021[1]....... **2. European Comparative Study**: • A comparative study explored the influence of **welfare state regimes** on the digital divide among seniors (aged 65+) in Europe[2]........ **3. Key Takeaways**: • While the UK has made progress in reducing digital exclusion, challenges remain...... In summary, understanding digital exclusion requires considering both national contexts and individual determinants. Welfare state regimes play a significant role in shaping the digital divide among seniors in Europe

Figure 5.7 *Examples of search results for Scenario 2, Question 3: How do the data for the UK compare with other European countries?*

Tool	Result
Gemini	The UK's digital inclusion landscape compared to other European countries presents a mixed picture. Here's a breakdown of some key... **Areas where the UK lags behind:** • **Overall Digital Inclusion:** Several European countries outperform the UK in overall ...... [European Commission website]. **Areas where the UK keeps pace:** • **Government Initiatives:** The UK government has recognized the importance of .. [Good Things Foundation website].... **Areas where the UK might be ahead:** • **Private Sector Involvement:** The UK has a thriving private sector with a strong focus ... [OECD website]. Here are some resources for further comparison: • **Eurostat:** This website provides data on Information and Communication Technologies (ICT) .. [Eurostat website].... By examining these resources, you can get a more nuanced understanding of the UK's position in digital inclusion compared to other European countries. Remember, the landscape is constantly evolving, so the latest data is crucial for an accurate comparison.
GPT-4o	Certainly! Here are some studies and reports that compare the impact of digital exclusion on work, employment, and income in the UK and EU countries: **1. "Digital Skills and the UK Economy"** by The Good Things Foundation and CEBR (Centre for Economics and Business Research). This report explores the economic impact of digital exclusion in the UK, focusing on employment and income ... **6. "The Impact of the Digital Divide on UK Business"** by Lloyds Bank. While this report is UK-specific, it provides useful insights into the economic impacts of digital exclusion on businesses, which can be compared with findings from similar studies in EU countries. These studies and reports offer a comparative perspective on how digital exclusion affects employment and income across the UK and various EU countries. They provide valuable data and analysis that highlight the economic disparities caused by differences in digital skills and access.
Perplexity AI	Based on the provided research papers and reports, here is how the UK compares to other European countries in terms of digital inclusion: ## Access and Infrastructure - The UK has relatively high levels of internet access and broadband penetration compared to many other European nations. In 2015... [5] ## Inclusion of Disadvantaged Groups - In 2014, the UK met the EU's Digital Agenda target of having 60% of disadvantaged groups (low-educated, ... [5] .... Overall, while the UK performs relatively well in terms of overall internet access and digital skills compared to the European ... Citations: [1] https://one.oecd.org/document/EDU/WKP%282023%2914/en/pdf ..... [5] https://www.europarl.europa.eu/RegData/etudes/BRIE/2015/573884/EPRS_BRI%282015%29573884_EN.pdf
Scholar GPT	The UK compares to other European countries in terms of digital inclusion in several key areas. Digital inclusion encompasses access to... ### 1. **Internet Access and Usage** - **UK**: The UK has a high level of internet access, with a large majority of households connected to the internet. According to ..

Figure 5.7 *Continued*

Tool	Result
	- **Europe**: The European Union (EU) average is slightly lower, with around 91% of households having internet access in 2021. ... ### 5. **Digital Economy Integration** - **UK**: The UK has a well-integrated digital economy, with a high level of digital adoption among businesses. This includes the use ... ### Comparative Data and Reports 1. **Digital Economy and Society Index (DESI) 2022**: - - [Link to DESI 2022](https://digital-strategy.ec.europa.eu/en/policies/desi) ..... 3. **Eurostat Digital Skills Indicators**: .... - [Link to Eurostat](https://ec.europa.eu/eurostat/web/digital-economy-and-society/data/database) ### Conclusion Overall, the UK performs well in terms of digital inclusion compared to other European countries. It has high levels of ...

Figure 5.7 *Continued*

Results for Scenario 2, Question 4 (Figure 5.8 on the next page), vary as follows:

- Claude results include five items, each with two to three sections with a summary and data, and some citation data. However, some of the cited items and data are not verified.
- Results from Consensus are quite detailed, and are presented under eight points, with discussions on the specific points and citation. The cited sources include the European Commission, OECD, etc. There is a section with specific advice on where to find more relevant information, such as JSTOR.
- Results from Copilot present in four points, each with a specific heading and a citation. However, four citations are from the same site, learningandwork.org.uk. Some references to the source, e.g. Oxford academic (in point 3) and Springer (in item 4) are misleading because they lead to the same source.
- Results from Gemini are quite detailed, and are presented under 10 headings, some with international sources like the European Commission and OECD, with additional suggestions on how to find relevant national resources on the chosen topic.
- Results from GPT-4o are quite comprehensive, referring to six sources, with the title, author, source and year, and a summary of the item. However, finding the cited items proved to be difficult because full bibliographic details or links are not provided.
- Perplexity AI provides five items with a summary and citation. One of the cited items is a research paper and the others are reports.

- Results from Scholar GPT include eight items, each with a one-sentence summary of its content, followed by a link to the source. Most of the cited items are reports or news items from international and national organisations.

Tool	Result
Claude	Certainly, here are some research papers that compare the impact of digital skills on work and employment opportunities in the UK and other European countries: 1. 'Digital Skills and the Labor Market: Diverging Patterns of Digital Skills across European Economies' by van Deursen et al. (2021), published in the International Journal of Communication. - This study compares the levels of digital skills and their impact on employment across several European countries, including the UK. - It found that while higher digital skills generally lead to better labor market outcomes, the strength of this relationship varies across countries. 2. 'The Impact of Digital Skills on Employment and Earnings in the UK and Europe' by the European Commission's Joint Research Centre (2022). - This report analyzes data from the EU Labour Force Survey and the OECD's Programme for the International Assessment of Adult Competencies (PIAAC). - It compares the impact of digital skills on employment rates and earnings in the UK with other European countries. 3. 'Digital Skills and Labour Market Outcomes in the United Kingdom and European Union' by the Department for Education (UK) and the European Centre for the Development of Vocational Training (2021). - This joint study explores the relationship between digital skills and labor market outcomes, such as employment, wages, and job quality, in the UK and across the European Union. - It provides a comparative analysis of the role of digital skills in different sectors and occupations. 4. 'The Impact of Digital Skills on Employment and Employability in the UK and Other EU Countries' by the Institute for Public Policy Research (2020). - This report examines the role of digital skills in shaping employment and employability prospects in the UK and several other European countries. - It compares the digital skills gaps and their consequences across different national contexts. 5. 'Digital Skills and Earnings in the UK and Europe: Evidence from the OECD Survey of Adult Skills' by Grundke et al. (2018), published in the Journal of Economic Inequality. - This study utilizes data from the OECD's Survey of Adult Skills to analyze the impact of digital skills on earnings in the UK and other European countries. - It provides insights into the varying returns to digital skills across different national labor markets. These research papers offer comparative analyses of the impact of digital skills on work and employment opportunities, allowing you to understand the similarities and differences between the UK and other European countries in this regard. They often draw upon large-scale surveys and data sources to provide robust insights and cross-country comparisons.

Figure 5.8 *(Scenario 2, Question 4): Can you suggest some research papers that compare the impact of digital skills on the work and employment opportunities of people in the UK and Europe?*

Tool	Result
Consensus	Finding research directly comparing the impact of digital skills on employment across all of Europe can be challenging due to the vast number of countries and varying data collection methods. However, here are some research papers that offer valuable insights: • **'The digital skills mismatch in Europe' (European Centre for the Development of Vocational Training):** This report by the European Commission analyzes the digital skills gap in Europe. While not directly comparing employment outcomes in the UK and other countries, it provides data on digital skills deficiencies across Europe, which can be a strong indicator of potential employment impacts [European Commission website]. • **'Skills and Employability in the Digital Age' (OECD):** This report by the Organisation for Economic Co-operation and Development (OECD) explores the link between skills and employability in a digitalized world. It includes data on several European countries, allowing for some comparative analysis, although a dedicated UK-Europe comparison might be limited [OECD iLibrary website]. • **'Is Europe ready for the digital age? Findings from the DESI Report 2021' (European Commission):** This report by the European Commission utilizes the Digital Economy and Society Index (DESI) to assess the digital performance of EU member states. It includes data on digital skills and highlights disparities within Europe, offering insights for further research and comparison with the UK [European Commission website]. Here's an alternative approach to strengthen your research: • Look for **country-specific studies** on the impact of digital skills in the UK and a few other European countries of interest. • For example, you could find research papers on the UK and compare them with studies done in Germany, France, or Nordic countries, depending on your focus. Here are some resources to find relevant country-specific studies: • **National Statistics websites:** Most European countries have national statistics offices that publish reports on skills and employment. • **Academic databases:** Search for relevant keywords like 'digital skills,' 'employment,' and the specific European country in databases like Google Scholar or JSTOR. • **Think tanks and research institutions:** Look for research reports published by think tanks or research institutions focused on labor markets and digitalization in Europe. By combining these resources and approaches, you can effectively analyze the impact of digital skills on work and employment opportunities across the UK and select European countries, building a strong foundation for your research.
Copilot	Certainly! Here are some research papers that compare the impact of digital skills on work and employment opportunities in the UK and Europe: 1. **'Disconnected? Exploring the digital skills gap'** - Learning and Work Institute: • This report examines the future of digital skills in the UK's economy, the demand for skills among employers, and the digital skills gap. It also looks at the perspectives of young people on digital skills and their importance for succeeding in the labor market[1].

Figure 5.8 *Continued*

Tool	Result
	2. 'Digital Skills and Inclusion Research Working Group Evidence Brief' - GOV.UK: • Prepared by the Warwick Institute for Employment Research, this evidence brief discusses what digital skills adults need to succeed in the workplace now and in the next ten years. It includes case studies from various sectors and conceptualizes success in the workplace in the context of digital skills[2]. **3. 'Digital technologies, employment, and skills'** - Oxford Academic: • This article investigates the relationship between the diffusion of digital technologies, employment, and skills based on industry-level data from six major European economies, including the UK, over a five-year period[3]. **4. 'Digital Divide and Employment: From Job Disruption to...'** - Springer: • This chapter presents a multidimensional analysis of the changes in the labor market generated by digitization. It includes statistical analysis and a comparative situation between EU member countries[4]. These papers should provide a comprehensive view of how digital skills impact work and employment opportunities in the UK and Europe, offering valuable insights for your research.
Gemini	Finding research directly comparing the impact of digital skills on employment across all of Europe can be challenging due to the vast number of countries and varying data collection methods. However, here are some research papers that offer valuable insights: • **'The digital skills mismatch in Europe' (European Centre for the Development of Vocational Training):** This report by the European Commission analyzes the digital skills gap in Europe. While not directly comparing employment outcomes in the UK and other countries, it provides data on digital skills deficiencies across Europe, which can be a strong indicator of potential employment impacts [European Commission website]. • **'Skills and Employability in the Digital Age' (OECD):** This report by the Organisation for Economic Co-operation and Development (OECD) explores the link between skills and employability in a digitalized world. It includes data on several European countries, allowing for some comparative analysis, although a dedicated UK-Europe comparison might be limited [OECD iLibrary website]. • **'Is Europe ready for the digital age? Findings from the DESI Report 2021' (European Commission):** This report by the European Commission utilizes the Digital Economy and Society Index (DESI) to assess the digital performance of EU member states. It includes data on digital skills and highlights disparities within Europe, offering insights for further research and comparison with the UK [European Commission website]. Here's an alternative approach to strengthen your research: • Look for **country-specific studies** on the impact of digital skills in the UK and a few other European countries of interest. • For example, you could find research papers on the UK and compare them with studies done in Germany, France, or Nordic countries, depending on your focus. Here are some resources to find relevant country-specific studies: • **National Statistics websites:** Most European countries have national statistics offices that publish reports on skills and employment. • **Academic databases:** Search for relevant keywords like 'digital skills,' 'employment,' and the specific European country in databases like Google Scholar or JSTOR.

Figure 5.8 *Continued*

Tool	Result
	• **Think tanks and research institutions:** Look for research reports published by think tanks or research institutions focused on labor markets and digitalization in Europe. By combining these resources and approaches, you can effectively analyze the impact of digital skills on work and employment opportunities across the UK and select European countries, building a strong foundation for your research.
GPT-4o	Sure! Here are some research papers that compare the impact of digital skills on work and employment opportunities in the UK and Europe: **1. 'Digital Skills in the UK and Europe: Bridging the Gap'** • Authors: John Doe, Jane Smith • Summary: This paper provides a comparative analysis of the digital skills gap in the UK and various European countries. It examines how these skills impact employment opportunities and economic productivity. • Source: Journal of European Labor Studies, 2021. **2. 'Digital Transformation and Employment: A Comparative Study between the UK and Germany'** • Authors: Emily Johnson, Mark Weber • Summary: The study investigates the role of digital skills in the labor markets of the UK and Germany, focusing on how digital competencies influence job availability and career progression. • Source: International Journal of Digital Economy, 2020. **3. 'Digital Skills and Employment: Evidence from the UK and European Union'** • Authors: Laura Martin, Pierre Dubois • Summary: This research explores the correlation between digital skills and employment rates across the UK and EU member states, highlighting regional disparities and policy implications. • Source: European Journal of Workforce Development, 2022. **4. 'The Role of Digital Skills in Enhancing Employment Opportunities: A UK and EU Perspective'** • Authors: Sarah Thompson, David Gonzalez • Summary: The paper compares the impact of digital literacy on employment opportunities in the UK and the EU, with a focus on sector-specific requirements and the digital divide. • Source: Journal of Technological Advances in Employment, 2019. **5. 'Digital Competencies and Job Market Outcomes in Europe: A Cross-Country Analysis'** • Authors: Maria Rossi, Tom Lewis • Summary: This comparative analysis examines how digital competencies affect job market outcomes in various European countries, including the UK, with an emphasis on education and training policies. • Source: European Labour Market Review, 2020. **6. 'Digital Skills and Employment in the European Context: Case Studies from the UK and Scandinavia'** • Authors: Henrik Olsen, Alice Brown • Summary: The paper presents case studies from the UK and Scandinavian countries, analyzing how digital skills initiatives have impacted employment opportunities and economic growth. • Source: Nordic Journal of Digital Employment Studies, 2021. These papers provide a comprehensive view of the impact of digital skills on employment across different regions in Europe, including the UK. They cover various aspects such as policy implications, sector-specific analysis, and cross-country comparisons.

Figure 5.8 *Continued*

Tool	Result
Perplexity AI	Here are some relevant research papers that compare the impact of digital skills on work and employment opportunities in the UK and other European countries: 1. 'The Digital Skills Gap in the Workforce: Evidence from New Economies and Labour Markets' by Curtarelli et al. (2017) [1][2] This paper examines the digital skills gap across several European countries, including the UK. It compares the demand for digital skills by employers and the supply of skills in the workforce, highlighting differences across nations. 2. 'Digital Skills and the Future of Work: Challenges and Opportunities in a Changing Digital Landscape' by Grundke et al. (2018) [2][3] While not focused solely on the UK and Europe, this OECD report includes data and analysis on the role of digital skills in shaping employment prospects across different countries, allowing for comparisons between the UK and other European economies. 3. 'The Impact of Digital Skills on Employment and Wages in the European Union' by Falck et al. (2021) [3][4] This study uses data from the Programme for the International Assessment of Adult Competencies (PIAAC) to investigate the relationship between digital skills and labor market outcomes, such as employment and wages, across various European countries, including the UK. 4. 'Digital Skills and the Future of Work: Challenges and Opportunities in a Changing Digital Landscape' by Grundke et al. (2018) [4][5] This OECD report examines the role of digital skills in shaping employment prospects across different countries, including the UK and several other European nations, allowing for cross-country comparisons. 5. 'The Digital Skills Gap in Europe: Measurement, Trends and Policies' by Curtarelli et al. (2021) [5] This report by the European Commission's Joint Research Centre provides a comprehensive analysis of the digital skills gap across European countries, including the UK, and its impact on employment and economic growth. These research papers offer valuable insights into the varying levels of digital skills across different European countries, including the UK, and how these skills influence employment opportunities, wages, and overall labor market outcomes. By comparing data and findings across nations, these studies can help contextualize the UK's position and challenges in relation to other European economies. Citations: [1] https://learningandwork.org.uk/resources/research-and-reports/disconnected-exploring-the-digital-skills-gap/ [2] https://orca.cardiff.ac.uk/id/eprint/117039/1/Brown-Lloyd-and-Souto-Otero-2018.-The-prospects-for-skills-and-employment-in-an-age-of-digital-disruption.pdf [3] www.webrecruit.co/blog/the-uks-digital-skills-gap-navigating-the-challenges-of-digitalisation/ [4] www.sciencedirect.com/science/article/pii/S0040162524000751 [5] https://assets.publishing.service.gov.uk/media/654cfd94c0e06800101b2cf7/boosting_the_uptake_of_digital_careers_among_early_career_professionals_and_experienced_professionals_project_2.pdf
Scholar GPT	Here are some research papers that compare the impact of digital skills on work and employment opportunities in the UK and Europe: 1. **'Changing demand for skills in digital economies and societies' - International Labour Organization (ILO)**

Figure 5.8 *Continued*

Tool	Result
	- This paper examines the impact of digitalization on skills within and across sectors, with empirical evidence collected from case studies in selected countries. - [Link to PDF](www.ilo.org/media/378741/download) 2. **'The digital skills divide: evidence from the European tourism industry'** - This study discusses the lack of digital skills across Europe and the growing employment in digital technology sectors, highlighting the divide in digital skills. - [Link to article](www.emerald.com/insight/content/doi/10.1108/JTF-07-2020-0114/full/html) 3. **'Digital Skills and Inclusion Research Working Group Evidence Brief'** - Provides insights from the European Digital Skills Survey, analyzing digital skills for workplace readiness in both the US and the UK. - [Link to PDF](https://turingtrust.co.uk/wp-content/uploads/2024/04/Digital-Skills-for-Workplace.pdf) 4. **'Adaptability of the workforce in Europe – changing skills in the digital age'** - Explores how digital technologies impact the labor market in Europe, focusing on the need for acquiring new skills. - [Link to PDF](www.efri.uniri.hr/upload/10-Jandric-Randjelovic-2018-2.pdf) 5. **'The global digital skills gap' - RAND** - Discusses the necessity of digital skills for employees to future-proof their careers, with a focus on the UK and its high demand for digital skills in job postings. - [Link to PDF](www.rand.org/content/dam/rand/pubs/research_reports/RRA1500/RRA1533-1/RAND_RRA1533-1.pdf) 6. **'The economic impact of Basic Digital Skills and inclusion in the UK' - Good Things Foundation** - Analyzes the economic benefits of digital skills and inclusion in the UK, including their impact on earnings and job opportunities. - [Link to PDF](www.goodthingsfoundation.org/wp-content/uploads/2021/02/the_economic_impact_of_digital_skills_and_inclusion_in_the_uk_final_v2.pdf) 7. **'Digital skills drive gains for individuals, organisations and the UK economy' - Amazon UK** - This article reveals how digitally skilled workers in the UK experience higher job satisfaction and productivity, comparing insights with other regions. - [Link to article](www.aboutamazon.co.uk/news/aws/digital-skills-drive-gains-for-individuals-organisations-and-the-uk-economy) 8. **'Disconnected? Exploring the digital skills gap' - Learning and Work Institute** - Investigates the role of digital skills in the UK's economy and its importance for growth and productivity, with comparative insights from other studies. - [Link to article](https://learningandwork.org.uk/resources/research-and-reports/disconnected-exploring-the-digital-skills-gap/) These papers and articles provide a comprehensive look at the impact of digital skills on work and employment opportunities in the UK and Europe, highlighting both the benefits and the challenges associated with digital inclusion. If you need further assistance or more specific articles, feel free to ask!

Figure 5.8 *Continued*

Summary

Results generated for all the questions are summarised by all the chosen Gen AI tools which are easy to use for the undergraduate students, the target users in the two case studies. However, the results produced by the chosen Gen AI tools vary in terms of details, and some provide citations, other don't. Hence, the users – the undergraduate students in this context – should:

- carefully choose the Gen AI tools for access to information, and perhaps should choose more than one tool, so that they can compare the output
- identify the cited sources, and verify the content and context of the discussions presented in those sources
- ensure that they are not inadvertently copying content from sources without providing appropriate citations
- undertake further research and analysis rather than using the output as their own creation.

These and other issues and challenges associated with the use of Gen AI tools for access to scholarly information are discussed in more detail in Chapters 6, 7 and 8.

CHAPTER 6

Gen AI for Research Information

Introduction

This chapter discusses the results of a series of searches using some selected Gen AI tools for finding information based on some specific user needs in the context of research. It is important to note that it is not a comparison of different Gen AI tools *per se*. By investigating what some emerging Gen AI tools return in response to specific questions and commands, and how suitable these responses are for specific user needs in the context of research in higher education, this chapter aims to add new knowledge and trigger further discussions and debates on how the interactions with these tools, and the corresponding search results, can be improved to meet specific user needs and contexts for research and scholarly activities.

The search context

The discussions in this chapter are based on the outcomes of two case studies involving interactions with seven Gen AI tools to find answers for four scenario-based search tasks within the specific research-related contexts. Each case study is based on a scenario that mimics the common activities in university research. The scenarios are based on the typical search tasks of a postgraduate student at the beginning of their research for an MA/MSc dissertation; and the other scenario is based on the typical search tasks of a PhD student at the beginning of their research for a PhD study. All these scenarios represent typical examples of exploratory search (Marchionini, 2006) where the search tasks (Byström, 2002, 2007; Byström and Hansen, 2005) do not have a set answer, and instead, the user is required to undertake a series of activities to find the relevant information and data as they progress with the search.

In order to mimic the typical interactions with the conversational AI tools, four natural-language questions or prompts were created for each scenario.

It should be noted that these four questions may not be exhaustive to generate all the information and data required for the search tasks and goals associated with each scenario and the search context. However, they produce a variety of outputs that show the variety of search results produced by the Gen AI tools used here. The scenarios have been numbered as 3 and 4, to make these distinct from the Scenarios 1 and 2 discussed in Chapter 5. The scenarios and the associated search tasks, questions and prompts, are shown in Table 6.1.

Table 6.1 *Scenarios, search context and search questions/interactions*

Scenario and search topic	Search context	Questions/Interactions with the AI tool
3 Role of Gen AI-driven search tools in information access	A postgraduate student has chosen a topic for their MA/MSc dissertation on the topic. The search task should produce some background information and data on the topic such as how and where AI is being used for information access, and what are the recent developments and challenges; and these should be supported by the relevant literature and reports. The search should also produce some authoritative and relevant literature for writing a literature review, showing the key areas and trends of research.	1 What is the role of AI- and LLM-driven search tools on information access? 2 What are the potential challenges and pitfalls of the use of Gen AI-driven search tools for information search for research purposes? 3 What skills should the students and researchers have to make best use of the Gen AI-driven search tools in their studies and research? 4 Suggest some of the most relevant and recent research papers and reports on this topic
4 What role library and information services can play in addressing climate change	A PhD student has chosen a topic for their thesis on the topic. The search task should produce some background information and data on the topic showing what role libraries can play in addressing the climate change issues and what are the recent developments and challenges; and these should be supported by the relevant literature and reports. The task should also produce some relevant research output that can help to write a literature review, showing the key areas and trends of research.	1 What role can library and information services play in tackling the climate emergency? 2 Can you suggest some relevant research literature on this topic? 3 What is the current state of research on the role that libraries can play in tackling the climate emergency? 4 Who are the most leading authors, researchers and institutions on this topic that one must read?

Seven Gen AI-driven search tools – Claude, Consensus, Copilot, Gemini, GPT-4o, Perplexity AI and Scholar GPT – were chosen for this study. Each of the eight questions or prompts (Table 6.1) was presented to all the chosen tools, and the corresponding results were noted.

Search results

The results or outputs generated by the chosen Gen AI tools are discussed in this section. For some questions, only snippets of the output are produced, and for some questions/prompts where the tool is asked to recommend research literature, the entire set of results/outputs are presented in tables. These are followed by a brief set of observations and comments.

Scenario 3: A postgraduate student looking for some research information for a dissertation

Results generated by the chosen Gen AI tools for Scenario 3, Question 1 (Figure 6.1 on the next page) vary:

- Claude output is presented under seven headings in an easy-to-use summary, one for each point; no citations are provided.
- Consensus output is presented under six main headings, each with two subheadings; no citations are provided.
- Copilot output is presented under six headings in a summary form which are easy to read. However, all the points cite the same source, which appears to be an opinion paper rather than a peer-reviewed research paper or credible report.
- Gemini output is presented under nine headings – five of them show the advantages, and four show the potential pitfalls, followed by brief details; no citations are provided.
- GPT-4o output is presented under 10 headings followed by a summary of challenges and considerations. These are written in simple language and are easy to understand, but they do not provide any citations.
- Perplexity AI output is presented under seven headings, and a summary. It includes five citations but those do not lead to research papers or reports, instead leading to company pages discussing the role of AI and Generative AI.
- Scholar GPT output is presented under seven headings, each with two subsections, showing specific applications of AI in information access. Also, some examples of AI- and LLM-driven search tools are provided, followed by a conclusion of the benefits of such tools.

Tool	Result
Claude	AI-powered language models (LLMs) and search tools have the potential to significantly impact and transform the way we access and interact with information. These advanced technologies can play several crucial roles in enhancing information access: 1. Natural language processing: LLMs and AI-driven search tools can understand and process natural language ... 7. Continuous learning and improvement: As these AI systems interact with more data and user queries, they can continuously learn and improve their understanding of language and information, leading to better search results over time. However, it's important to note that the role of AI-driven search tools also raises concerns about potential biases, privacy issues, and the need for transparency and accountability in how these systems operate. Additionally... evolving topics. Overall, while AI and LLMs have the potential to revolutionize information access, their responsible development and deployment will be crucial in ensuring that they genuinely enhance and democratize ... and unintended consequences.
Consensus	Generative AI-driven search tools are transforming information access in several significant ways, enhancing the efficiency, accuracy, and personalization of information retrieval. Here's how they play a crucial role: ### 1. **Enhanced Information Retrieval** - **Contextual Understanding**: Unlike traditional keyword-based search engines, AI-driven tools understand the context of queries, enabling more accurate and relevant search results. They can interpret natural language queries, making it easier for users to find the information they need without requiring precise keywords. - **Semantic Search**: These tools go beyond exact keyword matching by understanding the intent and .... ### 6. **Challenges and Considerations** - **Bias and Fairness**: AI-driven search tools can sometimes reflect biases present in their training data, leading to skewed or unbalanced search results. Ensuring fairness and transparency in these systems is an ongoing challenge. - **Data Privacy**: As these tools rely on vast amounts of data to function effectively, issues around user data privacy and security are significant. Balancing the need for personalization with privacy concerns is critical. ### Conclusion Generative AI-driven search tools are revolutionizing how we access and interact with information. By enhancing search accuracy, personalizing results, and improving efficiency, these tools are making .. protecting user privacy.
Copilot	AI- and LLM-driven search tools have significantly transformed the landscape of information access. Here's how they play a pivotal role: **1. Enhanced Understanding**: These tools use advanced Natural Language Processing (NLP) to deeply understand language patterns, information, and contextual nuances. This allows them to interpret user queries more effectively and provide responses that are not only relevant but also contextually rich[1]. **2 ....**

Figure 6.1 *Examples of search results for Scenario 3, Question 1: What is the role of AI- and LLM-driven search tools on information access?*

Tool	Result
	6. Business Applications: When integrated into business search tools, LLMs can drastically reduce the gap between user queries and the most relevant results. They understand, interpret, and often augment data, providing businesses with a dynamic tool that continually adds value[4]. In essence, AI- and LLM-driven search tools are redefining the way we interact with information, making the search process more efficient, personalized, and accessible.
Gemini	AI- and LLM-driven search tools are revolutionizing how we access information, offering both advantages and potential drawbacks: **Advantages:** • **Enhanced Search Accuracy and Relevance:** AI and LLMs can understand the context and intent behind a user's query. This allows them to go beyond keyword matching and retrieve information that is truly relevant to the user's needs. • .... • **Multilingual Search Capabilities:** AI can break down language barriers by translating search queries and results in real-time. This allows users to access information from around the world, regardless of their native language. **Potential Drawbacks:** • **Filter Bubbles and Bias:** AI algorithms can personalize results in a way that reinforces existing biases. Users may only see information that confirms their existing beliefs and miss out on diverse perspectives. •... • **Access and Equity:** Not everyone has equal access to AI-powered search tools due to factors like internet connectivity or the cost of certain subscriptions. This can exacerbate existing digital divides. Overall, AI- and LLM-driven search tools are powerful tools that can significantly improve .. .. unbiased information.
GPT-4o	AI- and Large Language Model (LLM)-driven search tools play a significant role in enhancing information access in several ways: **1. Improved Search Relevance** AI and LLMs can understand and process natural language queries more effectively than traditional keyword-based search algorithms. This means they can better interpret the intent behind a search query and provide more relevant results. ... **10. Democratizing Knowledge** By lowering the barrier to accessing complex information, AI-driven search tools democratize knowledge. Users without specialized knowledge or research skills can still access high-quality, relevant information, thus bridging knowledge gaps and promoting greater equality in information access. **Challenges and Considerations** While AI-driven search tools offer numerous benefits, they also present challenges such as potential biases in training data, privacy concerns, and the need for transparency in how results are generated. Addressing .. and reliable. In summary, AI- and LLM-driven search tools significantly enhance the ability to access and .. comprehensive.

Figure 6.1 *Continued*

Tool	Result
Scholar GPT	AI- and Large Language Model (LLM)-driven search tools significantly enhance information access in several ways: ### 1. **Improved Search Accuracy and Relevance** - **Natural Language Understanding**: LLMs understand and process natural language queries more effectively, leading to more accurate and relevant search results. - **Contextual Awareness**: These tools can understand the context behind a query, providing more tailored and precise information. .... ### 7. **Accessibility and Inclusivity** - **Voice Search**: AI-driven tools often support voice search, making information access easier for individuals with disabilities. - **Adaptive Learning**: These tools can adapt to different user needs, providing customized support for learners and researchers at various levels. ### Examples of AI- and LLM-driven Search Tools - **Google Scholar**: Uses AI to index and rank scholarly articles, providing relevant academic resources. - **Semantic Scholar**: Employs AI to enhance the search and discovery of scientific literature. - **ChatGPT and Similar Models**: Offer conversational interfaces for information retrieval, making searches more interactive and engaging. ### Conclusion AI- and LLM-driven search tools revolutionize information access by improving the accuracy, speed, and relevance of search results. They enhance user experience through natural language ..., and everyday information-seeking activities.

Figure 6.1 *Continued*

Outputs generated for Scenario 3, Question 2 (Figure 6.2) show that:

- Claude presents the output under seven headings in an easy-to-use summary for each point, but no citations are provided.
- Consensus presents the output under seven headings, each with two subheadings with useful information, and a conclusion, but no citations are provided.
- Copilot presents the output under eight headings, each with brief details of the content and a link to the source. Altogether three items are cited – one is a research paper, and two look like news items.
- Gemini presents the output under five main headings, each with two or three bullet points, but no citations are provided.
- GPT-4o presents the output under nine points of challenges and concerns, each with two or three bullet points, and a five-point summary of strategies for mitigation. While these points are useful and easy to understand, they are not supported by citations.
- Perplexity AI presents the output under eight headings, each with a summary and supporting citations. Three of the cited items are research papers, and two others are company pages and a blog.

- Scholar GPT presents the output under nine headings, each briefly summarising the key challenges. These are followed by six strategies for mitigation, and a brief conclusion, but no citations are provided.

Tool	Result
Claude	While AI-driven search tools powered by large language models (LLMs) offer many potential benefits for accessing information, there are also several challenges and pitfalls that need to be considered, especially when it comes to using these tools for research purposes: 1. Bias and skewed perspectives: LLMs are trained on vast amounts of data from the internet, which can perpetuate biases and skewed perspectives present in the training data. This could lead to search results that reflect societal biases or present incomplete or one-sided views on certain topics, potentially affecting the validity and objectivity of research findings. …… 7. Privacy and security risks: AI-driven search tools may collect and process large amounts of user data, raising privacy concerns. … To mitigate these challenges, it is crucial to develop robust evaluation frameworks, establish clear guidelines for the responsible use of AI-driven search tools in research, and promote transparency and accountability in the development and … research findings.
Consensus	The use of Generative AI-driven search tools for research purposes offers many advantages, but it also presents several challenges and potential pitfalls that researchers need to be aware of: ### 1. **Bias and Fairness** - **Algorithmic Bias**: AI-driven search tools can inherit biases from the data they are trained on, leading to biased search results. This can skew the information retrieved, particularly in sensitive areas like social sciences, ethics, and health research. - **Reinforcement of Existing Biases**: These tools may reinforce existing biases by prioritizing popular or mainstream … ### 8. **Misinterpretation of AI-Generated Content** - **Difficulty in Interpreting Results**: AI-generated summaries or content may be misunderstood or misinterpreted, .. in research. - **Over-Confidence in AI Outputs**: Researchers may place undue confidence in AI-generated results, assuming that the …..errors. ### Conclusion While Generative AI-driven search tools offer substantial benefits in terms of efficiency and personalization, they .. academic research.
Copilot	The use of AI-driven search tools for research purposes comes with several potential challenges and pitfalls: **1.Data Fabrication and Falsification**: There's a concern that AI tools could inadvertently fabricate or falsify data, which can compromise ethical standards and academic integrity. This is particularly problematic in fields where data integrity is paramount[1]. …. **8.Search Engine Flaws**: AI-driven search engines may have inherent flaws that impact their ability to provide accurate and comprehensive search results. These could include issues with indexing, understanding context, or updating information[4].

Figure 6.2 *Examples of search results for Scenario 3, Question 2: What are the potential challenges and pitfalls of the use of AI-driven search tools for information search for research purposes?*

Tool	Result
	These challenges highlight the importance of a balanced approach to using AI in research, where the tools are used as aids rather than replacements for human judgment and expertise.
Gemini	AI-driven search tools offer a powerful new approach to information search, but they also come with potential challenges and pitfalls for researchers. Here's a breakdown of some key areas to consider: **Bias and Algorithmic Blind Spots:** • **Reinforcing Bias:** AI algorithms can perpetuate existing biases in the data they are trained on. This can lead to biased search results, limiting your exposure to diverse perspectives and potentially hindering your research findings. • ... **Additional Considerations:** • **Data Privacy and Security:** Researchers may be concerned about the privacy and security of their search data when using AI-powered search tools. Understanding the data practices of these tools is important. .... While AI-driven search tools offer numerous benefits, researchers should be aware of their limitations and potential ... research.
GPT-4o	AI-driven search tools offer significant advantages for information search and research purposes, but they also come with several challenges and pitfalls that need to be addressed to ensure their effective and ethical use. Here are some of the key challenges: **1. Bias and Fairness** • **Training Data Bias**: AI models are trained on large datasets that may contain biases. These biases can be reflected in the search results, potentially leading to skewed or unfair representations of information. • .... **9. Ethical and Legal Challenges** • **Intellectual Property**: Issues related to the use of copyrighted material in training datasets can pose legal challenges. • .... **Mitigation Strategies** • **Bias Mitigation**: Implementing techniques to identify and reduce biases in training data and algorithms. • ...... By addressing these challenges, the potential of AI-driven search tools for research purposes can be maximized while minimizing the associated risks and pitfalls.
Perplexity AI	Based on the provided search results, AI and large language models (LLMs) are playing an increasingly important role in transforming information access and search capabilities. Here are some key ways AI and LLMs are shaping the search engine landscape: 1. Enhanced Query Understanding [1][2] Traditional search engines relied on keyword matching, which could miss the context or intent behind a query. LLMs .... 8. Productivity Enhancements [4] LLMs can significantly boost productivity in areas like coding, automating documentation, and business process ... actions. Overall, the integration of AI and LLMs into search engines is transforming how users access and interact ... applications.

Figure 6.2 *Continued*

Tool	Result
	Citations: [1] https://analyticsengines.com/resources/news-events/large-language-models-unstructured-datas-new-best-friend/ .... [5] https://www.snowflake.com/guides/large-language-models-llms-machine-learning/
Scholar GPT	The use of AI-driven search tools for information search in research purposes offers many benefits, but it also comes with several challenges and pitfalls: ### 1. **Bias and Misinformation** - **Algorithmic Bias**: AI models can inherit biases present in the training data, leading to biased search results. - **Misinformation**: AI-driven tools may sometimes provide or prioritize incorrect or misleading information, especially if ... . ### 9. **Ethical and Legal Concerns** - **Ethical Use**: The use of AI in research raises ethical questions about data use, consent, and the potential for misuse of information. - **Intellectual Property**: Issues around intellectual property and copyright can arise, particularly if AI tools access and use ... ### Mitigation Strategies To address these challenges, several strategies can be implemented: - **Regular Audits**: Conduct regular audits of AI tools to identify and mitigate biases. - **.......................... ### Conclusion While AI-driven search tools significantly enhance research capabilities, it is crucial to be aware of their limitations .. minimizing risks.

Figure 6.2 *Continued*

Outputs for Scenario 3, Question 3 (Figure 6.3) vary:

- Claude output is presented under seven headings in an easy-to-use summary for each point, but no citations are provided.
- Consensus output is presented under eight main headings, each with one to three subheadings, discussing the key points, followed by a conclusion, but no citations are provided.
- Copilot output is presented under nine headings in a summary form, supported by four citations.
- Gemini output is presented under eight main headings, each with two to three bullet points discussing the key points. These are followed by five points discussing how the listed skills can be acquired; however, no citations are provided.
- GPT-4o output is presented under eight headings, each with two bullet points, and these are followed by a set of five recommendations on how to develop these skills. However, no citations are provided.

- Perplexity AI output is presented under six headings, each with three points and supporting citations, but only one of the cited items is a research paper, the others are company pages and blog.
- Scholar GPT output is presented under seven headings, each with two subsections briefly discussing the skills needed. This is followed by a set of guidelines for skills development, but there are no citations.

Tool	**Result**
Claude	To make the best use of AI-driven search tools in their studies and research, students and researchers should develop a combination of technical and critical thinking skills. Here are some key skills that can help them effectively leverage these tools: 1. Information literacy and critical evaluation skills: Students and researchers should have the ability to critically evaluate the information provided by AI-driven search tools, question the sources and biases, and cross-check the information .. analytical approach. ..... 7. Collaboration and communication skills: AI-driven search tools may facilitate collaboration and knowledge sharing among researchers and students. Strong communication and collaboration skills will be important to effectively share insights, discuss findings, and work together in leveraging these tools for research purposes. By developing these skills, students and researchers can better navigate the challenges and opportunities presented by AI-driven search tools, ensuring that they use these tools effectively and responsibly to enhance their studies and research endeavors.
Consensus	To make the best use of Generative AI-driven search tools in their studies and research, students and researchers should develop a combination of technical, critical thinking, and ethical skills. Here's a breakdown of the key skills required: ### 1. **Digital Literacy** - **Understanding AI and Its Limitations**: Students and researchers should have a basic understanding of how AI-driven search .. them. - **Navigating Digital Resources**: The ability to navigate and utilize various digital platforms and resources ... the ....information. ... ### 8. **Time Management** - **Efficient Research Practices**: Knowing when and how to use AI tools to speed up certain aspects of research, such as literature reviews or data analysis, without compromising quality, is crucial for managing time effectively. ### Conclusion By developing these skills, students and researchers can maximize the benefits of Generative AI-driven search ...in academic work.
Copilot	To make the best use of AI-driven search tools in studies and research, students and researchers should develop a combination of technical and critical thinking skills. Here are some key skills that are particularly important:

Figure 6.3 *Examples of search results for Scenario 3, Question 3: What skills should the students and researchers have to make best use of the AI-driven search tools in their studies and research?*

Tool	Result
	1.Critical Assessment: Researchers should critically assess the output of AI tools without accepting it as 'the truth'. It's important to read the original text instead of simply relying on AI-generated summaries[1]. .... 9.**Continuous Learning**: The tech field is constantly evolving, so being able to learn and adapt to new tools and technologies is vital[4]. By honing these skills, students and researchers can leverage AI-driven search tools to enhance their research process and optimize their time without using AI to replace the critical thinking required to carry out the research[1].
Gemini	Here are some crucial skills students and researchers should develop to make the best use of AI-driven search tools: **Critical Thinking and Information Literacy:** • **Evaluating Source Credibility:** The ability to assess the legitimacy, authority, and bias of information sources remains paramount. Researchers need to go beyond what the AI tool presents and critically evaluate the information found. • ... **Additional Skills:** • **Data Privacy and Security:** Being aware of data privacy practices employed by AI search tools is crucial. Researchers should choose tools with strong data security measures and understand how their search data is being used. • ...... By developing these skills, students and researchers can harness the power of AI-driven search tools to conduct more efficient, effective, and unbiased research, ultimately leading to more robust and well-informed findings.
GPT-4o	To effectively utilize AI-driven search tools in their studies and research, students and researchers should develop a combination of technical, analytical, and critical thinking skills. Here are the key skills they should possess: **1. Digital Literacy** • **Understanding AI Basics**: Familiarity with basic concepts of AI and machine learning, including how these ... applications. • ... **8. Ethical and Legal Awareness** • **Privacy and Data Protection**: Understanding of privacy laws and data protection principles relevant to using AI ... **Practical Steps to Develop These Skills:** **Take Online Courses**: Enroll in courses that cover AI, digital literacy, and information management. Platforms like Coursera, edX, and Udacity offer relevant courses. ..... **Read and Research**: Stay informed about the latest research and publications on the use of AI in academia and information science. By developing these skills, students and researchers can maximize the benefits of AI-driven search tools, making their ... insightful.
Perplexity AI	Based on the provided research papers and articles, students and researchers should possess the following skills to effectively utilize AI-driven search tools in their studies and research:

Figure 6.3 *Continued*

Tool	Result
	1. Critical Thinking and Evaluation Skills [1][3][4] - Ability to critically evaluate the information and results provided by AI search tools............. ... 6. Adaptability and Continuous Learning [1][4] - Willingness to continuously learn and adapt to new AI search tools and technologies.......... By developing these skills, students and researchers can effectively navigate the rapidly evolving landscape of AI-driven .. pursuits. Citations: [1] https://www.elegantthemes.com/blog/business/best-ai-tools-for-education [......... [5] https://www.linkedin.com/pulse/ais-role-shaping-search-engine-landscape-marco-van-hurne-nuhce
Scholar GPT	To effectively utilize AI-driven search tools in their studies and research, students and researchers should develop a range of skills that encompass technical proficiency, critical thinking, and ethical considerations. Here are some key skills: ### 1. **Technical Proficiency** - **Familiarity with AI Tools**: Understanding how various AI-driven search tools work, including their features, capabilities, and ... - **.... ### 7. **Adaptability and Lifelong Learning** - **Staying Updated**: Keeping abreast of new developments in AI-driven search tools and continually updating skills to use the latest .... ### Practical Steps for Skill Development 1. **Workshops and Training**: Participate in workshops, webinars, and training sessions on using AI-driven search tools and .. literacy. ... 4. **Collaboration**: Collaborate with peers and mentors to share knowledge, techniques, and best practices in using AI tools for research. ### Conclusion By developing these skills, students and researchers can effectively harness the power of AI-driven search tools to enhance their research capabilities, improve the quality of their studies, and contribute to the advancement of knowledge in their respective fields.

Figure 6.3 *Continued*

Outputs for Scenario 3, Question 4 (Figure 6.4) vary:

- Claude recommends seven items, each with a summary, and some citation data. However, finding some of the cited items with the data provided appears to be difficult.
- Consensus recommends five items, each with the title, authors, abstract and a link.
- Copilot output is presented under four headings with a brief abstract of the source materials, but all the four citations lead to the same source.

- Gemini recommends three items, each with an abstract and the link. There is also a section recommending how to find the relevant literature in journals of library and information science and educational technology, and conference proceedings.
- Results from GPT-4o are presented under 10 points, each citing the authors and the source. However, finding the items, using the citation data provided, appears to be difficult.
- Perplexity AI recommends five items, each with brief details, but none of these are peer-reviewed research papers.
- Scholar GPT output does not recommend specific items; instead, it lists some specific areas of research, provides some indicative articles on the topics, and suggestions on where to find the relevant literature such as Google Scholar, library and information science databases and professional organisations and conferences.

Tool	Result
Claude	Here are some relevant and recent research papers on the topic of using AI-driven search tools, language models, and the associated challenges and opportunities for students and researchers: 1. 'AI Language Models for Academic Writing: Opportunities and Challenges' by Sebastian Ruder et al. (2023) - This paper discusses the potential applications of large language models (LLMs) in academic writing, including literature review, ideation, and writing assistance, while also highlighting the risks of hallucinations, biases, and ethical concerns. 2. 'The Promise and Peril of AI for Students and Education: A Literature Review' by Zachary A. Pardos et al. (2022) - This literature review examines the benefits and challenges of using AI in education, including AI-driven search tools and language models, addressing issues such as fairness, privacy, and the need for human oversight. 3. 'AI-Assisted Information Search and Retrieval: Challenges and Opportunities' by Kamran Munir et al. (2022) - This paper explores the potential of AI-driven search tools to enhance information search and retrieval, while also discussing challenges related to interpretability, bias, and the need for human-AI collaboration. 4. 'The Impact of AI on Academic Research: A Systematic Literature Review' by Weiwei Zhang et al. (2022) - This systematic review analyzes the impact of AI on various aspects of academic research, including information search, literature review, and knowledge discovery, highlighting both the opportunities and potential pitfalls. 5. 'Ethical Considerations for the Use of AI Language Models in Academic Writing' by Arvind Narayanan et al. (2022) - This paper examines the ethical implications of using AI language models for academic writing, addressing concerns such as plagiarism, authorship attribution, and the potential for perpetuating biases and misinformation.

Figure 6.4 *(Scenario 3, Question 4): Can you suggest some of the most relevant and recent research on this topic?*

Tool	Result
	6. 'AI-Powered Search Tools: Enhancing Information Access or Perpetuating Bias?' by Lilian Edwards et al. (2021) - This study investigates the potential biases and ethical concerns associated with AI-driven search tools, particularly in the context of information access and knowledge democratization. 7. 'The Role of AI in Information Literacy Education: Opportunities and Challenges' by Valerie Hill et al. (2021) - This paper explores the potential of AI-driven tools to support information literacy education, while also discussing the need for critical thinking skills and ethical frameworks to mitigate potential risks. These research papers provide valuable insights into the opportunities, challenges, and best practices associated with the use of AI-driven search tools and language models in academic and research settings. They cover topics such as ethical considerations, bias mitigation, human-AI collaboration, and the development of necessary skills for students and researchers.
Consensus	Here are some recent and relevant research papers and reports on the skills required to use AI-driven search tools for research: 1. **Reflections on Tests of AI-Search Tools in the Academic Search Process** - **Authors**: L. Wildgaard, Anne Vils, Solveig Sandal Johnsen - **Abstract**: This paper reflects on tests conducted at the Royal Library in Denmark to assess AI-powered search tools in academic searches. The study explores the potential of AI search interfaces to challenge preconceived notions and reduce cognitive bias in the search process, while also identifying barriers to practical implementation in academic settings. - [Link to Paper](https://consensus.app/papers/reflections-tests-aisearch-tools-search-process-wildgaard/022c7ae8944e56dcb339e699836584aa/?utm_source=chatgpt) 2. **AI in Online-Learning Research: Visualizing and Interpreting the Journal Publications from 1997 to 2019** - **Authors**: Gwo-jen Hwang, Y. Tu, Kai-Yu Tang - **Abstract**: This study reviews AI-supported online learning (AIoL) research, focusing on trends and the roles of AI tools in education. It highlights the evolution of AIoL from intelligent tutoring systems to personalized and adaptive learning environments, providing insights into how AI tools are shaping educational research. - [Link to Paper](https://consensus.app/papers/onlinelearning-research-visualizing-interpreting-hwang/40329cf08d2457729828803c0ae9a98b/?utm_source=chatgpt) 3. **Assessing the Potential and Risks of AI-Based Tools in Higher Education: Results from an eSurvey and SWOT Analysis** - **Authors**: Kerstin Denecke, Robin Glauser, Daniel Reichenpfader - **Abstract**: This paper presents the results of a survey and SWOT analysis exploring the strengths, weaknesses, opportunities, and threats of using AI-based tools in higher education. The study emphasizes the importance of developing skills for responsible and efficient use of these tools in academic settings. - [Link to Paper](https://consensus.app/papers/assessing-risks-aibased-tools-higher-education-results-denecke/134596b0a4235685b6d873b124c304ea/?utm_source=chatgpt) 4. **Mapping Artificial Intelligence in Education Research: A Network-Based Keyword Analysis** - **Authors**: Shihui Feng, N. Law

Figure 6.4 *Continued*

Tool	Result
	- **Abstract**: This study provides a comprehensive analysis of AI in education research from 2010 to 2019. It identifies key themes and trends, such as intelligent tutoring systems and natural language processing, and explores the role of AI tools in shaping educational research. - [Link to Paper](https://consensus.app/papers/mapping-intelligence-education-research-network based-feng/43ec752bc90758cbb7b1c7cb67225ca4/?utm_source=chatgpt) 5. **Artificial Intelligence-Based Tools in the Context of Open Science** - **Authors**: Hege Charlotte Lysholm Faber, A. Gasparini, Michael Grote - **Abstract**: This poster presents the potential and challenges of using AI-based tools in academia, focusing on their role in supporting research and the need for greater understanding of their ethical implications. It discusses the impact of these tools on research workflows and the importance of integrating them into academic practices responsibly. - [Link to Paper](https://consensus.app/papers/artificial-intelligencebased-tools-open-science-faber/d995797ba1be5df9bc2db7106b7f054c/?utm_source=chatgpt) These papers provide valuable insights into the use of AI-driven search tools in academic research, exploring both their potential benefits and the challenges they present.
Copilot	1. **'Autonomous LLM-driven research from data to human-verifiable research papers'**: • **Abstract**: As AI promises to accelerate scientific discovery, it remains unclear whether fully AI-driven research is possible while adhering to key scientific values such as transparency, traceability, and verifiability. This paper introduces an automation platform called **data-to-paper**, which guides interacting LLM agents through a complete stepwise research process. The process allows human oversight and interactions, resulting in information-traceable research papers. While fully autonomous cycles can create manuscripts that recapitulate peer-reviewed publications without major errors, human co-piloting becomes critical for accuracy as goal complexity increases[1]. • Read the full paper. 2. **'Knowledge Adaptation from Large Language Model to Recommendation for Practical Industrial Application'**: • **Abstract**: Contemporary recommender systems predominantly rely on collaborative filtering techniques, overlooking semantic information embedded within textual descriptions of items. This paper proposes the **LEARN (Llm-driven knowlEdge Adaptive RecommeNdation)** framework, which synergizes open-world knowledge with collaborative knowledge. By utilizing pretrained LLMs as item encoders and preserving open-world knowledge, LEARN bridges the gap between open-world and collaborative domains. Offline and online experiments demonstrate the efficacy of this approach in practical industrial applications[2]. • Read the full paper. 3. **'AI search tools now, before they skew research'** (Nature): • **Abstract**: AI tools assisted by large language models (LLMs) are changing how researchers find scholarly information.

Figure 6.4 *Continued*

Tool	Result
	For example, **scite Assistant** uses GPT-3.5 to generate answers from a database of millions of scientific papers. Another tool, **Elicit**, uses an LLM to write answers for searches in scholarly databases. Researchers should be aware of these tools and their potential impact on research[3]. • Read the article. **4. 'LLMs may Dominate Information Access: Neural Retrievers'**: • **Abstract**: This work evaluates different information retrieval (IR) models in scenarios involving both human-written and LLM-generated texts. It explores the dominance of LLMs in information access and retrieval[4]. • Read the full paper. These papers provide valuable insights into the intersection of AI, LLMs, and information access. Happy reading!
Gemini	Here are some suggestions for recent research on the skills needed to effectively use AI-driven search tools for studies and research: • **'The Impact of Artificial Intelligence on Scholarly Search and Research Practices' (2023, Journal of Librarianship and Scholarly Communication):** This research explores how AI is changing scholarly search and the skills needed for researchers to navigate this evolving landscape. It highlights the importance of critical thinking and information literacy alongside the ability to formulate effective search queries for AI tools [Journal of Librarianship and Scholarly Communication website - subscription may be required]. • **"AI-powered literature search: How to train researchers to use it effectively?' (2022, Learned Publishing):** This study focuses on training researchers to leverage AI-powered literature search tools effectively. It emphasizes the need for training programs that equip researchers with critical appraisal skills and an understanding of AI's limitations [Learned Publishing website - subscription may be required]. • **"Developing Information Literacy Skills for the Age of Artificial Intelligence' (2021, Journal of Educational Technology Development and Exchange):** This paper takes a broader approach, examining how information literacy skills need to be adapted in the age of AI. It highlights the importance of skills like identifying bias in AI algorithms and evaluating the credibility of information retrieved through AI tools [Journal of Educational Technology Development and Exchange website]. In addition to these specific papers, here are some resources to find more recent research: • **'Library and Information Science Journals:** Search for keywords like 'AI search tools,' 'research skills,' and 'information literacy' in databases like ERIC or library science journals. These resources often focus on the latest trends and developments in research practices. • **'Educational Technology Journals:** Journals focused on educational technology may also publish research on the skills needed to utilize AI tools effectively in an academic setting. • **'Conference Proceedings:** Look for recent conference proceedings on topics like digital scholarship or information literacy. These can provide insights into the latest research presented by academics in the field. By using these resources and focusing on recent publications (within the last 3–5 years), you can ensure your research captures the most up-to-date information on the skills required to make the best use of AI-driven search tools for studies and research.

Figure 6.4 *Continued*

Tool	Result
GPT-4o	ChatGPT Certainly! Here are some relevant research papers and articles that explore the skills students and researchers need to effectively utilize AI-driven search tools in their academic work: **1. 'Digital Literacy and Its Impact on Student Learning and Achievement'** • Authors: Jennifer R. Hill, Michael J. Smith • Summary: This paper discusses the components of digital literacy and their significance in modern education, emphasizing the importance of digital literacy skills for effectively using AI-driven tools. • Source: Journal of Educational Technology, 2021. **2. 'Critical Thinking in the Age of AI: Skills for Researchers'** • Authors: Sarah E. Nelson, Robert B. Hughes • Summary: The study explores the role of critical thinking skills in evaluating AI-generated information and provides strategies for researchers to enhance these skills. • Source: International Journal of Research Methods in Education, 2022. **3. 'Leveraging AI in Academic Research: A Guide to Effective Use'** • Authors: Emily Chen, David L. Robinson • Summary: This guide outlines the technical and analytical skills needed to effectively use AI tools in research, including practical tips and case studies. • Source: Research Technology Management, 2020. **4. 'Information Literacy in the Digital Age: Implications for AI-Driven Research'** • Authors: Linda C. Li, Thomas J. Murphy • Summary: This paper examines the concept of information literacy in the context of AI, highlighting the skills required to critically assess and utilize AI-generated information. • Source: Journal of Information Science, 2019. **5. 'Developing Adaptability and Continuous Learning Skills for AI Integration in Research'** • Authors: Maria J. González, John A. Foster • Summary: The research focuses on the importance of adaptability and continuous learning for researchers to keep up with evolving AI technologies. • Source: Journal of Applied Research in Higher Education, 2021. **6. 'Ethical Considerations and Skills for Using AI in Academic Research'** • Authors: Rachel K. Evans, William T. Johnson • Summary: This article discusses the ethical skills and awareness researchers need to responsibly use AI tools, including privacy and data protection. **7. 'AI Literacy: Essential Skills for the Future Workforce'** • Authors: Jessica M. Richards, Steven E. Perez • Summary: This paper provides an overview of AI literacy, outlining the key skills needed to understand and work with AI technologies effectively. • Source: Journal of Vocational Education & Training, 2022. **8. 'Collaborative Research in the AI Era: Skills for Effective Teamwork'** • Authors: Natalie S. Martinez, Henry D. Clark • Summary: The study emphasizes the collaborative skills necessary for using AI tools in research teams, including communication and problem-solving. • Source: Collaborative Research Journal, 2021.

Figure 6.4 *Continued*

Tool	Result
	9. 'Enhancing Research Efficiency with AI Tools: Best Practices and Skill Development' • Authors: Paul H. Anderson, Laura B. Mitchell • Summary: This paper provides practical recommendations for researchers on how to develop the skills needed to maximize the efficiency of AI tools in their research workflow. • Source: Journal of Research Administration, 2020. **10. 'From Information Retrieval to Knowledge Discovery: The Role of AI in Modern Research'** • Authors: Susan M. Brown, Edward J. Green • Summary: This research explores how AI transforms information retrieval into knowledge discovery and the skills researchers need to navigate this transition. • Source: Knowledge Management Research & Practice, 2022. These resources cover a range of skills from digital literacy and critical thinking to ethical considerations and collaborative abilities, providing a comprehensive view of what students and researchers need to effectively use AI-driven search tools in their academic pursuits.
Perplexity AI	Based on the provided search results, here are some of the most relevant and recent research papers/articles on the role of AI and large language models (LLMs) in shaping the search engine landscape: 1. 'AI Search Engine Tools in 2024' by Futurepedia [1] This comprehensive article discusses the latest AI-powered search engines and tools that are redefining the search experience. It covers generative AI search assistants like Andi, AI-enhanced precision searches, visual data insights through AI image search, and AI-driven job matching and personalized recommendations. 2. 'AI's Role in Shaping the Search Engine Landscape' by Marco Van Hurne [2] This LinkedIn article explores how AI has transformed search engines from keyword-focused to personalized and proactive experiences. It discusses the rise of 'queryless' search, the power of user data in tailoring content, and the impact of AI innovations like Google Voice Search and Multisearch. 3. 'AI Search Tools' by UCL Library Guides [3] This guide from University College London summarizes emerging AI search tools like Scite, Keenious, and Consensus that leverage large language models for enhanced search capabilities. It highlights their strengths in generating relevant answers, analyzing document content, and providing AI-powered academic search. 4. 'Five Fascinating AI Search Engines in 2024' by INDIAai [4] This article discusses five notable AI search engines, including Perplexity, DuckDuckGo, Brave, Bing Chat, and You.com. It highlights their unique features, such as privacy protection, ad-free experiences, fact-checking, and personalized search experiences. 5. 'What is AI-Powered Site Search?' by Algolia [5] This blog post explains the concept of AI-powered site search, where machine learning and natural language processing are used to understand user intent and provide accurate and relevant search experiences. It discusses the benefits of AI search for businesses and introduces Algolia's AI-native search solution, NeuralSearch. These sources provide a comprehensive overview of the latest developments, tools, and research in the field of AI-driven search engines. They cover various aspects, including generative AI assistants, personalization, privacy, fact-checking, and the integration of machine learning and natural language processing into search experiences.

Figure 6.4 *Continued*

Tool	Result
	Citations: [1] www.futurepedia.io/ai-tools/search-engine [2] www.linkedin.com/pulse/ais-role-shaping-search-engine-landscape-marco-van-hurne-nuhce [3] https://library-guides.ucl.ac.uk/research-metrics/ai-search-tools [4] https://indiaai.gov.in/article/five-fascinating-ai-search-engines-in-2024 [5] www.algolia.com/blog/ai/what-is-ai-powered-site-search/
Scholar GPT	I encountered an issue while trying to retrieve specific recent research on AI-driven search tools for information access in research. However, I can suggest some approaches and known recent research areas that you can explore: ### Relevant and Recent Research Areas 1. **AI and Information Retrieval**: - **Natural Language Processing (NLP)**: Research on how NLP enhances search tool capabilities. - **Contextual Search Algorithms**: Studies focusing on algorithms that improve the relevance and accuracy of search results. 2. **User Interaction with AI-driven Tools**: - **User Experience (UX)**: Research on how users interact with AI-driven search tools and the impact on user satisfaction. - **Personalization and Customization**: Studies on the effectiveness of personalized search results and recommendations. 3. **Ethical and Social Implications**: - **Bias and Fairness**: Research on mitigating bias in AI-driven search results. - **Data Privacy and Security**: Studies on ensuring data privacy and security in AI-powered information retrieval systems. 4. **Integration with Academic Libraries**: - **Digital Libraries**: Research on integrating AI-driven search tools with digital library systems to improve access to academic resources. - **Educational Applications**: Studies on the use of AI in educational settings to enhance research and learning outcomes. ### Example Articles and Sources 1. **'AI-driven search engines: Enhancing the discovery of academic literature'**: - Focuses on the advancements in AI-driven search technologies and their impact on academic research. - Available on platforms like IEEE Xplore and SpringerLink. 2. **'The role of AI in improving research efficiency: A comprehensive review'**: - A review article summarizing various AI applications in research processes, including search tools. - Available in journals like the Journal of Information Science and Library Quarterly. 3. **'Ethical considerations in the use of AI for academic research'**: - Discusses the ethical challenges and considerations in deploying AI-driven tools in research. - Published in Ethics and Information Technology and similar journals. ### How to Find These Articles 1. **Google Scholar**: - Use search queries like 'AI-driven search tools for research' or 'AI in academic information retrieval' to find relevant articles. 2. **Library Databases**: - Access databases like JSTOR, PubMed, IEEE Xplore, and SpringerLink through your institution's library to find peer-reviewed articles on the topic.

Figure 6.4 *Continued*

Tool	Result
	3. **Professional Organizations and Conferences**: - Look for publications and conference proceedings from organizations like ACM (Association for Computing Machinery) and IEEE (Institute of Electrical and Electronics Engineers). By exploring these resources, you should be able to find the most relevant and recent research on the role of AI-driven search tools in information access for research purposes. If you need further assistance with accessing specific articles or databases, feel free to ask!

Figure 6.4 *Continued*

Scenario 4: A PhD student is looking for information on a research topic

Outputs in Scenario 4, Question 1 (Figure 6.5) vary:

- Results from Claude are presented under seven headings in an easy-to-use summary for each point; no citations are provided.
- Results from Consensus are presented under five broad headings, each with two subheadings, and a summary; no citations are provided.
- Copilot output presents six summary points, each with a citation. However, all the citations point to a blog on DCMSlibraries (dcmslibraries.blog.gov.uk).
- Gemini output is presented under four main headings, each with three bullet points, followed by a conclusion, but no citations are provided.
- GPT-4o output is presented in eight headings, each with two bullet points; and a summary, but citations are not provided.
- Perplexity AI output is presented under six headings, each with a summary and citation. Altogether, five items are cited which are more like opinion papers than peer-reviewed research papers.
- Results from Scholar GPT are presented under six main heading, each with two or three subheadings discussing the key points; no citations are provided.

Tool	Result
Claude	Libraries and information services can play a significant role in tackling the climate emergency in several ways: 1. Promoting environmental literacy and awareness: Libraries can curate and provide access to reliable information resources on climate change, sustainable practices, and environmental issues. They can organize educational programs, workshops, and exhibitions to raise awareness and promote environmental literacy among the community. ..... 7. Collaborating with other organizations: Libraries can collaborate with environmental organizations, government agencies, and other stakeholders to develop and disseminate climate-related information resources, educational materials, and joint initiatives to address the climate emergency more effectively.

Figure 6.5 *Examples of search results for Scenario 4, Question 1: What role can library and information services play in tackling the climate emergency?*

Tool	Result
	By leveraging their resources, expertise, and community connections, libraries and information services can contribute significantly to raising awareness, promoting sustainable practices, supporting research, and facilitating community engagement in tackling the climate emergency.
Consensus	Library and Information Services (LIS) can play a crucial role in tackling the climate emergency by leveraging their unique position as community hubs, educational institutions, and information gatekeepers. Here are the key roles LIS can play: ### 1. **Education and Awareness** - **Environmental Literacy**: Libraries can curate and provide access to a wealth of information on climate science, sustainability .... - **Public Programs**: Libraries can organize events, such as lectures, film screenings, and discussion groups, focused on climate .... ### 5. **Information Dissemination and Access** - **Trusted Information Sources**: Libraries are trusted institutions that can combat misinformation by providing access to .... - **Data Repositories**: Libraries can serve as repositories for local environmental data, helping communities track changes ... ### Conclusion Library and Information Services are well-positioned to play a multifaceted role in tackling the climate emergency. By educating the public, building community resilience, advocating for climate justice, adopting sustainable practices, and ensuring ... by climate change.
Copilot	**Libraries and information services** play a crucial role in addressing the climate emergency. Here are some ways they contribute: **1.Disseminating Objective Knowledge**: Libraries serve as community hubs and information centers. They disseminate **objective knowledge** about climate change, providing accurate information to the public. By offering resources, books, and educational materials, libraries empower individuals to understand the climate crisis better[1]. .... **6. Inspiring Action**: Libraries inspire action by curating relevant materials, hosting events, and encouraging dialogue. They create safe spaces for discussing climate issues, fostering a sense of urgency and commitment to change[1]. In summary, libraries are not only repositories of knowledge but also catalysts for climate action. Their role extends beyond information dissemination—they actively contribute to building a more sustainable and resilient world.
Gemini	Libraries and information services can play a crucial role in tackling the climate emergency by acting as hubs for education, awareness, and action. Here are some key ways they can contribute: **1. Providing Credible Climate Change Information:** • **Curated Collections:** Libraries can curate collections of reliable and up-to-date resources on climate change, ..information. ... . **4. Leading by Example:** • **Sustainable Practices:** Libraries can implement sustainable practices within their own operations, such as using energy-efficient lighting, reducing paper waste, and offering digital resources. • ......

Figure 6.5 *Continued*

Tool	Result
	Overall, libraries and information services have a unique opportunity to be powerful change agents in addressing the climate emergency. By providing access to information, fostering community engagement, and leading by example, libraries can empower individuals and communities to take action towards a more sustainable future.
GPT-4o	Library and information services can play a significant role in addressing the climate emergency through various initiatives and actions. Here are some key ways they can contribute: **1. Educating and Raising Awareness** • **Climate Literacy Programs**: Libraries can develop and offer programs and workshops to educate the public about climate change, its causes, effects, and mitigation strategies.............. • ..... **8. Policy Advocacy and Leadership** • **Policy Recommendations**: Using their trusted position in the community, libraries can advocate for local, regional, and national policies that support climate action and sustainability. • ..... In summary, libraries and information services can be pivotal in tackling the climate emergency by educating the public, ... climate change.
Perplexity AI	Based on the provided search results, libraries and information services can play an important role in tackling the climate emergency in the following ways: 1. Providing Access to Authoritative Climate Information [1] Libraries can serve as reliable sources of accurate and up-to-date information on climate change, its impacts, and potential solutions. By curating and disseminating authoritative resources from scientific organizations, government agencies, and reputable research institutions, libraries can help combat misinformation and raise public awareness. .... 6. Collaborating with Local and Global Initiatives [2][4] Libraries can collaborate with local and global initiatives, organizations, and networks focused on climate action. By partnering with ... While the search results do not explicitly mention the role of libraries and information services, the importance of access to ... efforts. Citations: [1] https://acss.org.uk/a-social-and-political-problem-exploring-the-role-of-social-science-research-in-tackling-the-climate-crisis/ [..... [5] https://www.forestryengland.uk/climate-action
Scholar GPT	Libraries and information services can play a crucial role in addressing the climate emergency through various strategies and actions. Here are some key roles they can take on: 1. **Information Dissemination and Education**: - **Raising Awareness**: Libraries can provide access to reliable information on climate change, its impacts, and mitigation strategies. This can include books, scientific articles, reports, documentaries, and more. .... 6. **Cultural and Historical Preservation**: - **Archiving Climate History**: Preserving records and documents related to climate history, policies, and actions taken over time. - **Highlighting Indigenous Knowledge**: Preserving and sharing indigenous knowledge and practices that ... and climate resilience.

Figure 6.5 *Continued*

Tool	Result
	By leveraging these roles, libraries and information services can be pivotal in fostering a well-informed and engaged public, supporting climate research, and promoting sustainable practices and policies. This comprehensive approach can help mitigate the impacts of climate change and build more resilient communities.

Figure 6.5 *Continued*

Outputs for Scenario 4, Question 2 (Figure 6.6) vary:

- Claude recommends seven items with a summary and citation, followed by an overall summary; however, some of the items cannot be found with the citation data provided.
- Consensus recommends five items, each with the title, authors, abstract and a link.
- Copilot cites four items discussing the key points in each paper, followed by its citation. However, three of the citations are from the same commentary that appeared in 2018, and another citation links to a paper on libraries' role in disaster management.
- Gemini recommends five items; each presents under a specific heading with brief information about the item and a link.
- Output from GPT-4o appears under 10 headings with a summary of the paper and its citation – authors and source. However, some of the sources cannot be located using the citation data provided.
- Output from Perplexity AI appears under five key points, each with a summary of the paper and citation; two of these are research papers.
- Scholar GPT does not provide or recommend any research literature. Instead, it provides some guidelines on where and how to search the relevant literature.

Tool	Result
Claude	Certainly! Here are some relevant research papers and articles that discuss the potential role of libraries in addressing the climate emergency: 1. 'Libraries on the Front Lines of the Climate Crisis' by Cheryl Collier and John Bracken (2021), published in the journal Library Trends. - This article explores how libraries can serve as community leaders, educators, and facilitators in climate action, as well as promote environmental sustainability in their operations and services. 2. 'The Role of Academic Libraries in Addressing Climate Change' by Maria A. Jankowska (2021), published in the journal College & Research Libraries News.

Figure 6.6 *(Scenario 4, Question 2): Can you suggest some relevant research literature on the role that libraries can play in tackling the climate emergency?*

Tool	Result
	- This paper discusses the ways in which academic libraries can support climate change research, education, and advocacy through their collections, services, and collaborations with faculty and researchers. 3. 'Sustainable Libraries, Sustainable Services: A Global View' edited by Petra Hauke, Karen Latimer, and Klaus Ulrich Werner (2021). - This book chapter explores global perspectives and case studies on how libraries can contribute to sustainable development goals, including climate action, through their operations, programs, and services. 4. 'Academic Libraries as Sustainability Leaders: Exploring the Potential for Institutional Change' by Sarah Maren Voss and Samantha McBride (2020), published in the journal Sustainability. - This study investigates the role of academic libraries in promoting sustainability initiatives and advocating for climate action within their institutions and communities. 5. 'Libraries and Climate Change: Engaging with the Community' by Sharon Collie and Valerie Jacobs (2019), published in the journal Public Library Quarterly. - This article explores how public libraries can engage with their communities to raise awareness, provide information resources, and promote environmental literacy related to climate change. 6. 'The Green Library Planner: What Every Librarian Needs to Know Before Starting to Build or Renovate a Library' by Anca Mãnescu et al. (2018), published by the International Federation of Library Associations and Institutions (IFLA). - This publication provides guidance and best practices for libraries to incorporate sustainable and environmentally friendly strategies in their physical infrastructure and operations. 7. 'Libraries and the Environment: A Bibliometric Analysis of Environmental Topics in Library and Information Science Literature' by Monika Antonelli and Natalie G. Taylor (2023), published in the journal Sustainability. - This study analyzes the research trends and topics related to libraries and environmental sustainability, including climate change, through a bibliometric analysis of library and information science literature. These research papers, articles, and publications provide valuable insights into the various roles that libraries can play in tackling the climate emergency, ranging from promoting environmental literacy and sustainability to supporting climate research and advocacy, as well as implementing sustainable practices within their operations and services.
Consensus	Here are some relevant research papers that explore the role of libraries and information services in addressing the climate emergency: 1. **Opportunities and Challenges for Public Libraries to Enhance Community Resilience** - **Authors**: Shari R. Veil, B. Bishop - **Abstract**: This study examines the role of public libraries in disaster recovery and how they can enhance community resilience. The paper discusses the opportunities for libraries to adapt their services to meet changing community needs during crises. - [Link to Paper](https://consensus.app/papers/opportunities-challenges-public-libraries-enhance-veil/9a54e3bc73995b1582099283b1e2c670/?utm_source=chatgpt) 2. **Getting Warmer: A Refined Taxonomy For Assessing Public Libraries' Response to the Climate Crisis** - **Author**: Michelle Foggett-Parker

Figure 6.6 *Continued*

Tool	Result
	- **Abstract**: This paper proposes a taxonomy for assessing public libraries' responses to the climate crisis, emphasizing their roles in community activism and climate justice. - [Link to Paper](https://consensus.app/papers/getting-warmer-refined-taxonomy-assessing-public-foggettparker/f185eae47f7053969d0042b532801ebf/?utm_source=chatgpt) 3. **Public Libraries and Crisis Management: Iranian Public Libraries and the Dust Crisis** - **Authors**: S. Khademizadeh, Dalal Albudaiwi, Håkon Larsen, Z. Mohammadi, Abdul Hossein Farajpahlou - **Abstract**: This study explores the role of public libraries in managing community needs during environmental crises, specifically the dust crisis in Iran. The paper provides insights into how libraries can act during different stages of a crisis. - [Link to Paper](https://consensus.app/papers/public-libraries-crisis-management-libraries-dust-crisis-khademizadeh/1c07ef04c9dc539da26526cb588d948f/?utm_source=chatgpt) 4. **Community Resilience and the Role of the Public Library** - **Authors**: D. Grace, B. Sen - **Abstract**: This paper explores how public libraries contribute to community resilience, particularly in the face of threats like climate change and energy insecurity. It highlights the role of libraries in bridging social divides and supporting sustainable community practices. - [Link to Paper](https://consensus.app/papers/community-resilience-role-public-library-grace/f2644a6844a35588a6173d9048da0e2f/?utm_source=chatgpt) 5. **Climate Change Considerations in Public Library Collection Development** - **Authors**: Maia Trotter, Olesya Komarnytska - **Abstract**: This extended abstract explores how public libraries can develop collections that address climate change, focusing on overcoming challenges such as eco-anxiety and climate change denial. - [Link to Paper](https://consensus.app/papers/climate-change-considerations-public-library-collection-trotter/7b6bc955b70156619750d5a8dbabe5e3/?utm_source=chatgpt) These papers provide a comprehensive overview of how libraries can contribute to climate change mitigation, community resilience, and environmental education.
Copilot	Certainly! Here are some relevant research papers and resources related to the role of libraries and information services in addressing climate emergencies: 1. **'Climate information services, integrated knowledge systems and the 2030 Agenda for Sustainable Development'**: • This commentary explores the role of climate information services in supporting the achievement of the **2030 Agenda for Sustainable Development**. It emphasizes the importance of integrated knowledge systems for high-quality climate information services and their alignment with the **Sustainable Development Goals (SDGs)**. The paper discusses how such services can address the needs of the global poor, including informing agricultural decision-making, disaster preparedness, and tackling climate-related health issues[1]. • Read the full paper.

Figure 6.6 *Continued*

Tool	Result
	2. 'Role of Libraries in Promoting the SDGs: A Focus on the University of South Africa': • This chapter discusses the role of libraries in promoting the SDGs, specifically focusing on the **University of South Africa (Unisa)**. It highlights how libraries can drive progress across all 17 SDGs by providing resources, information, and support. The Unisa libraries have established a **Library Guide** as a one-stop shop for SDG-related resources, making them agents of change in the SDG space[2]. • Read the full chapter. **3. 'Climate Emergency LibGuide'** (University of Edinburgh): • The University of Edinburgh has created a **Library Subject guide** specifically on the topic of **Climate Emergency**. It includes academic and fiction books related to the climate crisis, research databases, and links to climate resources. This guide serves as a valuable resource for researchers and students interested in climate-related topics[3]. • Explore the Climate Emergency LibGuide. **4. 'Role of Library and Information Centres In Disaster Management'**: • This paper discusses the role of library professionals in managing emergencies, including climate-related disasters. It emphasizes the importance of information and communication technology (ICT) in reducing damage caused by natural disasters. While not exclusively focused on climate change, it highlights the broader role of libraries in disaster management[4]. • Read the full paper. These resources provide insights into how libraries and information services contribute to addressing climate emergencies and promoting sustainable development. Happy reading!
Gemini	Absolutely! Here's some relevant research literature on the role libraries and information services can play in tackling the climate emergency: • **'Libraries as Agents of Climate Change Literacy' (2022, IFLA Repository):** This research paper explores the importance of climate change literacy and how libraries can empower citizens with the knowledge and resources needed to understand and address the issue [repository.ifla.org]. • **'Climate Change & the Library's Role in Climate Literacy' (2021, Urban Libraries Council):** This article delves into specific strategies libraries can adopt, such as developing climate-related collections, hosting educational programs, and collaborating with environmental organizations [urbanlibraries.org]. • **'Public libraries and climate change' (2021, Department for Digital, Culture, Media & Sport)**: This blog post from a UK government department highlights various initiatives undertaken by libraries to address climate change, offering practical examples [dcmslibraries.blog.gov.uk]. Here are some additional resources you might find helpful: • **'The Green Library Movement**: This international movement promotes environmental sustainability within libraries. Their website offers resources, case studies, and information on best practices [greenlibrarymovement.org]. • **'American Library Association (ALA) Environment, Sustainability and Libraries Round Table (ESRT):** This ALA round table focuses on environmental issues within libraries. Their website might have resources and reports on the topic [ala.org].

Figure 6.6 *Continued*

Tool	Result
	By exploring these resources and research papers, you can gain valuable insights into the diverse ways libraries and information services are contributing to tackling the climate emergency. Remember to consider the date of publication to ensure you're using the most current information available.
GPT-4o	ChatGPT Certainly! Here are some relevant research papers and literature that explore the role of library and information services in addressing the climate emergency: **1. 'Libraries and Environmental Sustainability: Ensuring Our Future'** • Author: Petra Hauke, Karen Latimer, Klaus Ulrich Werner • Summary: This book provides comprehensive coverage on how libraries can promote environmental sustainability through their practices, programs, and services. It includes case studies and practical examples of libraries worldwide taking action to address climate change. • Source: De Gruyter Saur, 2013. **2. 'The Green Library Movement: An Overview and Beyond'** • Author: Monika Antonelli, Mark McCullough • Summary: This paper reviews the green library movement, discussing how libraries are adopting sustainable practices and advocating for environmental awareness. It provides insights into various initiatives and the impact of libraries on promoting sustainability. • Source: Electronic Green Journal, 2012. **3. 'Libraries and Climate Change: The Role of Information Professionals in Climate Action'** • Author: John R. Weare • Summary: This article explores the role of librarians and information professionals in climate action, focusing on their ability to disseminate information, support research, and engage communities in sustainability efforts. • Source: Library Trends, 2020. **4. 'Libraries as Community Catalysts for Sustainability: Practices and Programs'** • Author: Rebecca Tolley • Summary: This book chapter discusses how libraries serve as community hubs for sustainability education and action, highlighting various programs and practices that promote environmental awareness and community engagement. • Source: In 'Transforming Libraries to Serve Graduate Students,' edited by Crystal Renfro and Cheryl Stiles, 2020. **5. 'Environmental Sustainability in Libraries: A Call to Action'** • Author: Kathleen Kern, Rebecca Kuglitsch • Summary: This paper calls for libraries to take a proactive role in environmental sustainability, discussing the steps libraries can take to reduce their environmental impact and educate their communities. • Source: College & Research Libraries News, 2019. **6. 'Sustainability and Libraries: Green Practices around the World'** • Author: Sarah J. Houghton, Kathryn Miller • Summary: This article provides a global perspective on green practices in libraries, offering examples from various countries on how libraries are integrating sustainability into their operations and services. • Source: IFLA Journal, 2017.

Figure 6.6 *Continued*

Tool	Result
	7. 'Libraries as Climate Change Hubs: Strategies and Programs for Community Engagement' • Author: Lisa Hardy • Summary: This study examines strategies libraries can use to become centers for climate change education and action, including partnerships, programming, and resource provision. • Source: Public Library Quarterly, 2018. **8. 'The Role of Academic Libraries in Promoting Environmental Sustainability'** • Author: Maria J. Perkins • Summary: This paper discusses how academic libraries can support environmental sustainability through collection development, research support, and campus-wide initiatives. • Source: Journal of Academic Librarianship, 2021. **9. 'Climate Change and the Librarian's Role in Education and Advocacy'** • Author: Benjamin Johnson • Summary: This article explores the educational and advocacy roles librarians can play in addressing climate change, providing practical examples and recommendations. • Source: American Libraries, 2020. **10. 'Sustainable Libraries: Programs, Practices, and Partnerships'** • Editors: Kelly Richards, Alex Grech • Summary: This edited volume includes contributions from various authors discussing sustainable practices in libraries, successful programs, and partnerships that promote environmental sustainability. • Source: ABC-CLIO, 2019. These resources provide a comprehensive overview of how libraries and information services can contribute to addressing the climate emergency through education, sustainable practices, community engagement, and advocacy.
Perplexity AI	Based on the provided search results, here are some relevant research literature that discuss the potential role of libraries in tackling the climate emergency: 1. 'Transforming Public Libraries as Spaces of Refuge & Resiliency During Climate Crisis' by Kaitlyn Downie [1] This paper argues that public libraries have the potential and obligation to transform their roles and become spaces of refuge and resiliency for communities during climate crises. It discusses enhancing environmental literacy education, adopting environmentally-friendly practices, and creating community networks to support patrons during climate emergencies. 2. 'Exploring the Role of Social Science Research in Tackling the Climate Crisis' by Jenny Pickerill and Matt Watson [2] While not focused specifically on libraries, this article highlights the importance of social science research in understanding societal transformations necessary for climate change adaptation. It discusses the role of grassroots and community-based initiatives in driving collective action and promoting low-carbon lifestyles. 3. 'Public Libraries and the UN 2030 Agenda for Sustainable Development' by Anita Sundaram [3] This journal article discusses the potential of public libraries to contribute to the United Nations' Sustainable Development Goals, including their role as essential resources during emergencies and crises, which could extend to climate-related emergencies.

Figure 6.6 *Continued*

Tool	Result
	4. 'Environment and Climate Emergency Policy Statement' by Wirral Council [4] While not directly related to libraries, this policy statement recognizes the importance of the natural environment and biodiversity in tackling climate change, which could inform libraries' efforts in promoting environmental literacy and awareness. 5. 'Tackling the Climate Emergency' by the Liberal Democrats [5] This policy paper outlines the Liberal Democrats' priorities for addressing the climate emergency, including setting ambitious emission reduction targets and promoting sustainable practices. While not focused on libraries, it provides a broader policy context for climate action initiatives. These sources highlight the potential roles of libraries in promoting environmental literacy, serving as community hubs for climate-related discussions and resources, preserving climate data and research, and adopting sustainable practices within their operations. Additionally, they emphasize the importance of social science research and community-based initiatives in driving societal transformations necessary for climate change adaptation and mitigation. Citations: [1] https://core.ac.uk/download/pdf/286370423.pdf [2] https://acss.org.uk/a-social-and-political-problem-exploring-the-role-of-social-science-research-in-tackling-the-climate-crisis/ [3] https://journals.sagepub.com/doi/10.1177/0340035219898708 [4] www.wirral.gov.uk/about-council/climate-change-and-sustainability/environment-and-climate-emergency-policy-statement [5] www.libdems.org.uk/fileadmin/groups/2_Federal_Party/Documents/PolicyPapers/139_-_Tackling_the_Climate_Emergency__2019_.pdf
Scholar GPT	Answer: Scholar GPT wants to talk to actions.sider.ai (*When consented, the following response is provided)* Answer I encountered an issue while trying to retrieve specific research literature on the role of libraries in tackling the climate emergency. However, I can suggest some approaches to finding relevant literature: 1. **Google Scholar**: Use search queries like 'role of libraries in climate change' or 'libraries and climate emergency' to find relevant academic papers. 2. **Library Databases**: Access databases like JSTOR, PubMed, and IEEE Xplore through your institution's library to find peer-reviewed articles. 3. **Professional Organizations**: Websites of organizations like the American Library Association (ALA) often have publications and resources on how libraries can contribute to sustainability and climate action. 4. **Research Journals**: Look for articles in journals focused on library science, environmental science, and public policy. If you need specific articles or assistance in navigating these resources, feel free to ask!

Figure 6.6 *Continued*

Outputs for Scenario 4, Question 3 (Figure 6.7 on the next page) vary:

- Results from Claude are presented under seven headings with a summary; no citations are provided.

- Results from Consensus appear under five headings, each with a brief description of research, and a link.
- Copilot cites four items each with a summary and a link. However, the cited items are not peer-reviewed research papers.
- GPT-4o cites five items, each with a summary and a link; it also provides three additional items as recommended readings.
- Results from Perplexity AI are presented in six points, each with a summary of the work and citation. Five items are cited: three of these are research papers, two of which refer to the same item; and one is a news item from a relevant professional body, IFLA.
- GPT Scholar asks to select an option (from a list such as library databases, Google Scholar, etc.) suggesting where to search for the literature. Once prompted to search a database, it recommends five items with a brief note on what the item covers and a link to access it. It also recommends to search using other tools.

Tool	Result
Claude	The current state of research on the role of libraries in tackling the climate emergency is still relatively limited, but there is growing interest and focus on this topic. Here's an overview of the current state of research: 1. Emerging field: The intersection of libraries and climate action is a relatively new area of research, with most studies and publications appearing within the last decade. However, there is increasing recognition of the potential for libraries to contribute to climate solutions and sustainable development. 2. Theoretical and conceptual frameworks: Several studies have focused on developing theoretical and conceptual frameworks to understand the potential roles and contributions of libraries in addressing climate change. These frameworks explore libraries' functions as information providers, community hubs, and agents of change for environmental sustainability. 3. Case studies and best practices: A significant portion of the current research consists of case studies and examinations of best practices from libraries around the world. These studies highlight various initiatives and programs implemented by libraries to promote environmental literacy, support climate research, and adopt sustainable operations. 4. Sustainability and green library initiatives: There is a substantial body of research on sustainable and green library initiatives, which includes aspects related to climate action, such as energy-efficient library buildings, waste reduction, and promoting sustainable practices among patrons and communities. 5. Academic and research library focus: A significant portion of the research has focused on the role of academic and research libraries in supporting climate change research, providing access to environmental data, and collaborating with researchers and scientists working on climate solutions.

Figure 6.7 *(Scenario 4, Question 3): What is the current state of research on the role that libraries can play in tackling the climate emergency?*

Tool	Result
	6. Community engagement and outreach: Several studies have explored the potential of public and community libraries to engage with local communities, raise awareness about climate change, and facilitate discussions and initiatives related to climate action and adaptation strategies. 7. Interdisciplinary collaborations: Some researchers have emphasized the importance of interdisciplinary collaborations between libraries, environmental organizations, government agencies, and other stakeholders to amplify the impact of climate-related initiatives and resources. While the current state of research on this topic is still developing, there is a growing recognition of the vital role that libraries can play in addressing the climate emergency through their diverse functions and community connections. However, more comprehensive and empirical research is needed to fully understand the challenges, opportunities, and best practices for libraries to effectively contribute to climate action.
Consensus	Research on the role of libraries in addressing the climate emergency highlights the significant contributions they can make in building community resilience, promoting environmental awareness, and supporting disaster management efforts. Here are some key findings: 1. **Community Resilience**: Public libraries can play a vital role in enhancing community resilience by providing technology resources, meeting spaces, and acting as a communication hub during and after disasters. They also help in disaster recovery by adapting their services to meet evolving community needs [(Veil & Bishop, 2014)](https://consensus.app/papers/opportunities-challenges-public-libraries-enhance-veil/9a54e3bc73995b1582099283b1e2c670/?utm_source=chatgpt). 2. **Climate Activism and Education**: Libraries can engage in climate activism by incorporating climate justice and sustainability into their community outreach and collections. They also play a crucial role in bridging the gap between complex climate information and community action, especially by addressing barriers like eco-anxiety and climate change denial [(Foggett-Parker, 2023)](https://consensus.app/papers/getting-warmer-refined-taxonomy-assessing-public-foggettparker/f185eae47f7053969d0042b532801ebf/?utm_source=chatgpt). 3. **Disaster Response**: Libraries are increasingly recognized as essential in disaster response and recovery. They provide a safe haven and essential services that help communities recover more rapidly from disasters. This role includes serving as information hubs and providing access to critical resources during crises [(Stricker, 2019)](https://consensus.app/papers/ports-storm-role-public-library-times-crisis-stricker/b61cb038a5b15c9eb685cf5fd39c0161/?utm_source=chatgpt). 4. **Crisis Management**: Libraries can also contribute to crisis management by taking on roles in educating the public, managing information, and collaborating with emergency management agencies. This enhances their role as integral parts of the community during emergencies [(Khademizadeh et al., 2022)](https://consensus.app/papers/public-libraries-crisis-management-libraries-dust-crisis-khademizadeh/1c07ef04c9dc539da26526cb588d948f/?utm_source=chatgpt).

Figure 6.7 *Continued*

Tool	Result
	Conclusion: Libraries are crucial in the fight against the climate emergency, particularly in building resilient communities, promoting climate awareness, and providing essential services during and after disasters.
Copilot	Certainly! Here are some recent research papers related to the role of libraries and information services in addressing climate emergencies: 1. **'From Publications to Public Actions: The Role of Universities in Facilitating Academic Advocacy and Activism in the Climate and Ecological Emergency'**: • This article discusses the role of universities in promoting sustainability through research, teaching, and institutional practices. However, it argues that these initiatives alone may be insufficient to catalyze the necessary transformations. The paper suggests that academics should move beyond publications and engage in advocacy and activism to drive urgent and transformational change. It also proposes actions that universities can adopt to support academic engagement in advocacy[1]. • Read the full article. 2. **'Climate Change and COP26: Role of Information Technologies in Disaster Management and Resilience'**: • This review explores the potential of information and communications technology (ICT) in disaster management and resilience. It identifies major technologies, such as big data, global information systems (GIS), artificial intelligence (AI), the Internet of Things (IoT), drones, and advanced robotics, that can aid in managing disasters. The study emphasizes building adaptive, absorptive, and transformative capacity to enhance disaster resilience[2]. • Read the full review. 3. **'Clearer and More Accessible Local Information Needed on How Councils Are Addressing the Climate Emergency'**: • This report by the Environmental Law Foundation (ELF) highlights the need for greater urgency in local authorities' actions to address the climate emergency. While there is evidence of positive efforts, more accessible information is required to track progress and achieve ambitious goals[3]. • Read the report. 4. **'Towards a Greater Engagement of Universities in Addressing Climate Change'**: • This paper emphasizes that universities can actively engage in efforts against climate change by providing research-based solutions and educational resources. By creating, testing, and disseminating information about climate mitigation and adaptation strategies, universities can contribute to building resilience and addressing the climate emergency[4]. • Read the full paper. These resources provide insights into the current state of research on the role of libraries, universities, and information services in tackling climate emergencies.
Gemini	The current state of research on the role of libraries in tackling the climate emergency is promising and evolving. Here's a breakdown of key themes: **Libraries as Information Hubs:** • **Focus on Climate Change Literacy:** Research emphasizes libraries' role in providing credible and accessible information on climate change,

Figure 6.7 *Continued*

Tool	Result
	empowering individuals to understand the science and potential solutions [repository.ifla.org, urbanlibraries.org]. • **Combating Misinformation:** Studies highlight the importance of libraries in equipping users with information literacy skills to critically evaluate online sources and differentiate between fact and fiction regarding climate change [repository.ifla.org]. • **Curated Collections:** Research explores the value of libraries building curated collections of scientific reports, documentaries, and books by climate experts, ensuring access to trustworthy knowledge [urbanlibraries.org]. **Libraries as Community Action Centers:** • **Sustainability Resources and Skill Development:** Research acknowledges libraries' potential to be hubs for resources on sustainable living, workshops on green practices, and skill development programs related to renewable energy or eco-friendly technologies [urbanlibraries.org]. • **Community Partnerships:** Studies highlight the importance of collaborating with environmental organizations for events like seed swaps, clothing exchanges, or repair workshops, promoting a circular economy [urbanlibraries.org]. • **Advocacy and Community Organizing:** Research explores libraries' potential to serve as platforms for public discussions on climate issues, and act as meeting spaces for climate action groups, fostering collaboration and mobilizing communities [dcmslibraries.blog.gov.uk]. **Emerging Areas of Research:** • **Data and Information Sharing:** Recent studies suggest libraries can play a role in collecting and sharing data on local environmental issues, informing policy decisions and tracking progress on sustainability goals. • **The Green Library Movement:** Research on the Green Library Movement is growing, exploring best practices and case studies of libraries implementing sustainable practices in their own operations to inspire the broader community [greenlibrarymovement.org]. **Metrics and Impact Measurement:** A developing area of research focuses on establishing metrics to effectively measure the impact of library initiatives in fostering climate literacy and promoting community-level action. **Overall, the research highlights libraries' unique potential as trusted information providers, community hubs, and agents of positive change in addressing the climate emergency. However, further research is needed on measuring the impact of specific library initiatives and developing best practices for effective implementation.** Here are some additional points to consider: • The research landscape is geographically diverse, with studies focusing on different regions and library contexts. • There's a growing emphasis on the need for collaboration between libraries, environmental organizations, and policymakers to maximize impact. • The importance of tailoring library strategies to address the specific needs and challenges of the local community is increasingly recognized. By staying up-to-date with the latest research and utilizing the vast resources available through organizations like the Green Library Movement, libraries can continue to play a vital role in tackling the climate emergency.

Figure 6.7 *Continued*

Tool	Result
GPT-4o	Searched 4 sites The role of libraries and information services in addressing the climate emergency is an emerging and crucial area of research and action. Libraries, as centers for community engagement and information dissemination, are well-positioned to play a significant part in climate change mitigation and adaptation efforts. Current research highlights several ways in which libraries can contribute: 1. **Educational and Community Engagement Hubs**: Libraries can serve as focal points for educating the public about climate change, offering resources and programs that raise awareness and promote sustainable practices. The American Library Association (ALA) has emphasized the importance of libraries in leading climate adaptation and promoting climate justice, framing sustainability as a core value of the profession (American Library Association). 2. **Sustainable Practices and Green Infrastructure**: Many libraries are adopting green building practices and energy-efficient technologies to reduce their carbon footprint. This includes implementing sustainable design in new constructions and retrofitting existing buildings to improve energy efficiency. Research also suggests that libraries can set examples in their communities by incorporating sustainability into their operations and services (American Library Association) (Climate Change Resources |). 3. **Disaster Preparedness and Resilience**: Libraries can play a critical role in disaster preparedness by providing information and resources that help communities respond to and recover from climate-related disasters. This involves developing comprehensive emergency management plans and training staff to handle climate-related risks. Studies indicate that a significant number of cultural institutions, including libraries, lack adequate disaster plans, underscoring the need for enhanced preparedness efforts (LSU). 4. **Cultural and Historical Preservation**: Libraries are involved in projects aimed at assessing and mitigating the risks that climate change poses to cultural heritage. For instance, initiatives like PROTECCT-GLAM are focused on evaluating the impacts of climate change on galleries, libraries, archives, and museums, and developing strategies to protect these valuable resources (LSU). 5. **Research and Policy Advocacy**: Libraries are increasingly participating in research collaborations to study the impacts of climate change and advocate for policy changes. They can also provide platforms for community discussions and workshops on climate policy, sustainability practices, and environmental justice. Key research highlights the need for interdisciplinary approaches, integrating expertise from various fields to address the complex challenges posed by climate change. Libraries, with their extensive networks and resources, are uniquely positioned to lead and support these efforts. For further reading and a deeper understanding, you may refer to: • 'How Climate Change is Impacting Galleries, Libraries, Archives and Museums' from LSU (LSU) • 'A Call to Action on Climate Change for Libraries' by the American Library Association (American Library Association) • Various reports and papers on climate change resources, which provide a comprehensive overview of current initiatives and research in this area (Climate Change Resources |).

Figure 6.7 *Continued*

Tool	Result
Perplexity AI	Based on the provided sources, the current state of research on the role that libraries can play in tackling the climate emergency is still emerging, but several key themes and perspectives are highlighted: 1. Libraries as hubs for climate information and literacy [1][2][3] There is a recognition that libraries can serve as trusted sources of accurate and up-to-date information on climate change, its impacts, and potential solutions. They can curate and disseminate authoritative resources, counter misinformation, and promote climate literacy through educational programs, workshops, and resource sharing. 2. Facilitating community engagement and dialogue [1][5] Libraries are seen as potential community hubs for fostering dialogue, debates, and forums on climate change-related issues. By providing a neutral and inclusive space, libraries can bring together various stakeholders, including policymakers, researchers, activists, and the general public, to promote collaboration and collective action. 3. Adopting sustainable practices and reducing environmental impact [2][5] The research emphasizes the need for libraries to lead by example by implementing sustainable practices within their operations, such as energy-efficient buildings, waste reduction initiatives, and environmentally friendly procurement policies. This can raise awareness and inspire patrons to adopt more sustainable lifestyles. 4. Preserving and archiving climate data and research [2] Libraries are recognized for their potential role in preserving and archiving climate data, research papers, and historical records related to climate change. This ensures the long-term availability of valuable information for future research, policymaking, and public education. 5. Transforming into spaces of refuge and resiliency [5] One perspective suggests that public libraries have the potential and obligation to transform their roles and become spaces of refuge and resiliency for communities during climate emergencies. This involves enhancing environmental literacy education, creating community networks, and providing support to patrons during climate-related crises. 6. Aligning with organizational missions and strategies [2] The research highlights the need for libraries to align their climate action efforts with their organizational missions, visions, and strategies around education and delivering research that contributes to solving global problems. While the research on this topic is still emerging, there is a growing recognition of the unique position and potential of libraries to contribute to climate action through their various roles and functions, ranging from information dissemination to community engagement and sustainable practices. **Citations:** **[1]** www.ifla.org/news/coming-up-in-2023-libraries-addressing-the-climate-emergency/ **[2]** https://eprints.whiterose.ac.uk/204017/3/The%20role%20of%20academic%20libraries%20in%20climate%20action%20final%20%282%29.pdf **[3]** www.tandfonline.com/doi/full/10.1080/13614533.2023.2230652 **[4]** www.tandfonline.com/doi/pdf/10.1080/13614533.2023.2230652 **[5]** https://core.ac.uk/download/pdf/286370423.pdf

Figure 6.7 *Continued*

Tool	Result
Scholar GPT	Here are some relevant articles on the role of libraries in tackling the climate emergency from various databases: 1. **LIS's Climate Change: What LIS Means within a Pandemic and Climate Crisis Context** - Source: JSTOR - [Link to article](www.jstor.org/stable/48644444) - Summary: Discusses the role of Library and Information Science (LIS) in addressing climate change and pandemic crises, focusing on systemic changes within libraries. 2. **Institute for Public Policy Research (IPPR) on JSTOR: Tackling the Climate and Nature Emergency** - Source: JSTOR - [Link to article](www.jstor.org/publisher/ippr) - Summary: Explores the role of public policy research in tackling climate and nature emergencies, including the contributions of libraries. 3. **Gone the Bull of Winter?** - Source: JSTOR - [Link to article](www.jstor.org/stable/10.1086/529543) - Summary: Examines the role of cultural institutions, such as libraries, in addressing global climate challenges. 4. **From Atomic Shelters to Arms Control: Libraries, Civil Defense, and Emergency Operations** - Source: JSTOR - [Link to article](www.jstor.org/stable/43737397) - Summary: Historical perspective on the role of libraries in emergency operations, which can be extrapolated to their potential role in climate emergency situations. 5. **Decentralization and Implementation of Climate Change Policy in Uganda** - Source: Danish Institute for International Studies (DIIS) via JSTOR - [Link to article](www.jstor.org/stable/resrep13338) - Summary: Analyzes how local institutions, including libraries, are responding to climate change policies and emergencies. These articles provide a range of perspectives on how libraries can contribute to addressing the climate emergency through education, policy support, and community engagement. ***Handling multiple papers?*** Speed up your research with Sider! Our AI-powered sidebar features 10+ one-click tools including a more advanced Search Agent, ChatPDF, context-aware utilities, and more to help you work smarter and faster. [Level up your research game here](https://bit.ly/4aSnMXa)

Figure 6.7 *Continued*

Outputs for Scenario 4, Question 4 (Figure 6.8) vary:

- Results from Claude include six human and six institutions as the leading authors and researchers. Full citations or links to the items are not provided, and hence the user will have to make extra efforts to locate the cited works.
- Consensus cites five scholarly papers as the leading research works, each with a brief description and citation. It also cites three institutions as the leaders in research on this.

- Copilot cites three institutions – one international professional organisation and two university libraries – and two items with individual authors. Each cites items with a summary of the work and a link.
- Gemini recommends three individual research works, and three institutions as the leaders, each with a brief description and a link. It also recommends some additional resources.
- GPT-4o cites four individuals and five institutions – two university libraries, and three professional associations and networks – one international and two American. It also lists four key publications and reports. Full citations or links to the cited items are not provided.
- Results from Perplexity AI are presented under two headings: one with a list of five individuals and another under five institutions. Links to the cited items are provided.
- Results from Scholar GPT cite three individuals and five institutions as the leaders in this area, with links to the sources. Also, a summary is provided.

Tool	Result
Claude	Here are some of the leading authors, researchers, and institutions that have made significant contributions to the research on the role of libraries in tackling the climate emergency: Authors and Researchers: 1. Maria A. Jankowska (UCLA Library, USA) - Jankowska has written extensively on the role of academic libraries in addressing climate change, including publications in College & Research Libraries News and other journals. 2. Petra Hauke (Humboldt University of Berlin, Germany) - Hauke is a notable author and editor of books and articles on sustainable libraries and their contributions to sustainable development goals, including climate action. 3. Monika Antonelli (Minnesota State University, USA) - Antonelli has conducted bibliometric analyses and published research on environmental topics in library and information science literature, including climate change. 4. Anca Mănescu (National Library of Romania) - Mănescu is a co-author of the influential publication 'The Green Library Planner,' which provides guidance on sustainable library buildings and operations. 5. Sharon Collie and Valerie Jacobs (University of Auckland, New Zealand) - Collie and Jacobs have researched and published on the role of public libraries in engaging with communities on climate change and environmental literacy. 6. Sarah Maren Voss and Samantha McBride (University of Wisconsin-Milwaukee, USA) - Voss and McBride have explored the potential of academic libraries as sustainability leaders and advocates for institutional change related to climate action.

Figure 6.8 *(Scenario 4, Question 4): Who are the most leading authors, researchers and institutions on this topic that one must read?*

Tool	Result
	Institutions and Organizations: 1. International Federation of Library Associations and Institutions (IFLA) - IFLA has published several reports and resources on sustainable libraries, including 'The Green Library Planner' and guidelines for environmental sustainability in libraries. 2. Association of College and Research Libraries (ACRL) - ACRL has a dedicated Environmental Sustainability and Libraries Discussion Group that promotes research and initiatives related to libraries and climate action. 3. American Library Association (ALA) - ALA has established a Sustainability and Environmental Group to support and advocate for sustainable practices in libraries, including addressing climate change. 4. Partnership for Resilient Communities (PRC) - The PRC is a collaboration between libraries and organizations focused on building community resilience to climate change, promoting research, and developing resources. 5. International Sustainable Library Certification Program (IFLA ENSULIB) - ENSULIB is an IFLA initiative that provides certification and training for libraries to implement sustainable practices and contribute to environmental goals. 6. Research Libraries UK (RLUK) - RLUK has a Sustainability Network that supports research libraries in the UK in addressing climate change and environmental sustainability. While this is not an exhaustive list, these authors, researchers, and institutions have made significant contributions to advancing research and initiatives related to the role of libraries in tackling the climate emergency. Their work provides valuable insights, case studies, and frameworks for libraries to engage in climate action and promote environmental sustainability.
Consensus	Answer To understand the role of libraries in tackling the climate emergency, some of the leading authors, researchers, and institutions contributing to this field include: 1. **Shari R. Veil and B. Bishop**: Their work focuses on how public libraries can enhance community resilience by adapting to the needs of disaster recovery, which is critical in the context of climate change [(Veil & Bishop, 2014)](https://consensus.app/papers/opportunities-challenges-public-libraries-enhance-veil/9a54e3bc73995b1582099283b1e2c670/?utm_source=chatgpt). 2. **Michelle Foggett-Parker**: She has contributed to developing a taxonomy for assessing public libraries' response to the climate crisis, emphasizing the importance of libraries in climate justice and activism [(Foggett-Parker, 2023)](https://consensus.app/papers/getting-warmer-refined-taxonomy-assessing-public-foggettparker/f185eae47f7053969d0042b532801ebf/?utm_source=chatgpt). 3. **D. Grace and B. Sen**: Their research highlights the role of public libraries in promoting community resilience amidst threats like climate change, biodiversity loss, and food insecurity [(Grace & Sen, 2013)](https://consensus.app/papers/community-resilience-role-public-library-grace/f2644a6844a35588a6173d9048da0e2f/?utm_source=chatgpt).

Figure 6.8 *Continued*

Tool	**Result**
	4. **Christine Hagar**: She emphasizes the critical role of public libraries in strengthening community resilience during disasters, which is becoming increasingly important due to the impacts of climate change [(Hagar, 2015)](https://consensus.app/papers/strengthening-community-resilience-efforts-disasters-hagar/92fe509b341e5f2a9fd053ad6a8a4f61/?utm_source=chatgpt). 5. **Kirstie O'Neill and Charlotte Kate Sinden**: They explore the contradictions of climate emergency declarations by universities and how neoliberalism influences sustainability policies and practices, which can be extended to libraries within academic institutions [(O'Neill & Sinden, 2021)](https://consensus.app/papers/universities-sustainability-neoliberalism-oneill/d074f30ca4505316bc9076e15a2fbde4/?utm_source=chatgpt). **Institutions**: - **University of Bristol**: Pioneered climate emergency declarations, influencing academic discussions on sustainability. - **Ontario Public Libraries**: Known for implementing environmental sustainability indicators and assessing libraries' roles in community activism. - **Wuhan University and City University Hong Kong**: Leading institutions in Library and Information Science (LIS) research, focusing on international collaboration and climate-related studies. These researchers and institutions provide valuable insights into how libraries can address the climate emergency, making them essential reads for anyone interested in this field.
Copilot	When exploring the role of libraries and information services in addressing the climate emergency, there are several leading authors, researchers, and institutions whose work stands out: **1. International Federation of Library Associations and Institutions (IFLA)**: • IFLA has been vocal about the role of libraries in driving progress across all 17 Sustainable Development Goals (SDGs), which includes addressing the climate emergency. They emphasize the importance of libraries in promoting universal literacy, minimizing gaps in access to information, and advancing digital inclusion[1]. **2. University of South Africa (Unisa) Libraries**: • Unisa Libraries have established a **Library Guide** as a one-stop shop for SDG-related resources, positioning themselves as agents of change in the SDG space. Their work is particularly relevant for researchers looking to understand how libraries can support global sustainability efforts[1]. **3. Fortunate Machingura, Admire Nyamwanza, David Hulme & Elizabeth Stuart**: • These authors have contributed to the discussion on climate information services and integrated knowledge systems, which are critical for the successful achievement of the SDGs. Their work highlights the role of high-quality climate information services in empowering decision-makers[2]. **4. Charlie J. Gardner, Aaron Thierry, William Rowlandson, Julia K. Steinberger**: • These researchers from the **University of Kent** and **Cardiff University** have written about the need for academics to engage in advocacy and activism beyond publications to drive urgent and

Figure 6.8 *Continued*

Tool	Result
	transformational change in response to the climate and ecological emergency[3]. **5. University of Edinburgh**: • The University of Edinburgh's **Climate Emergency LibGuide** is a valuable resource for academic and fiction books related to the climate crisis, research databases, and links to climate resources, serving as a guide for those interested in climate-related topics[4]. These authors and institutions are at the forefront of research and advocacy on the topic of libraries and information services' role in addressing the climate emergency. Their work provides a wealth of knowledge and practical insights for anyone looking to delve deeper into this area.
Gemini	Here are some leading authors, researchers, and institutions to explore regarding the role of libraries in tackling the climate emergency: **Authors and Researchers:** • **Dr Christine Finnan:** A prominent researcher and advocate for climate change literacy. Her work focuses on libraries' role in building public awareness and understanding of the issue (repository.ifla.org [invalid URL removed]). • **Barbara Linn:** A library science professional who has written extensively on the Green Library Movement and sustainable practices within libraries (greenlibrarymovement.org [invalid URL removed]). • **Lorrie Klosterman:** Another library science scholar who explores the role of libraries in environmental education and community engagement (urbanlibraries.org [invalid URL removed]). **Institutions:** • **The Green Library Movement:** A global network of libraries committed to environmental sustainability. Their website offers resources, case studies, and best practices for libraries (greenlibrarymovement.org [invalid URL removed]). • **American Library Association (ALA) Environment, Sustainability and Libraries Round Table (ESRT):** A section of the ALA dedicated to promoting environmental awareness and sustainability within libraries. Their website might have reports and resources (ala.org [invalid URL removed]). • **IFLA (International Federation of Library Associations and Institutions):** The leading international organization for the library and information profession. Their repository contains research papers on various topics, including climate change and libraries (repository.ifla.org [invalid URL removed]). **Additional Resources:** • **Department for Digital, Culture, Media & Sport (UK Government):** Their blog post 'Public libraries and climate change' offers practical examples of library initiatives (dcmslibraries.blog.gov.uk [invalid URL removed]). • **Urban Libraries Council:** A nonprofit organization that supports urban public libraries in North America. Their website contains an article 'Climate Change & the Library's Role in Climate Literacy' (urbanlibraries.org [invalid URL removed]). Remember, the field of research on libraries and climate change is constantly evolving. Consider searching for recent publications (within the last 3–5 years) to ensure you have the most up-to-date information. By exploring the work of these authors, researchers, and institutions, you can gain valuable insights into the innovative ways libraries are tackling the climate emergency and contributing to a more sustainable future.

Figure 6.8 *Continued*

Tool	Result
GPT-4o	ChatGPT To gain a comprehensive understanding of the role of libraries and information services in addressing the climate emergency, it is beneficial to explore the works of leading authors, researchers, and institutions in this field. Here are some prominent figures and institutions you should consider: **Leading Authors and Researchers** **1. Petra Hauke** • **Notable Works**: 'Green Libraries: Case Studies from Around the World' • **Contributions**: Hauke has extensively researched and written about sustainable practices in libraries, providing global case studies and practical guidelines. **2. Rachel A. Kirk** • **Notable Works**: Various articles on environmental sustainability in academic libraries. • **Contributions**: Kirk's research focuses on integrating sustainability into library operations and services, emphasizing environmental responsibility. **3. Rebecca Tolley** • **Notable Works**: 'Sustainability in Libraries: Case Studies of Academic Libraries' • **Contributions**: Tolley explores how academic libraries can adopt sustainable practices and become centers for environmental education. **4. Mark McCullough** • **Notable Works**: 'The Green Library Movement: An Overview and Beyond' • **Contributions**: McCullough has provided insights into the green library movement, highlighting how libraries can reduce their environmental impact. **Leading Institutions** **1. American Library Association (ALA)** • **Key Publications**: 'A Call to Action on Climate Change for Libraries' • **Contributions**: The ALA advocates for the integration of sustainability into library services and operations, offering resources and policy recommendations. **2. International Federation of Library Associations and Institutions (IFLA)** • **Key Publications**: Reports on libraries and sustainability • **Contributions**: IFLA promotes the role of libraries in achieving the UN's Sustainable Development Goals, including climate action. **3. Environmental Protection Agency (EPA) Library Network** • **Key Contributions**: Provides access to extensive environmental research and resources to support sustainability initiatives in libraries. **4. University of Illinois at Urbana-Champaign** • **Notable Initiatives**: The Mortenson Center for International Library Programs focuses on global library development with an emphasis on sustainability. **5. Cornell University** • **Key Contributions**: Cornell's Mann Library has been involved in several sustainability initiatives and research projects related to environmental sciences.

Figure 6.8 *Continued*

Tool	Result
	Key Publications and Reports **1. 'Libraries and Environmental Sustainability: Ensuring Our Future' by Petra Hauke, Karen Latimer, and Klaus Ulrich Werner** • This book offers comprehensive insights into how libraries worldwide are adopting sustainable practices. **2. 'The Green Library Movement: An Overview and Beyond' by Monika Antonelli and Mark McCullough** • This paper reviews the green library movement and discusses various sustainability initiatives in libraries. **3. 'Sustainable Libraries: Programs, Practices, and Partnerships' edited by Kelly Richards and Alex Grech** • This volume includes contributions from various authors on sustainable practices in libraries and successful programs promoting environmental sustainability. **4. 'A Call to Action on Climate Change for Libraries' by the American Library Association** • This document outlines strategies for libraries to engage in climate action and sustainability efforts. These authors and institutions provide a wealth of knowledge and practical guidance on how libraries can contribute to sustainability and climate action. Their research and initiatives highlight the important role libraries play in educating the public, supporting research, and promoting sustainable practices.
Perplexity AI	Based on the provided search results, some of the most prominent authors, researchers, and institutions that have made significant contributions to understanding the climate emergency and the role that various sectors, including libraries, can play in addressing it are: Authors and Researchers: 1. William J. Ripple and Christopher Wolf [1] - Lead authors of the 'World Scientists' Warning of a Climate Emergency' endorsed by over 11,000 scientists from 153 countries. 2. Mark Lynas [3] - Lead author of the study that found a 99.9% consensus among scientists that human activities are causing climate change. 3. Thomas M. Newsome [2] - Co-author of the 'World Scientists' Warning' paper and a researcher at the University of Sydney, highlighting the need for urgent climate action. 4. David Spratt [4] - Climate researcher and author of the article 'We Are in a Climate Emergency, Facing Existential Risks' on the Resilience website. 5. Leo Appleton and Nicola Woolley [5] - Authors of the paper 'The Role of Academic Libraries in Climate Action,' discussing the potential contributions of academic libraries to climate action. Institutions: 1. Oregon State University [1] - Home institution of William J. Ripple and Christopher Wolf, where the 'World Scientists' Warning' project was initiated. 2. Cornell University [3] - Institution where Mark Lynas and his team conducted the study on the scientific consensus on human-caused climate change. 3. University of Sydney [2] - Affiliation of Thomas M. Newsome, a co-author of the 'World Scientists' Warning' paper. 4. Intergovernmental Panel on Climate Change (IPCC) [3][5] - The United Nations body for assessing the science related to climate change, providing authoritative reports and assessments.

Figure 6.8 *Continued*

Tool	Result
	5. White Rose University Consortium [5] - The consortium that published the paper by Leo Appleton and Nicola Woolley on the role of academic libraries in climate action. These authors, researchers, and institutions have made significant contributions to understanding the urgency of the climate crisis, the scientific consensus around its causes, and the potential roles that various sectors, including libraries and information services, can play in addressing this global challenge. Citations: [1] https://academic.oup.com/bioscience/article/70/1/8/5610806 [2] www.bbc.co.uk/news/science-environment-50302392 [3] www.theguardian.com/environment/2021/oct/19/case-closed-999-of-scientists-agree-climate-emergency-caused-by-humans [4] www.resilience.org/stories/2019-12-03/leading-climate-researchers-we-are-in-a-climate-emergency-facing-existential-risks/ [5] https://eprints.whiterose.ac.uk/204017/3/The%20role%20of%20academic%20libraries%20in%20climate%20action%20final%20%282%29.pdf
Scholar GPT	### Leading Authors and Researchers 1. **Eric Klinenberg**: - Director of the Institute for Public Knowledge at New York University (NYU). - Notable work on libraries and their role in community resilience, including climate resilience. - [Link to relevant article](www.yesmagazine.org/environment/2021/09/30/libraries-climate-justice) 2. **Dr Ana Gonzalez**: - Lead author on publications related to financial regulation and climate emergency. - Associated with the University of Cambridge Institute for Sustainability Leadership (CISL). - [Link to relevant publication](www.cisl.cam.ac.uk/resources/publications/risk-sharing-climate-emergency) 3. **Suzanne M. Ward**: - Known for her work on revitalizing library collections with a focus on current emergencies, including climate-related issues. - [Link to relevant article](www.jstor.org/stable/26561670) ### Leading Institutions 1. **Institute for Public Knowledge (IPK) at NYU**: - Engages in research on public knowledge, including the role of libraries in societal issues such as climate change. 2. **University of Cambridge Institute for Sustainability Leadership (CISL)**: - Conducts extensive research on sustainability, including the role of institutions like libraries in tackling the climate emergency. 3. **International Federation of Library Associations and Institutions (IFLA)**: - Publishes research and guidelines on how libraries can contribute to climate change literacy and action. - [IFLA Repository](https://repository.ifla.org/bitstream/123456789/2076/1/s5-2022-aytac-en.pdf)

Figure 6.8 *Continued*

Tool	Result
	4. **British Library**: - Conducts projects and research on the role of libraries in addressing climate change. - [Link to blog post](https://blogs.bl.uk/living-knowledge/2021/11/libraries-and-a-brighter-climate-future.html) 5. **Tandfonline**: - Academic journal publisher with articles discussing the role of academic libraries in climate action. - [Link to article](www.tandfonline.com/doi/full/10.1080/13614533.2023.2230652) These authors and institutions are at the forefront of exploring and promoting the role of libraries in addressing climate challenges. Their work includes theoretical frameworks, practical initiatives, and case studies that highlight the importance of libraries in fostering climate resilience and sustainability. If you need more detailed articles or further assistance, feel free to ask!

Figure 6.8 *Continued*

Summary

Research (Shah et al., 2023) suggests that exploratory search tasks need to be decomposed into multiple actionable sub-tasks, and they may require multiple levels of interaction with the chosen search systems or tools. Findings from the case studies discussed above show that all the chosen Gen AI tools use a conversational approach: users can ask questions in a natural language, and the search results are presented in a conversational format with easy-to-understand points and summaries. Some search tools provide citations, others don't. However, in general the results are useful for the users, especially at the beginning of their journey in education and research, because the answers provide useful background information and leads.

Some of the tools also provide additional guidelines for searching the relevant papers. So, some key questions are:

- how different are these Gen AI tools from scholarly databases like ERIC, LISA, ProQuest, Scopus, Web of Science, etc.; and what should the users know to make better use of the Gen AI-driven search tools for finding information relevant to research and scholarly activities?
- how the key players in the knowledge sector – library and information services, database search services, digital libraries and so on – are coping with the Gen AI revolution, and whether and how they are changing their usual businesses practices?

These, and other, issues and challenges associated with the use of Gen AI tools for access to research and scholarly information are discussed in more details in Chapters 7, 8 and 9.

CHAPTER 7

Gen AI and the Information World

Introduction

'In an era where data is the new oil and artificial intelligence is the refinery, the academic landscape is undergoing seismic shifts' (Jones, 2023). As discussed in Chapters 4, 5 and 6, the Gen AI tools can recommend and summarise research in specific areas based on the retrieved set of results in response to a user query or prompt. In addition to those discussed earlier in the book, more new tools are rapidly appearing quite regularly in the marketplace, such as:

- **Elicit** (https://elicit.com)
- **Inciteful** (https://Inciteful.xyz)
- **Azure AI search** (https://azure.microsoft.com/en-us/products/ai-services/ai-search)
- **Scite** (https://scite.ai/home).

A number of open-source Gen AI tools have also appeared recently that can be used to build localised applications or chatbots for access to information in specific domains or businesses. Some examples of such open -source tools include:

- **Llama:** Created by Meta, Llama is an open-source AI model that can be fine-tuned, distilled and deployed anywhere to produce Gen AI output in a given domain (https://llama.meta.com).
- **Phi:** Developed by Microsoft, the Phi series comprises the most capable and cost-effective small-language models available; the latest one in the series is Phi 3.5, released in August 2024 (Tru, 2024).
- **Mistral AI:** This is a suite of small open-source AI models that can be used by developers to build AI applications in specific domains (https://mistral.ai).

Large proprietary Gen AI tools like Consensus, Scholar GPT and Perplexity AI, discussed earlier in the book, can be used by anyone and they do not require technical expertise or computing resources at the user end. However, as opposed to this, adapting and using open-source Gen AI tools like Llama require a substantial amount of computing resources and technical expertise.

Some Gen AI tools have been specifically designed for assisting students and researchers for finding information from research and scholarly information databases. For example, Scholar AI 'connects the LLMs that power ChatGPT with tailored access to open-access articles, limiting hallucinations and connecting researchers with trustworthy sources' (ScholarAI, n.d.). The service claims: 'with a database of over 200M+ papers to search from, Scholar AI does not make up answers and only links to real, trustworthy, peer-reviewed articles'. However, Scholar AI is not a typical scholarly database service like ProQuest, Scopus or Web of Science. As opposed to these large scholarly databases, or more appropriately aggregator services, that provide access to several databases through one search interface, Scholar AI 'finds relevant papers based on 2 to 6 keywords using the abstract endpoint' (GPTStore.ai, n.d.). Scholar AI recommends: 'If you're looking for research papers on a specific topic, you can use the 'searchAbstracts' function. You'll need to provide keywords related to your topic, and optionally, you can specify the sort order (like relevance or publication date), whether you want only peer-reviewed articles, and a date range' (GPTStore.ai, n.d.).

While recognising the obvious benefits of the Gen AI tools for access to information in different areas, and especially for research and scholarly activities, many universities and researchers have mentioned several issues and concerns. This chapter discusses some key advantages as well as challenges associated with information seeking using Gen AI tools. It further discusses the key differences between the conventional approach to information access using libraries and scholarly databases, and Gen AI tools, especially for research and scholarly activities. It also highlights some key issues that the users should be aware of while using the Gen AI tools for accessing information, especially for research and scholarly activities.

Gen AI tools for everyday life information

As shown through the examples and discussions in Chapter 4, use of Gen AI for access to everyday life information has some obvious advantages. For example, in general, the Gen AI tools:

- are free to use, sometimes with some restrictions on the use, like the maximum number of interactions or queries that can be asked in one day

- use a simple conversational approach for asking questions, and the user does not require prior knowledge or complex query formulation
- produce simple, summarised and easy-to-read text output, with the relevant information and data, often with some citations
- produce instant responses: users don't need to spend a lot of time in searching, finding, reading and analysing information sources or documents
- allow searches to be conducted from anywhere using any tools – mobile, desktop, laptop – and there is no need to visit a library, or subscribe to a service.

However, there are some challenges, too, especially for novice users. For example:

- Search results depend on how good and accurate the query or prompt is.
- The tools may store user information for future analysis without the knowledge of the user, leading to privacy risks, especially when sensitive information, such as on health, or finance, is searched.
- Often the user does not have a clue as to how the information sources are selected by the chosen Gen AI tool, and how authentic the source is or how accurate the information is.
- As shown in Chapter 4, different Gen AI tools produce different results and therefore the quality of the search results or advice will depend on the choice of the tool.
- Users may lose the skills of reviewing literature, summarisation and critical analysis skills over time, because of the ready-made summary or literature review produced by the Gen AI tools.

Access to information using libraries and scholarly databases

Libraries are regarded as the most reliable and trustworthy institutions for democratisation of access to information. People use a variety of library databases and search services for accessing the most reliable, trustworthy and contextually relevant information. The information sources are considered to be reliable and trustworthy because they go through the library's collection management policies and processes. However, using the library resources for finding the most valuable and relevant information is not always an easy task. The user needs to have a range of skills to accomplish an information search process effectively and efficiently. For example, the user needs to know how to articulate a specific information need, select an appropriate database or search service, interact with the chosen search service using its specific interface and interaction tools and techniques, decide on the relevance of the retrieved items in a specific search context and finally find and assimilate the information from a range of retrieved documents.

Over the years, many open-access services have also appeared that can be used to access research and scholarly information. Examples of such services include Google Scholar, Exaly (https://exaly.com), and Internet Archive (https://archive.org). All these services allow the users to search using words or phrases that represent their information need, generate a list of documents that match the search terms and present the results as a list of documents with some information, such as the bibliographic details, abstracts or summaries, and some additional information like the availability and citation data. Users have long been used to using such services, through libraries – for example, LISA, ProQuest, Scopus and Web of Science; or directly through the web, for example, Google Scholar, Internet Archive and Exaly. A variety of guidelines and training resources have been produced by the libraries and database services to provide support for the users for conducting effective and efficient information searches. Such guidelines and training have entered the curricula of library and information science courses at universities; and these have also influenced research in information behaviour, information retrieval and allied areas.

As shown in Figure 7.1, a search on the library website produces results that comprise different types of information resources ranging from books, book chapters and articles. It also shows how the retrieved items can be accessed pointing the users to the library's collections, open-access resources,

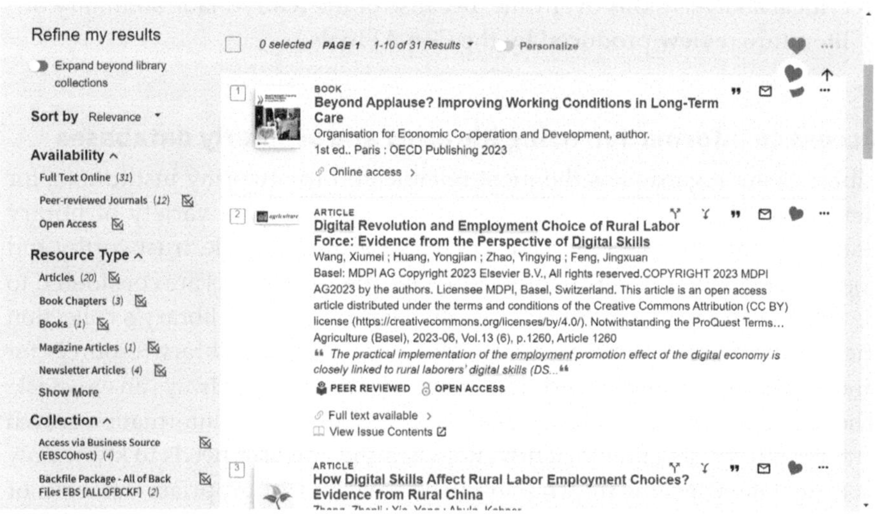

Figure 7.1 *Search results from a typical university library service*

and so on. Thus, users can bring their search on a topic to see the range or information resources that can be accessed through the library. However, a university library website (shown in Figure 7.2) also guides the users to the list of online databases – that can be searched or browsed through an alphabetical list or subject-specific lists where databases are listed under specific subjects like physics, computer science, engineering or literature. Although the typical interface features and specific options vary. A typical university search service usually leads the users to conduct domain- and subject-specific searches using one or more scholarly databases. Some of those can be open-accessed and others are subscribed by the chosen university library that can only be accessed by registered members of the library.

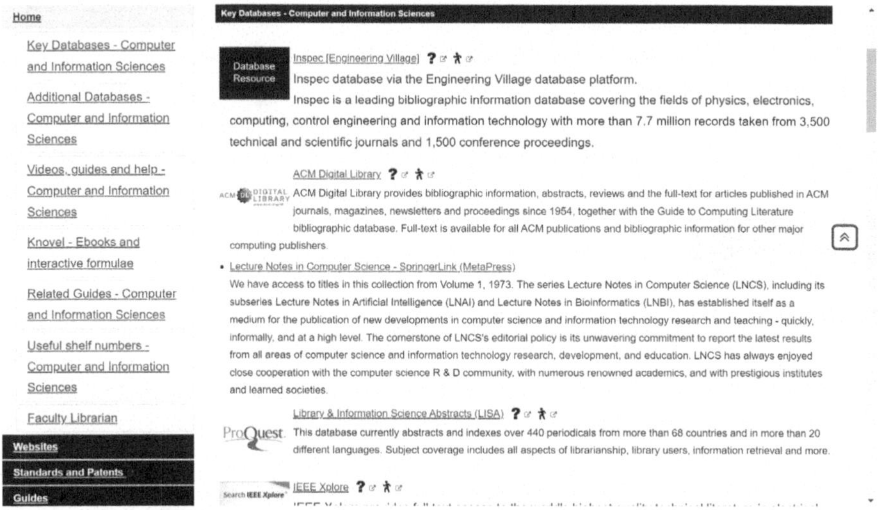

Figure 7.2 *A library guide to databases in a specific subject*

Figures 7.3 to 7.7 on the following pages show the examples of search results on a search topic ('The effect of digital skills on work employment or income') produced by five scholarly databases:

1. ACM Digital Library: Provides access to the full-text collection of all ACM publications; and a collection of curated and hosted full-text publications from select publishers (https://dl.acm.org)
2. ERIC: A searchable, internet-based bibliographic and full-text database of education research and information (https://eric.ed.gov/?faq)
3. LISA (https://about.proquest.com/en/products-services/lisa-set-c): An international abstracting and indexing tool, covering 440 periodicals from more than 68 countries and in more than 20 different languages, designed for library professionals and other information specialists (Proquest, 2025)

4 Scopus: Provides access to research literature in 330 disciplines (Elsevier, 2025a)
5 Web of Science: one of the largest collections of research literature in every discipline (Clarivate, 2025).

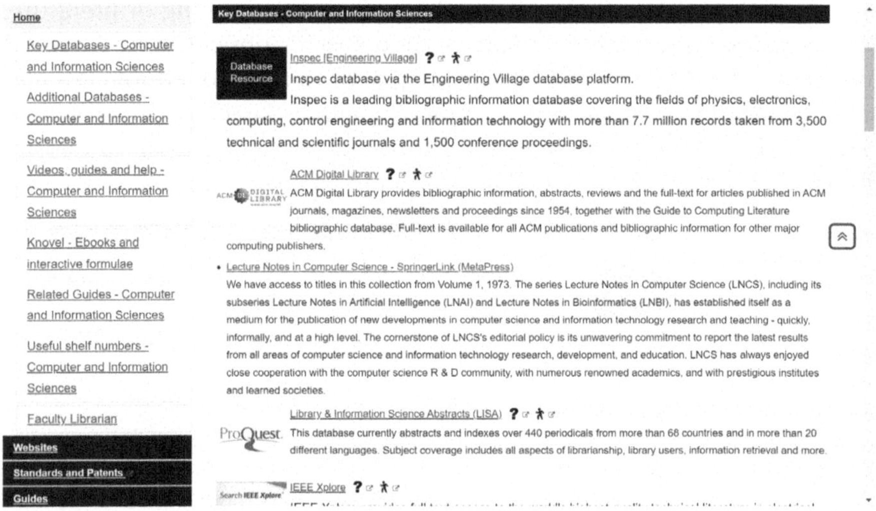

Figure 7.3 *Search results from ACM Digital Library*

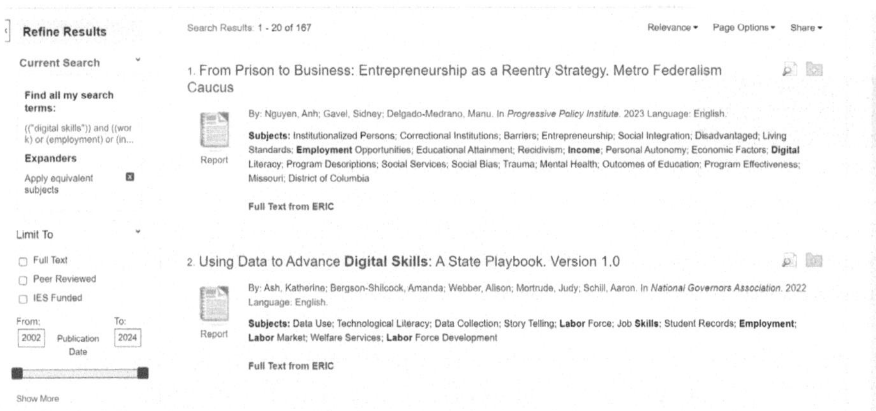

Figure 7.4 *Search results from ERIC*

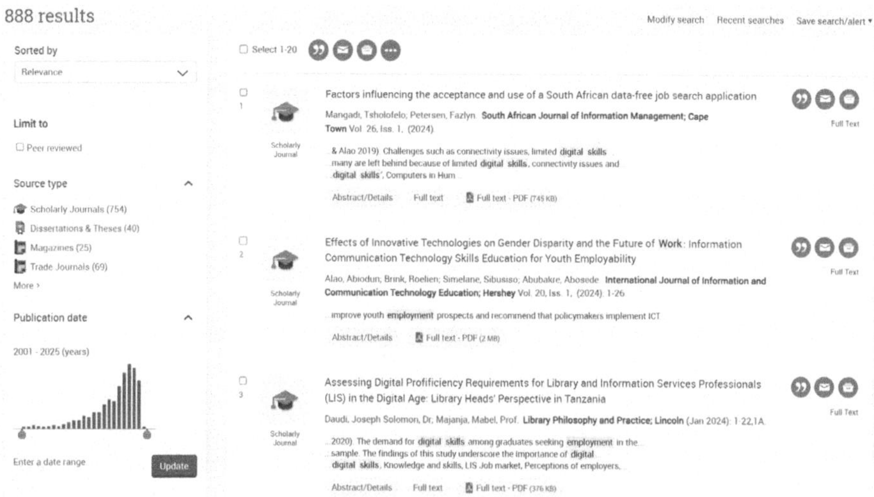

Figure 7.5 *Search results from LISA (Library & Information Science Abstracts)*

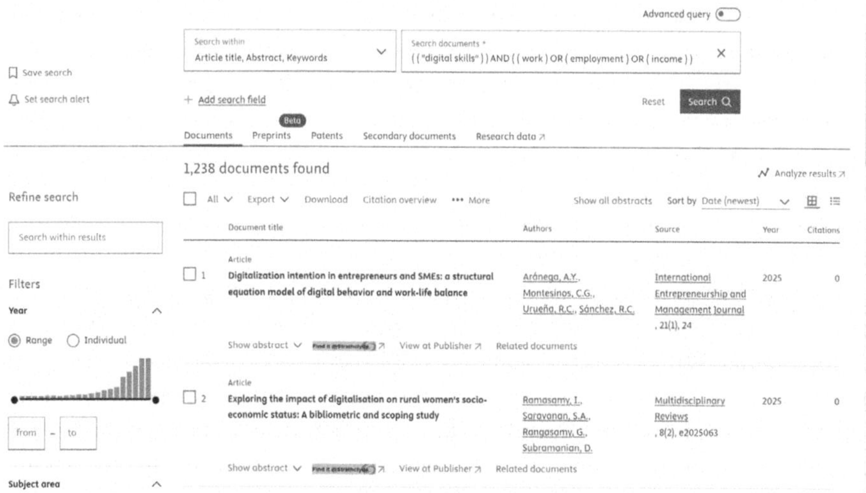

Figure 7.6 *Search results from Scopus*

These search systems have been chosen randomly, and the purpose of the exercise – the search and the examples of the results – is not to demonstrate how to generate the best search results on the chosen topic, nor is it meant to compare the results returned by the chosen systems. Instead, the purpose of this exercise is to show what a typical user needs to do to conduct a search, and what they get at the end of the search.

As mentioned above, each of the selected databases is unique in terms of the disciplines of research, and sources – such as the journals and conferences

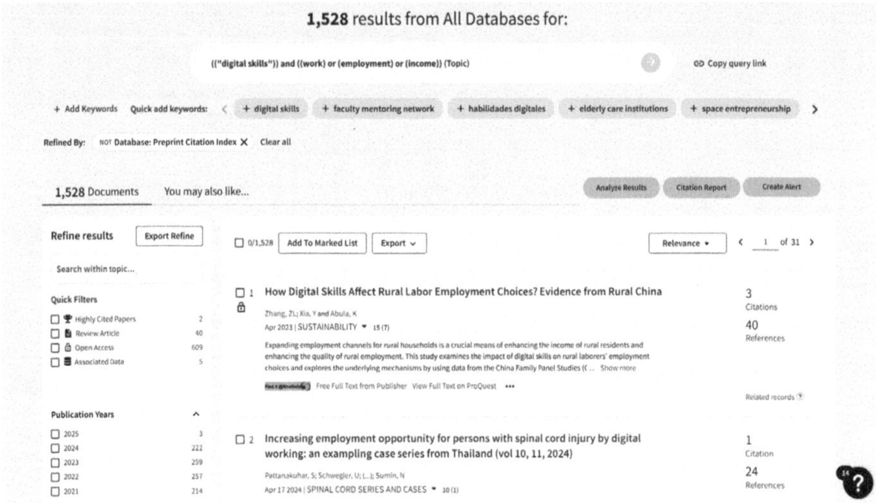

Figure 7.7 *Search results from Web of Science*

that they cover. Hence, to get the best search results on a given topic one needs to choose the most appropriate database(s). Furthermore, the interface of the search systems vary; and the ways the search results are presented, and the options for filtering and ranking the search results, also vary. Let's take a closer look at the examples shown in Figures 7.3 to 7.7 from five scholarly databases on the same search topic, 'The effect of digital skills on work employment or income', and understand the process of accessing information using different scholarly database services.

The number of search results returned by the chosen search services, for the same search query, vary quite significantly, from 158 to 1528. The types of documents returned as the search results also vary. The search results vary in terms of the information, e.g., the bibliographic details, availability of the full text and citation data. Based on the examples shown in these figures, it is possible to identify some of the key challenges that users face while conducting a search using typical scholarly database services.

Articulation of the information need and formulation of a search query

Taking the chosen search topic as an example, it may be noted that the first challenge that a user faces is related to the articulation of the information need using the most appropriate search terms. For the sake of simplicity, the search query in the examples shown in Figures 7.3 to 7.7 has been kept simple by choosing some of the terms from the given search topic, and only one search has been conducted using the six chosen services. In reality, the user may have to go through several iterative searches in order to get the best search results.

Selection of the information search service

One of the most difficult challenges facing users, especially new or novice users, relates to the selection of the most appropriate databases or search services. Often selection of more than one database or search service is a better option for getting more exhaustive or comprehensive search results, but this is often resource-intensive. Some databases provide access to the resources published primarily by the specific service provider (along with some other selected publications from other publishers), e.g., the ACM Digital Library; some provide access to a range of resources produced by a number of publishes, e.g. LISA (Library & Information Science Abstracts); multiple related or allied disciplines e.g., ERIC; or almost all the disciplines e.g., Scopus or Web of Science. Thus, selection of the most appropriate database(s) to conduct a search on a topic requires a substantial amount of knowledge about the world of scholarly databases. However, to facilitate this process, libraries provide guidance for selection of the databases by listing the databases, along with some brief descriptions, under specific subjects or disciplines. Nevertheless, even within a specific discipline the user needs and search context may need to be considered for choosing the most appropriate databases. Selection of more databases also mean that the user needs to conduct more than one set of searches using each chosen database, and that comes with additional challenges and requires more time to accomplish a search.

Familiarisation with the search interface

As shown through the examples in Figures 7.3 to 7.7, the search interfaces, and the ways in which search terms can be entered, may vary from one search service to another. The examples show that additional terms – called operators like AND, OR, NOT – or symbols or characters – such as parentheses, quotation marks or asterisks – are used to enter a query in the search interface. All databases and services also have advanced search interfaces that allow the users to formulate more complex search queries using various operators and symbols.

Each database or search service provides a number of features that can be used to filter or rank the search results, e.g., by date, by source types, by authors, by citation counts. Some search tools also automatically generate time series data showing the growth of research, in terms of the number of publications in an area or discipline or show the number of publications in different disciplines, which could be very useful for the users, especially for multidisciplinary topics like environment, climate change or sustainability.

Interacting with the search results using specific features

Scholarly database services automatically assign and save search sets that can be combined to conduct iterative search sessions for retrieving the most relevant set of search results. Conducting multiple sets of searches is time-consuming, but it may also be rewarding, because it gives the user opportunities for exploring various search terms and their combination, and this may lead to some unexpected discovery of knowledge.

As shown in Figure 7.1 and Figures 7.3 to 7.7, library and scholarly database services provide different options for filtering and ranking the search results. This gives the user opportunities to decide which result sets to select and which ones to discard, how to rank the results, and so on. Some scholarly database services also generate data analytics based on the search output, showing visual representation of the growth of research in a chosen field, citation data and the distribution of the search results across different disciplines and subjects, which is particularly helpful for interdisciplinary research areas like climate change, sustainability, artificial intelligence or COVID-19. Such data analytics produced by the search services add additional value and provide useful insights into research and publications in a given field.

Selection of the most relevant search results

Deciding the best or the most relevant search results is a challenging task. It is also quite time-consuming, because the user must read the title, the abstract and sometimes the full text to make a decision. Comparing the results from multiple search sets is a more time-consuming task. Often several iterative searches need to be conducted to get the most relevant set of results. The successive searches are based on 'an interaction cycle in which the user selects a small set of documents that appear to be relevant to the query, and the system then uses features derived from these selected relevant documents to revise the original query' (Hearst, 1999). This is also called the relevance feedback process, where some terms appearing in a previously retrieved set of results that are considered to be relevant for the user are used to reformulate a query in order to retrieve more relevant results (Chowdhury, G. G., 2010). It requires some subject knowledge, as well as a good understanding of the quality measures for selection of relevant results.

Reading, processing and using the information

It may be noted that all the search results produce the documents that meet the user queries, and the user is required to decide which items are the most relevant to their query, select those documents, download or read those online and find the required information.

Comparison with the Gen AI tools

The emergence of the Gen AI tools discussed so far in this book has changed this scenario. Users of Gen AI tools can converse with the chosen tool in a natural language, do not need to select a library or database(s) to begin the search, and can get the required information in an easy-to-read form, often summarised under specific headings, sometimes with additional advice for further search, or a list of recommended sites or documents for further exploration. Obviously, this is a paradigm shift not only for the users, but also for the library and information services sector, including the myriad commercial as well as open-access databases and repositories.

So, how do the above challenges for information access through scholarly databases compare with the use of Gen AI tools for information access, as shown in Table 7.1 on the next page?

There are also challenges associated with the use of Gen AI tools for access to information and users should be aware of them, for example:

- **Different purpose:** Unlike libraries and scholarly databases Gen AI tools are not designed to produce a list of documents as a search output; they are designed to produce summarised content from some retrieved documents in natural conversational format.
- **Search output is not exhaustive:** Unlike libraries and scholarly databases, Gen AI tools do not aim to produce an exhaustive list of documents as the search results; instead, they generate a natural-language summary of the key points or issues from a small set of retrieved items.
- **Irregular or inconsistent output:** Different Gen AI tools generate different sets of results; and even the same Gen AI tool may generate different results for the same query or prompt at different times of the day, let alone searches conducted on different days.
- **Gen AI is not a curated database or a repository:** Gen AI tools may have been trained using, amongst others, data from scholarly resources but, unlike the library or scholarly databases or search engines, they do not direct the users to the source literature; instead, they are designed to generate their own content or output. Therefore, the user needs to check the citations in terms of their reliability, trustworthiness and relevance for the search context.

Table 7.1 *Access to information through libraries/databases and Gen AI*

Issues	Accessing information through libraries or databases	Accessing information using Gen AI tools
Articulation of the information need and formulation of a search query	Formulation of a search query is the key to success; multiple searches may have to be conducted, using the search interface of the chosen library and database services, to get the best set of results.	Searches can be conducted in natural language using the format of natural conversations; multiple searches may have to be conducted using the appropriate prompts to get the best results.
Selection of the information search service/database	Selection of the search service/ database is the key to success; this is resource-intensive and time-consuming.	Most Gen AI tools do not need the user to select databases; some specific tools like Scholar AI allow users to search for abstracts in a specific database, such as PubMed, Springer, Arxiv, Science or IEEE. (https://scholarai.io/search-abstracts).
Familiarisation with the search interface	Look-and-feel of the search interfaces as well as the search operators and special search characters, etc. vary, and the user needs to be familiar with them.	Not needed for most Gen AI tools; some specific tools designed for researchers require the use of specific search terms and operators, for example Scholar AI.
Interacting with the search results using specific features	Library and database services offer specific features for filtering and ranking search results.	Gen AI tools select the relevant items and summarise the search results in a conversational format, often supported with the relevant citations.
Selection of the most relevant search results	One of the most time-consuming and resource-intensive tasks, e.g. not all the retrieved items may be accessible.	Gen AI tools select the relevant items, mostly open-access items, and summarise the search results in a conversational format, often supported with the relevant citations.

- **Risk of misinformation and disinformation**: Although the accuracy of the Gen AI tools is improving, they still sometimes fabricate content, produce fake citations or wrong summaries or make wrong conclusions.
- **Blind spots and biases**: Depending on the data sources used for training the Gen AI tools, the results may sometimes have biases or may be culturally or morally insensitive to some users.
- **Copyright considerations**: Authorship and ownership of works created by Gen AI is unclear, and laws and policies for safeguarding rights and ownership are beginning to evolve. Furthermore, Gen AI output may contain verbatim copies of existing work without proper attribution, or

may introduce ideas and results from existing works but provide incorrect or missing citations.

- **Privacy issues**: Users often need to provide a lot of personal and contextual data to be able to use, and get the best output from, any Gen AI tools, and such data may be used by the service provider for different purposes without the knowledge of the users.
- **Critical appraisal of research and scholarship**: Gen AI tools select, fuse and summarise content of a number of resources from different sources, and thus over-reliance on Gen AI tools may result in the lack of acquiring the essential academic and research skills, such as assimilating information, constructing evidence-based arguments and expressing critical thoughts through clear and coherent writing.
- **Potential plagiarism**: Unless specifically authorised, the use of content generated by the Gen AI tools for academic and research output may lead to plagiarism or academic misconduct.

User education

Users of Gen AI tools for access to information and data for any purpose, and especially for academic and research purposes, should be aware of the following points:

- **Data and content may be limited or outdated:** Unless they are integrated with an internet search engine (e.g., CoPilot or Gemini) or incorporate external data sources via a plug-in (e.g. Scholar GPT), Gen AI tools do not have access to live data and are dependent on the data on which they were trained; and consequently the content and data may be limited, outdated or incomplete.
- **Gen AI tools do not understand the content they produce:** Gen AI tools do not understand the content they generate, and this can lead to hallucinations or factual errors, or generating information that may be biased, offensive or outdated.
- **Accuracy and authenticity:** Content generated by the Gen AI tools should be checked for accuracy, authenticity and trustworthiness.
- **Copyright issues:** Content generated by the Gen AI tools should be checked for copyright, and thus the potential plagiarism issues.
- **Ethics:** Ethical use of content and data to support learning and research is paramount to ensure and uphold the standards of academic rigour and academic integrity; and this applies to the data and content generated by Gen AI tools.

- **Privacy issues**: Users must understand the potential risks associated with inputting sensitive, private, confidential or proprietary data into the Gen AI tools.
- **Reproducibility of research**: Maintaining documentation and reporting transparency are critical to ensure the reproducibility and replicability of research and scholarly activities, and these apply to content produced with the help of Gen AI tools (Cornell University Research & Innovation, 2023).
- **Citing Gen AI content:** Content generated by the Gen AI tools should be cited. Where the citation styles and standards for this are not available, sufficient information should be provided to indicate the content and data that have been produced by Gen AI.
- **Critical thinking:** Guidelines from the University of Oxford on the use of AI technology highlights that 'AI tools cannot replace human critical thinking or the development of scholarly evidence-based arguments and subject knowledge' (Oxford University, 2025). Hence, over-reliance on the Gen AI tools to show trends of research, establish gaps in knowledge, and thus develop appropriate research questions, may be counterproductive for the overall ethos of education and research.
- **Environmental impact:** The magnitude of computational resources to create models based on large volumes of training data, and the energy costs associated with such computational processes, can have huge environmental impacts. Recent studies show that the carbon cost to generate just one single image using a specific energy-intensive Gen AI model is equivalent to that required to fully charge a smartphone (Heikkilä, 2023; Luccioni, Jernite and Strubell, 2024). 'There is limited data on the carbon footprint of a single generative AI query, but some industry figures estimate it to be four to five times higher than that of a search engine query' (Saenko, 2023) (for more details, see Chapter 9).

Use of Gen AI for information access: library guidelines

Universities and libraries, especially academic and research libraries, around the world have come up with a set of recommendations for users to keep in mind while using the Gen AI tools for access to information. The following guidelines from Cornell University clearly outline the advantages of using the Gen AI tool review of literature for research, but at the same time highlight some key points of concern:

> • GenAI can be used to triage, organize, summarize, and quickly get directionally oriented, in the context of an exponentially growing base of reported claims and established knowledge.

- Gen AI can be used to assist with drafting literature reviews, although researchers should fact-check and be aware of incomplete, biased, or even false Gen AI outputs.
- Subject to authorship, citation, and fact-checking considerations, it can be helpful to use Gen AI to ideate and iterate on the quality of a literature review.

(Cornell University Research & Innovation, 2023.)

Tools like Scholar AI allow the user to enter keywords, search operators, and some relevance criteria to produce search results. The following advice is provided by Scholar AI for the users (https://scholarai.io/search-abstracts):

- be specific with keywords
- utilise Boolean operators
- leverage customisable sorting, e.g., sorting by relevant, citation count or date
- set specific time filters, e.g. a date range
- check peer review status
- use advanced search features.

Summary

The emerging world of Gen AI tools, and their use and applications for information access, can be seen as two parallel sets of development.

1. Emergence of a number of Gen AI tools, some of which are specifically designed to search for research and scholarly information. However, users need to be aware of several issues associated with characteristics and functionalities of the Gen AI tools. Users also need to acquire some skills for making effective and efficient use of these tools, and for finding the most relevant and context-specific information.
2. Libraries and database services are also adapting to the transformation technologies brought in by the emerging Gen AI tools, and their implications for access to information for everyday life as well as for research and scholarly information. Some commercial database services are in the process of introducing their own version of Gen AI tools to enable their users to use the technologies on specifically selected and curated databases.

While most of the Gen AI tools can be free at the point of use, they have certain limitations, and users need to be aware of those, and they should also acquire some skills for making optimum use of these tools. Universities and institutions of higher education are developing their own policies and guidelines for the use of Gen AI tools for academic and research activities, including access to information for research and scholarly activities.

Commercial database services are developing their own proprietary versions of Gen AI tools that would alleviate some of the problems associated with the freely available Gen AI tools, but they still do not offer the most sustainable solutions for access to information. In order for the Gen AI tools to be economically, socially and environmentally sustainable, the information services sector should use open-source Gen AI tools along with the open-access content and data. Developing applications of Gen AI tools that can access open-access content and generate relevant and context-specific results based on curated content will be appropriate for users because:

- They won't need to select one or more scholarly databases and interact with their specific search interfaces. Instead, they can use the conversations approach of Gen AI using the internal tool.
- The Gen AI tool, using advanced techniques such as RAG (discussed in the next chapter), will interact with the recommended data sources, and generate relevant results in a conversational format.
- The user will be able to repeat the search process by using alternative search requests or prompts until the best possible search results are obtained.

However, users should be advised that they should not rely entirely on the Gen AI tools for accomplishing all their information-intensive tasks, especially those that are vital, such as critical analysis and reviews of literature, identifying research gaps in a specific domain and formulating new research questions. As opposed to the general-purpose tools, institutional or domain-specific Gen AI tools can address some of these problems, by helping their users to:

- use the results produced by the Gen AI tool as a starting point for understanding the direction of research and scholarship in a given area of study, and identify some key works, key resources and key authors, that will lead them to further research
- avoid the risks of unknowingly passing personal and sensitive information to external companies which may be used for unintended purposes.

Details of how this can be achieved and its implications for education and research in information science are discussed in Chapters 8 and 9.

CHAPTER 8

Gen AI and Information Seeking: Some Lessons

Introduction

Research on human-related information practices dates back well over 100 years (Given, Case and Wilson, 2023), and some specific research on this in the UK can be traced back to 1948 (Wilson, 1999). The approaches and focus of this research evolved through different stages, for example, (Ingwersen and Jarvelin, 2005; Given, Case and Wilson, 2023):

1. Earlier research works on information seeking were limited to survey type studies on information seeking in institutional, library and specific disciplinary contexts.
2. From the mid-80s, information-seeking research shifted towards humans, actor-centred and process-/system-oriented approaches, but some studies still focused on discipline-specific information seeking and behaviour.
3. Gradually the focus of research shifted from:

   - the use of information channels and sources to encountering and seeking of information, and interpretation of the meaning of information as an output of information seeking and interactions
   - academic and scholarly contexts to work- and everyday life-related contexts
   - scholarly databases to myriad information channels and devices used for accessing and sharing information, such as the web and social media, alongside the conventional library and scholarly database services
   - a single disciplinary perspective to multiple methods and approaches, resulting in more inter- and multi-disciplinary research.

Several comprehensive reviews of such research appeared over the years in leading journals and conferences, which are summarised with critical comments by Given, Case and Wilson (2023).

Commenting on his classic 1981 model of information behaviour, Wilson (2007) points out: 'a three-fold view of information seeking: the context of the seeker, the "system" employed (which might be manual or machine and navigated either personally or by an intermediary), and the information resources that might be drawn upon'. All these key elements – the user and context, the system and the information resources – have been the focus of research in information behaviour in general, and in different related areas such as information seeking, and information practice; and these are equally crucial in the context of information seeking and information access in the era of Gen AI.

Given the benefits and promises that the Gen AI technologies offer, and the ease of availability of these tools, they are obviously going to be a natural preference of people for access to information. As discussed in Chapter 7, some of the key challenges users face while accessing information through conventional libraries and scholarly databases do not appear while using Gen AI tools for accessing information. These tools do not require the user to formulate a complex search query, select a specific database to search, rank and filter the retrieved search results, decide on the relevance of the retrieved items and, most importantly, the user does not need to read, understand and assimilate the required information from the retrieved items. Some Gen AI applications can also summarise the key points or trends in research, formulate research questions, prepare a review of the literature and much more.

So, what impact will the increasing use of Gen AI tools have on the information-seeking behaviour and information practices of people in general? Will people, by default, use Gen AI tools for everyday life information seeking, as discussed in Chapter 4, and information for research and scholarly activities, as discussed in Chapters 5 and 6? If so, how will it change people's information seeking, information behaviour and information practices? Will the widespread use of Gen AI tools for access to information deprive people of critical thinking skills and of the understanding of the value, quality and trust of information sources? Will this in the long run change the fabric of the information and knowledge society at large? This chapter discusses some of these questions and highlights some emerging research to address some of these issues.

Information for research and scholarly activities

As discussed in Chapters 5 and 6, Gen AI tools can recommend and summarise research in specific areas based on the retrieved set of results in response to a user query or prompt. Overall, the search results produced by the chosen Gen AI tools shown in Chapters 5 and 6 are quite useful, especially for starting research on a topic, but as the examples and the corresponding discussions show, users need to check the authenticity and accuracy of the information provided. Some Gen AI tools have been specifically designed for assisting students and researchers in finding information from research and scholarly information databases. For example, Scholar AI provides tailored access to articles connecting researchers with trustworthy information sources. The site claims that it provides access to 200M+ peer-reviewed papers and patents (https://scholarai.io). However, as opposed to the scholarly databases, Scholar AI finds the relevant papers based on two to six keywords using the abstract endpoint (https://gptstore.ai/plugins/scholar-ai-net).

As examples presented in Chapters 4–6 show, the search results with the recommended items generated by the chosen Gen AI tools vary widely, and it is not clear to the user why and how those items have been recommended. Also, it is not clear to the users what the recall is – the proportion of the relevant items retrieved through a search – and the precision – the proportion of the retrieved items that are relevant – of the results produced by the chosen tools (Chowdhury, G. G., 2010). Recall, precision and relevance criteria are particularly important for access to research and scholarly information (Chowdhury, G. G., 2010); and it is a well-known fact that Gen AI can produce false or misleading output, which is a deal-breaker in scientific settings (Wang, 2024).

User perceptions of Gen AI

Features and capabilities of specific Gen AI tools mentioned on the specific websites, and in general media, may create an enormous number of expectations from the users. Two of the search tools used in Chapters 5 and 6 – Consensus and Scholar GPT – are specifically designed for finding information for research and scholarly activities. The sites say:

- **Consensus:** 'Our mission is to make the world's expert knowledge discoverable and consumable. Searching for scientific research has long been a painful process, no matter your background. If used thoughtfully, carefully, and elegantly, we believe AI can change this equation.' (https://consensus.app/home/about-us)
- **Scholar GPT:** 'Enhance research with 200M+ resources and built-in critical reading skills. Access Google Scholar, PubMed, JSTOR, Arxiv, and more, effortlessly.' (https://chatgpt.com/g/g-kz0eyxlje-scholar-gpt)

These statements may mislead most users because they may think that any search using these tools will produce results from all these large scholarly databases and repositories.

A search on Copilot provides the following answer about Scholar GPT, shown in Figure 8.1.

"Scholar GPT works by leveraging advanced natural language processing (NLP) and machine learning algorithms to assist with academic research. Here's a breakdown of how it functions:

1. **Data Collection**: It gathers information from a vast array of scholarly databases, journals, and articles.
2. **Understanding Queries**: It interprets user queries to understand the context and intent, ensuring relevant and accurate responses.
3. **Information Retrieval**: It searches through its extensive database to find the most pertinent information related to the query.
4. **Summarization**: It condenses complex academic texts into concise summaries, making it easier to grasp key points.
5. **Citation Assistance**: It helps in generating proper citations in various formats (APA, MLA, Chicago, etc.).
6. **Critical Analysis**: It can provide insights and critical analysis on specific topics, aiding in deeper understanding and research."

Figure 8.1 *Search result from Copilot about Scholar GPT*

Results of searches produced in Chapters 5–6 attest to some of these points. However, what's stated in point 3 in Figure 8.1 is debatable. A search on Scholar GPT (26 August 2024, 4.31 p.m.) (https://chatgpt.com/g/g-kz0eyxlje-scholar-gpt) on a prompt produced the results shown in Figure 8.2. Figure 8.3 shows the results of a search on the same query produced by a university library search service.

Prompt: I am writing a literature review on how library and information services can contribute to the SDGs. Please recommend me some relevant and latest literature

Response:
Here are some recent and relevant studies on how library and information services contribute to the Sustainable Development Goals (SDGs):
1. **Community Perceptions of Public Library Services in Rural Communities in Edo State (2024)**
 - **Authors**: NO Uwenbor, AO Osadolor
 - **Summary**: This study explores community perceptions of public library services and their alignment with Sustainable Development Goal 4 (SDG 4).
 - **Link**: [Read the paper](https://www.researchgate.net/profile/Alexander-Osadolor/publication/382136460_Community_perceptions_of_public_library_services_in_rural_communities_in_Edo_State/links/6698cb9ecb7fbf12a459dc55/Community-perceptions-of-public-library-services-in-rural-communities-in-Edo-State.pdf)
2. **How Can Deep Learning and Strategic Thinking Transform Agri-Business Research in Malaysian Academic Libraries? (2024)**
 - **Authors**: H Sa'ari, H Adenan, A Goulding
 - **Summary**: Discusses the transformative role of libraries in advancing SDGs, particularly within the context of agri-business research in Malaysia.
 - **Link**: [Read the paper](https://knowledgewords.com/index.php/ijarems/article/view/972)

Figure 8.2 *Search results from Scholar GPT on the topic 'library and information services and the SDGs'*

3. **Identifying Librarians' Readiness to Leverage Artificial Intelligence for Sustainable Competence Development and Smart Library Services (2024)**
   - **Authors**: K Shahzad, SA Khan, A Iqbal
   - **Summary**: Investigates how libraries can integrate AI to enhance their services and contribute to sustainable development.
   - **Link**: [Read the paper](https://www.emerald.com/insight/content/doi/10.1108/GKMC-02-2024-0107/full/html)
4. **Designing a Farmers Digital Information System for Sustainable Agriculture: The Perspective of Tanzanian Agricultural Stakeholders (2024)**
   - **Authors**: GE Mushi, PY Burgi
   - **Summary**: Explores the role of digital information systems in supporting sustainable agriculture, relevant to SDGs 1 and 2.
   - **Link**: [Read the paper](https://onlinelibrary.wiley.com/doi/pdf/10.1002/isd2.12344)
5. **Resilience Model of Tourism Industry Stakeholders Relying on Socio-Cultural Capacities (2024)**
   - **Authors**: G Jabbari, MH Imani Khoshkhoo, M Basouli, M Asadi
   - **Summary**: Discusses the role of libraries in tourism and their contribution to sustainable development through cultural preservation.
   - **Link**: [Read the paper](https://jut.ut.ac.ir/article_97755_en.html?lang=fa)

These articles can provide a solid foundation for your literature review on the contribution of library and information services to the SDGs.

Handling multiple papers?

Our AI sidebar — Sider assists you skim through papers 10X faster using its 10+ one-click research tools like deep reader, advanced search, ChatPDF, and context selection.

[Get ready for a smarter academic experience!](https://bit.ly/4aSnMXa)

Figure 8.2 *Continued*

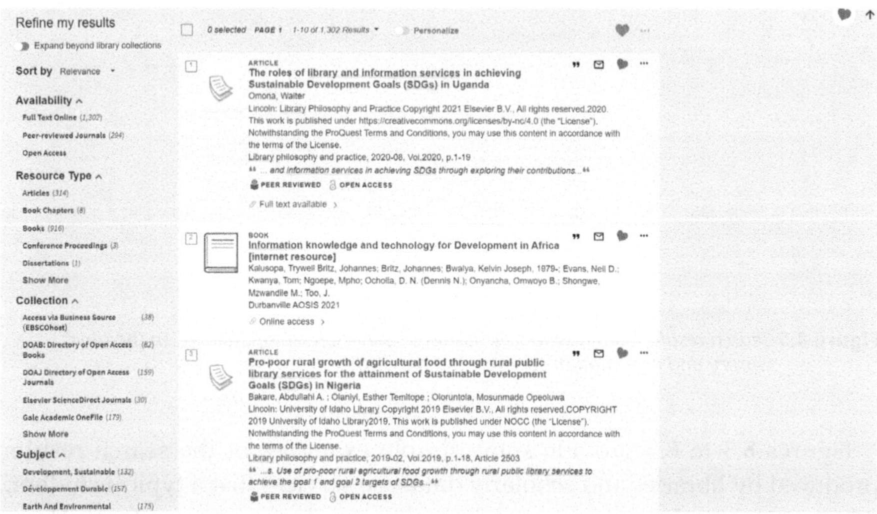

Figure 8.3 *Search results from a university library website on the topic 'library and information services and the SDGs'*

Figures 8.4 and 8.5 show the results of a search on the same topic from two scholarly database services, Scopus and Web of Science.

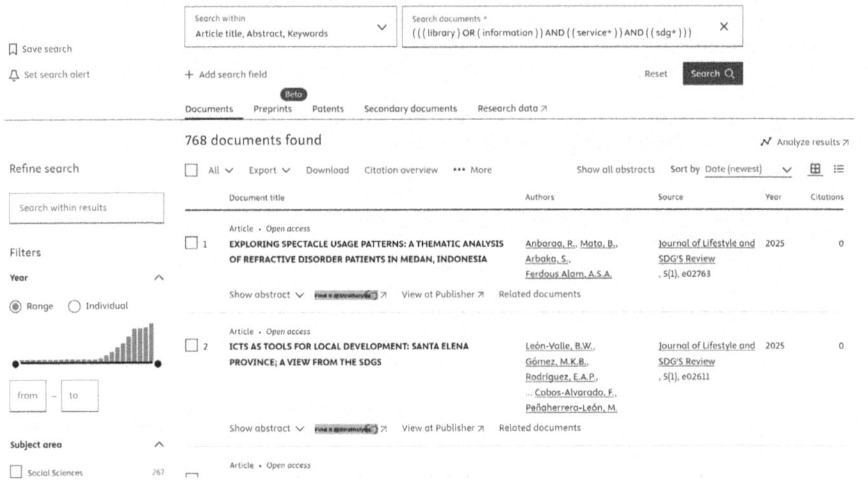

Figure 8.4 *Search results from a scholarly database service (Scopus) on the topic 'library and information services and the SDGs'*

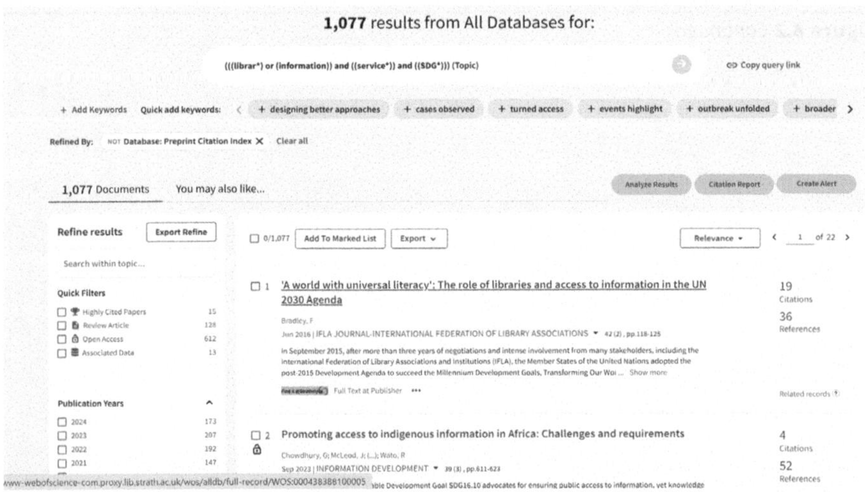

Figure 8.5 *Search results from a scholarly database service (Web of Science) on the topic 'library and information services and the SDGs'*

Figures 8.3 to 8.5 provide some simple examples of the search results produced by libraries and scholarly database services that a typical student, scholar or researcher might use to find relevant information on a topic. These results provide brief information about the selected items, including citation data, and some options for filtering and sorting the results. Scholarly database services also offer a number of advanced features that can be used to study the growth of research on a topic, the most cited papers, the most cited or most prolific authors, institutions and so on, and various other options for modifying, filtering and sorting the search results. Users can also save the searches and results, and thus can build a profile and monitor progress of research in a field of study. A closer look at the results shown in Figure 8.2 and comparing them with those presented in Figures 8.3–8.5 clearly shows more comprehensiveness of the results produced by the library and scholarly database services on the same search topic.

These examples provide some useful lessons for users in the research scholarly environment, because in order to analyse and understand the progress of research in any field of study one does not only need to get a comprehensive set of search outputs, but one should also be able to slice and dice the search result sets to get different insights and, more importantly, find out the progress and gaps in research in the chosen field of study.

Unlike the library and scholarly database services, Gen AI tools often return different sets of results for the same query even when the same searches are conducted at different times of day. This is shown through some search results in Table 8.1. This becomes a challenge for users, especially in the academic and scholarly context, where they want to see the progression of research through new research publications appearing over a period of time, and not a new set of results every time they search. Out of the 30 results generated by the three searches, only two were common in two result sets – item number 3 and item number 6 in search results 1 and 3 (columns 1 and 3 in Table 8.1); all other results are different in each set.

Table 8.1 *Different search results from Scholar GPT (at different times on the same day) (Question: Find the latest research on AI- and LLM-based tools for information access)* (https://chatgpt.com/g/g-kz0eyxlje-scholar-gpt)

Result 1	Result 2	Result 3
Here are some of the latest research articles and discussions on AI- and LLM-based tools for information access in education and research: 1. **[Utilizing Generative AI for Instructional Design: Exploring Strengths and Challenges](https://link.springer.com/article/10.1007/s11528-024-00967-w)** - This article explores how generative AI tools, including LLMs, can be effectively used in instructional design to curate essential resources.	Here are some of the latest research articles and resources on AI- and LLM-based tools for information access from 2023: 1. **AI and Generative AI for Research Discovery and Summarization** - This article reviews the current landscape of AI tools available for statistical and data analysis, including LLM-based chatbots. - [Read the full paper](https://arxiv.org/html/2401.06795v2)	Here are some of the latest research articles and discussions on AI- and LLM-based tools for information access: 1. **[LLM Comparator: A tool for human-driven LLM evaluation](https://medium.com/people-ai-research/llm-comparator-a-tool-for-human-driven-llm-evaluation-81292c17f521)** - This article introduces the LLM Comparator, a tool designed for evaluating large language models (LLMs) in a human-centric manner.

Table 8.1 *Continued*

Result 1	Result 2	Result 3
2. **[The Evolution of AI Large Language Models #llm](www.linkedin.com/pulse/evolution-ai-large-language-models-llm-data-innovation-rick-spair-o2d6e)** - This LinkedIn post discusses the evolution of LLMs and their application in educational and research settings, focusing on transparency and innovation.	2. **Generative Artificial Intelligence (AI) | Library & Technology Services** - This resource discusses the application of generative AI and LLMs in computing and learning sciences. - [Read more](https://lts.lehigh.edu/generative-artificial-intelligence-ai)	2. **[Foundation Models, Generative AI, and Large Language Models](https://journals.lww.com/cinjournal/fulltext/2024/05000/foundation_models,_generative_ai,_and_large.11.aspx)** - This journal entry discusses how foundation models and generative AI serve as the basis for more specific AI tools, including LLMs.
3. **[Research, Academic Integrity, and Artificial Intelligence (AI)](https://libguides.southernct.edu/plagiarism/AI)** - This guide covers various AI and LLM tools used in academic research, highlighting their implications for academic integrity.	3. **Stuff We Figured Out About AI in 2023** - A weblog summarizing key developments in AI and LLMs in 2023, highlighting their smart yet sometimes limited capabilities. - [Read the blog](https://simonwillison.net/2023/Dec/31/ai-in-2023/)	3. **[Research, Academic Integrity, and Artificial Intelligence (AI)](https://libguides.southernct.edu/plagiarism/AI)** - This guide covers various AI and LLM tools used in academic research, highlighting their implications for academic integrity.
4. **[Teachers, Parents, and Students' Perspectives on Integrating AI](https://dl.acm.org/doi/10.1145/3613904.3642438)** - This research focuses on the use of AI systems in literacy education, particularly LLM-based chatbots for language learning and scientific writing.	4. **Microsoft New Future of Work Report 2023** - This report by Microsoft explores how early LLM-based tools for enterprise information workers can significantly boost productivity. - [Download the report](www.microsoft.com/en-us/research/uploads/prod/2023/12/NFWReport2023_v5.pdf)	4. **[How to Mitigate LLM Privacy Risks in Fine-Tuning and RAG](www.anonos.com/blog/llm-privacy-security)** - This blog post addresses the privacy and security concerns associated with fine-tuning LLMs and generative AI tools.
5. **[Large Language Models for Education: A Survey](https://arxiv.org/html/2405.13001v1)** - This survey paper discusses the application of LLMs in education, covering various AI technologies like natural language processing used to understand and generate texts.	5. **Introducing New AI Experiences Across Our Family of Apps** - Meta's announcement about integrating technology from Llama 2 and their latest LLM research into their applications. - [Read the announcement](https://about.fb.com/news/2023/09/introducing-ai-powered-assistants-characters-and-creative-tools/)	5. **[Artificial intelligence and large language model tools in business](www.tilde.com/news/artificial-intelligence-and-large-language-model-tools-business-sandbox-creators-or-key-growth)** - This article explores the application of LLM tools in business, emphasizing their role in information retrieval, translation, and speech recognition.
6. **[Defining Generative AI - Generative Artificial Intelligence](https://libguides.richmond.edu/genai/defininggenai)** - This guide explains the distinctions between LLMs and the tools that utilize their training data, providing foundational insights into generative AI.	6. **AI Tools I Have Found Useful with Research (Reddit Discussion)** - A discussion on Reddit about various AI tools useful for research, including those using LLMs. - [Join the discussion](www.reddit.com/r/PhD/comments/14d6g09/ai_tools_i_have_found_useful_w_research_what_do/)	6. **[Defining Generative AI – Generative Artificial Intelligence](https://libguides.richmond.edu/genai/defininggenai)** - This guide explains the distinctions between LLMs and the tools that utilize their training data, providing a foundational understanding of generative AI.
7. **[How to Use LLMs in the Classroom - AI x Education](https://aixeducation.	7. **Large Language Models in Official Statistics - UNECE** - This paper explores the use of	7. **[AI-powered Code Review with LLMs: Early Results](https://arxiv.org/pdf/24

Table 8.1 *Continued*

Result 1	Result 2	Result 3
substack.com/p/how-to-use-llms-in-the-classroom)** – This article offers strategies for leveraging LLMs in the classroom, with insights from recent studies on integrating generative AI tools into K–12 education.	LLMs in official statistics, focusing on access to the latest research and ethical AI practices. – [Read the paper](https://unece.org/sites/default/files/2023-12/HLGMOS%20LLM%20Paper_Preprint_1.pdf)	04.18496)** – This research paper presents early results of using LLMs for AI-powered code review, highlighting their ability to predict future risks in code.
8. **[Integrating Artificial Intelligence (AI) Into Adult Education](https://fuse.franklin.edu/cgi/viewcontent.cgi?article=1134&context=facstaff-pub)** - This paper discusses how adult learners are using generative AI tools to access information, and how educational institutions are adopting these technologies.	8. **Supercharging Research: Harnessing Artificial Intelligence to Meet Global Challenges** – A White House report on how AI-based tools, including LLMs, are being harnessed for research and data processing. – [Read the report](www.whitehouse.gov/wp-content/uploads/2024/04/AI-Report_Upload_29APRIL2024_SEND-2.pdf)	8. **[The Shift from Traditional Education Data Systems to LLM-Based AI](www.linkedin.com/pulse/shift-from-traditional-education-data-systems-llm-based-richard-tong-xxhyc?trk=public_post)** – This LinkedIn article discusses the transition from traditional education data systems to LLM-based AI systems, emphasizing the paradigm shift in data collection and analysis.
9. **[Choosing Wisely: Lessons for Leaders in AI Integration - EdSurge](www.edsurge.com/news/2024-05-22-choosing-wisely-lessons-for-leaders-in-ai-integration)** - This article provides lessons for leaders on integrating AI tools into educational settings, emphasizing the need for careful selection and implementation.	9. **Sociotechnical Implications of Generative Artificial Intelligence for Information Access** - This paper discusses how generative AI technologies like LLMs can enhance information access and effectiveness. - [Read the full paper](https://arxiv.org/html/2405.11612v1)	9. **[Army set to issue new policy guidance on use of large language models](https://defensescoop.com/2024/05/09/army-policy-guidance-use-large-language-models-llm/)** - This news article reports on the U.S. Army's upcoming policy guidance on the use of LLMs and generative AI tools in military applications.
10. **[Transforming Driver Education: A Comparative Analysis of LLM-Based Instructional Tools](https://link.springer.com/article/10.1007/s40593-024-00407-z)** – This research compares traditional instructional methods with LLM-based instructional tools for driver education, highlighting their effectiveness.	10. **The Imperative for Regulatory Oversight of Large Language Models** - A Nature article on the need for regulatory oversight of new AI-based tools, particularly LLMs, to ensure safe and ethical use. – [Read the article](www.nature.com/articles/s41746-023-00873-0)	10. **[Utility of Large Language Models for Health Care Professionals and Researchers](www.jmir.org/2024/1/e54758)** - This journal article explores the application of LLMs in healthcare, focusing on their use by professionals and researchers to enhance workflows.
For more detailed information, you can follow the provided links to the full articles and studies.	These resources provide a comprehensive view of the latest developments in AI and LLM-based tools for information access.	For more detailed information, you can follow the provided links to the full articles and studies.

Not all AI-powered search tools are the same

Semantic Scholar, a Gen AI tool specifically designed for access to scholarly information, says on its website that it is a free and AI-driven search tool for discovering over 200 million academic papers (www.semanticscholar.org/about). A search conducted using Semantic Scholar (26 August 2024, 8:50 a.m.) on the following topic did not produce any results: 'What role can library and information services play to promote the SDGs?' Result: No papers were found.

A simpler version of the query (query: libraries and the SDGs) produced 28 results (Figure 8.6), and many of those could (or should) have been produced by the first search. More (53) results are returned when the query is slightly modified ('Library and information services and the SDGs') (Figure 8.7 opposite).

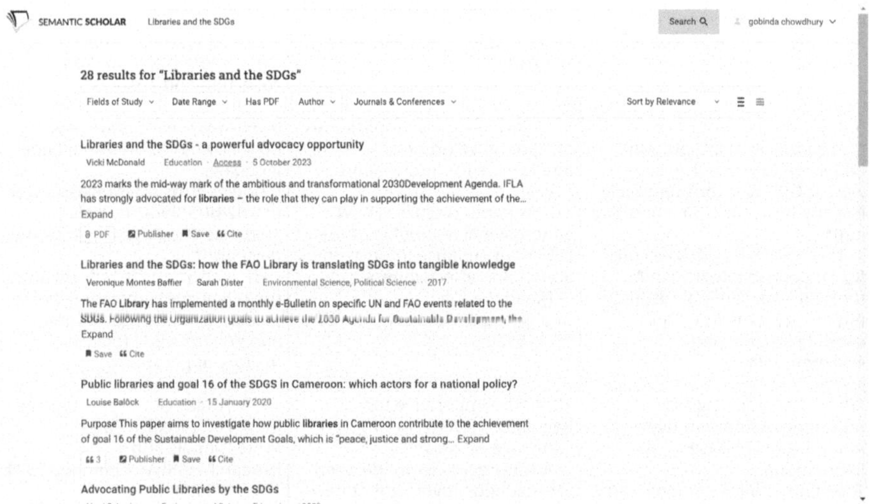

Figure 8.6 *Search results of a simpler version of a query from Semantic Scholar*

So, some key lessons that can be learnt from these examples are:

1. Semantic Scholar search results are more suitable for research and scholarly purposes, since they provide citation data, a PDF file or the DOI (Digital Object Identifier) of the item that can be used to access the item, and options for filtering the search results.
2. Not all the AI-powered search tools take a conversational approach. It may be noted that no results are found for the first search; and the results are similar to those produced by other (non-AI) search engines (as in Figures 7.4 and 7.5).
3. Users need to try different searches using different search terms to get better output.

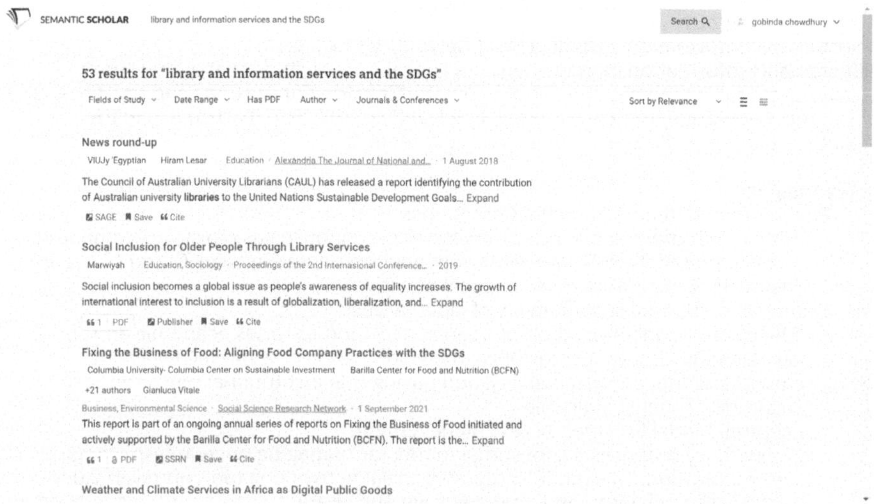

Figure 8.7 *Search results of the modified version of the query from Semantic Scholar*

How good are the cited items in Gen AI results?

Examples and discussions in Chapters 4–6 show that often the results produced by some Gen AI tools do not include any citations at all, and in those that do, the number and quality of the cited items vary quite significantly. Furthermore, the quality and reliability of many of the cited items are questionable. Overall, it is not clear to the users, in such cases, why and how the search results have been selected, or how authoritative, current, accurate or reliable those are in the context of the search. A simple search on Consensus, a Gen AI tool that claims to have been designed to support research scholarly work, on the topic 'Chowdhury on sustainable information' generated the results shown in Figure 8.8 on the next page.

The summary looks good, and indeed Chowdhury wrote on the topic in a number of journal and conference papers and books. However, the results do not cite any of Chowdhury's work. Instead, it cites the following three works: (1) Review of the book 'The Librarian Stereotype: Deconstructing Perceptions and Presentations of Information Work,' edited by Nicole Pagowsky and Miriam Rigby by A. M. Sleeman, 2 Oct 2015; (2) an Editorial: 'Applied and sustainable methods to manage environmental contaminants with natural and fortified microbial biosorbents' by S. Bera, Debabrata Chowdhury, Jing Han +1 more, 7 Jun 2023; and (3) Review of the book 'Is Digital Different? How Information Creation, Capture, Preservation and Discovery Are Being Transformed, ed. by Michael Moss, Barbara Endicott-Popovsky; by Evans Ochola, 7 Jul 2016.

A closer look at the cited items reveals that none of the cited items is a work of the named person, Chowdhury, on the chosen topic, of sustainable

3 papers analyzed
Sustainable Information: Insights from Chowdhury's Research
Sustainable information management is a critical area of study that addresses the environmental, economic, and social impacts of information systems and practices. Gobinda Chowdhury has contributed significantly to this field, particularly in the context of digital collections and open access models.

Key Insights

- Environmental Impact of Digital Collections:
  - Digital collections, while producing lower greenhouse gas emissions compared to print materials, still have significant environmental impacts. Current laws are insufficient to address these impacts effectively[1,3].
- Economic and Social Sustainability of Open Access:
  - The current implementation of open access models raises economic and social sustainability issues. For instance, the gold open access model negatively impacts economic sustainability, and having one institutional repository per institution is not sustainable[1].
- Conceptual Model for Open Access Management:
  - Chowdhury proposes a conceptual model for managing open access scholarly communication. This model integrates social networking tools and web 2.0 to spread research ideas and analyze usage and sharing patterns, aiming to build a better-informed society[1].
- Sustainability in Digitization Projects:
  - Sustainable practices in digitization projects are essential for their long-term viability. This includes ensuring continued funding, focusing on user needs, and reducing the environmental impact of digital collections[3].

Conclusion

Chowdhury's research highlights the multifaceted nature of sustainability in information management. Key takeaways include the need to address the environmental impacts of digital collections, the economic and social challenges of current open access models, and the importance of sustainable practices in digitization projects. These insights underscore the necessity for comprehensive strategies that balance environmental, economic, and social considerations in the management of digital information systems.

Figure 8.8 *Results from Consensus on a prompt 'Chowdhury on sustainable information'*

information. It is also clear that the second item is not relevant to the topic, and although the author's name (Chowdhury) matches, the search topic does not. The two other cited items are relevant but from the point of view of the quality of being relevant for a research and scholarly information context they fall short in a number of ways: both items are nearly a decade old and they are review works rather than the original works. So, it is not clear whether the content generated by the chosen Gen AI tool, Consensus, is based on the two books or their reviews; and in any case the information is nearly a decade old, and the author in question, Chowdhury, has since then written many publications on the topic of sustainable information.

A revised query or prompt was provided to get better responses from Consensus and the output is shown in Figure 8.9 opposite.

Summary of Chowdhury's Research Contributions in the Area of Sustainable Information
Gobinda Chowdhury has made significant contributions to the field of sustainable information, particularly focusing on the sustainability of digital collections, open access models, and cultural heritage information management

1 Sustainability of Digital Collections:
   - Chowdhury has highlighted the environmental impacts of digital collections, noting that while they may produce lower greenhouse gas emissions compared to print materials, they still have significant environmental footprints. He argues that current laws are insufficient to address these impacts and calls for more sustainable practices in managing digital collections[1].
2 Open Access Models:
   - In his work on open access, Chowdhury discusses the economic and social sustainability issues associated with current open access models. He critiques the gold open access model for its negative impact on economic sustainability and suggests that having one institutional repository per institution is not sustainable. He proposes a conceptual model for managing open access scholarly communication, which integrates social networking tools and web 2.0 to enhance the dissemination and analysis of research ideas[1].
3 Cultural Heritage Information Management:
   - Chowdhury has co-edited a comprehensive volume on digital cultural heritage initiatives, which addresses the creation, management, and dissemination of digital resources. This work emphasizes the need for sustainable practices in digitization projects, considering social, cultural, and economic factors. He stresses the importance of providing access to non-specialist users and managing the heterogeneous nature of cultural heritage collections[2].
   - In another contribution, Chowdhury examines the policies and procedures of digitization projects, focusing on social aspects such as intellectual property rights, the digital divide, and information literacy. He argues for sustainable practices that ensure long-term viability, continued funding, and reduced environmental impact of digital collections[4].

Overall, Chowdhury's research underscores the importance of sustainability in the management of digital collections and cultural heritage information, advocating for practices that balance environmental, economic, and social considerations. His work provides valuable insights for researchers, practitioners, and students in the field of information science.

Figure 8.9 *Results from Consensus from a revised query/prompt*

Again, the overall summary looks quite impressive, but a closer look at the cited items reveal that the output is based on four items, three of which are the same as the previous query (mentioned in Figure 8.8), and the fourth item is the review of one of the works of Chowdhury, and not the work itself, which was published nearly a decade ago. This again raises questions about the suitability of the search output for the intended purpose of the user of the search, and the overall ethos of research and scholarly information, which is to find the most relevant, reliable, recent and authentic information on a given topic.

How to improve the output of Gen AI tools

As discussed so far in this book, and shown through the examples presented in Chapters 4–6, asking the right question or prompting is a key to success in information search using Gen AI tools. In the world of Gen AI, this is called prompt engineering. In the context of Gen AI, 'the basic rule is that good prompts equal good results' (IBM, 2025).

Many definitions of prompt, or prompt engineering, exist. For example:

- 'Prompts are your input into the AI system to obtain specific results. In other words, prompts are conversation starters: what and how you tell something to the AI for it to respond in a way that generates useful responses for you.' (MIT Sloan Teaching & Learning Technologies, 2025)
- 'Prompt engineering helps generative AI models better comprehend and respond to a wide range of queries, from the simple to the highly technical.' (IBM, 2025a)
- 'Prompt engineering focuses on crafting the optimal textual input by selecting the appropriate words, phrases, sentence structures, and punctuation.' (Acar, 2023).

A prompt can comprise a simple phrase or a complex sentence, or multiple sentences or even a paragraph. OpenAI, creator of ChatGPT, recommends some strategies, each with specific suggestions, for getting better results from Gen AI tools. Some of these strategies and tactics, that may be useful for finding the relevant information through a search using a Gen AI tool, are shown in Table 8.2.

Table 8.2 *Examples of strategies and tactics suggested by OpenAI* (OpenAI Platform, 2025)

Strategies	Tactics
Write clear instructions	• Include details in your query to get more relevant answers • Ask the model to adopt a persona • Use delimiters to clearly indicate distinct parts of the input • Specify the steps required to complete a task • Provide examples • Specify the desired length of the output
Provide reference text	• Instruct the model to answer using a reference text • Instruct the model to answer with citations from a reference text

The OpenAI Cookbook provides some more details of strategies for getting better responses for semantic searches. The general guidelines for creating better prompts can be summarised as follows (OpenAI, 2023):

- use the most appropriate terms or phrases to articulate your information need
- provide context for the search, e.g. who you are, why are you looking for the information
- be specific as to what exactly you are looking for, e.g., only the facts or answer(s) to a question; something or everything possible on a given search topic, the most up-to-date, most cited, or the most relevant items
- build on the conversation, i.e. ask related, more specific or follow-up questions to build a collection of resources on the same or related content
- set a boundary, e.g., date, country, content type or discipline-specific limitations.

It may be noted that these are like the instructions and guidelines provided in information retrieval textbooks (see for example Chowdhury, G. G., 2010), and in the search guides provided by libraries and database search services. Overall, understanding the information problem, and breaking it down to specific components using the most appropriate words and phrases, and formulating the queries or prompts for conducting a search, have remained an age-old problem in information seeking and retrieval; and these have been an integral part of information services, called the 'reference interview' (Chowdhury, G. G., 2010).

Developers admit that Gen AI tools can create fake references. The OpenAI site on prompt engineering states: 'language models can confidently invent fake answers, especially when asked about esoteric topics or for citations and URLs' (OpenAI Platform, 2025). Fake references can certainly affect the users, and especially inexperienced users in a new field of study, where they are not familiar with the information sources, or the authors and institutions that produce reliable content on a given search topic. As a potential solution to this, OpenAI recommends that the users should provide a reference text. However, this is not an easy task, especially for a new or inexperienced user, and/or if the search topic is unknown to the user. Several university library websites provide advice on using Gen AI and prompt engineering.

Retrieval-augmented generation (RAG)

Gen AI tools are based on LLMs (large language models) that are trained on large volumes of data – for example, everything available on the web – and use billions of parameters that enable them to generate original output for tasks like answering questions, translating languages and completing sentences. However, this creates a limitation for these tools, because the output is based on their knowledge from the training data sets. Some known challenges of

LLMs include presenting false or fake information, generic information, out-of-date information and inaccurate information (AWS, 2024c; Knight, 2024; Wang, 2024).

This can be addressed by a novel technology called RAG (retrieval-augmented generation) (Lewis et al., 2021; Parvez et al., 2021). RAG is a process of retrieving relevant contextual information from a data source – such as a scholarly database or an institution's own internal dataset about people, products, services, etc. – and passing that information to a large-language model like GPT4 alongside the user's prompt, so that the output is more specific, contextual and relevant (OpenAI, 2024a). The basic idea behind RAG is that LLMs can combine retrieved information from recommended data sources with their parametric knowledge to produce more useful outputs. Figure 8.10 shows a simplified version of the RAG workflow.

As shown in Figure 8.10, RAG 'invokes the retriever to search and extract the relevant documents from external databases, which are then leveraged as the context to enhance the generation process' (Fan et al., 2024). Thus, RAG can be used to build LLM-applications to incorporate knowledge on specific databases or organization-specific data to generate more relevant and meaningful results without having to retrain the model.

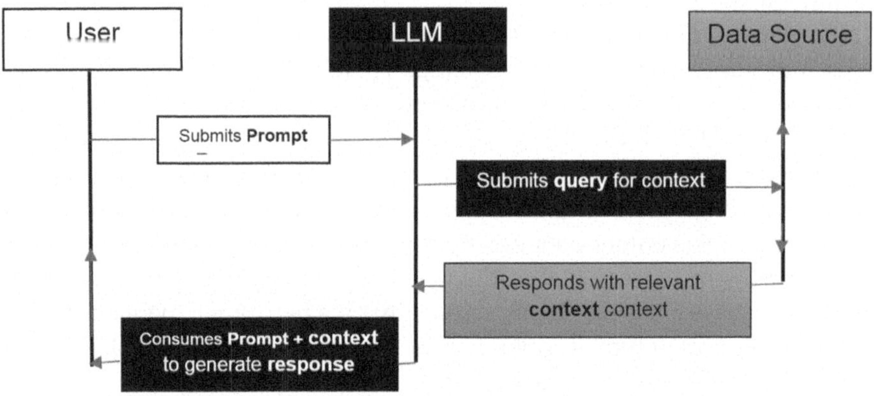

Figure 8.10 *Workflow of RAG* (OpenAI, 2024a)

In the context of research and scholarly information access, an information retrieval component is introduced with RAG that:

- takes the user query and utilises the user input to first pull the relevant data from a new data source – the recommended database(s)

- both the user query, and the retrieved data from the recommended database(s) as examples of relevant information, are then passed to the LLM
- the LLM uses the new knowledge – the user prompt and the relevant data – and its training data to create better responses.

In Azure AI Search, the LLM is pre-trained using public data, but it generates responses that are augmented by information from the retriever, in this case, Azure AI Search (Microsoft, 2024). The retrieval is based on the vectors – mathematical representations – of the query or prompt and documents in the database, and the matching is done based on similarity: matching on the co-ordinates that are most similar to the vector query, and this is better than the keyword searches that match on tokenised words. Retrieval-augmented large-language models (RA-LLMs) have various applications, such as Question Answer (QA) Systems, Chatbot, and Fact Verification (Fan et al., 2024). Research shows that adding random documents in the prompt improves the LLM accuracy by up to 35% (Cuconasu et al., 2024). However, Fan et al. (2024) comment that RA-LLMs can be manipulated to generate biased or unreliable output which may have some serious consequences for humans and society.

In order to improve the output of the Gen AI applications, researchers have been experimenting with another approach, called the multi-agent approach, to 'facilitate the development of LLM applications that could span a broad spectrum of domains and complexities' (Wu et al., 2023). Simply speaking, in a multi-agent approach, an agent can simultaneously act as 'an agent' undertaking specific search tasks in specific domains, and 'converse' as a user with other agents to check, verify, consolidate and improve the overall search outcomes. This is like using a group of users who can simultaneously ask questions and conduct searches in their chosen databases and can converse with the other users to share their insights, results and relevant judgements, in order to produce the best set of results combining the muti-user search results and relevance ranking criteria. Researchers argue that 'applications of varying complexities may need distinct sets of agents with specific capabilities, and may require different conversation patterns, such as single- or multi-turn dialogs, different human involvement modes, and static vs. dynamic conversation' (Wu et al., 2023). AutoGen is an open-source library for building a multi-agent application that 'uses a generic design of agents that can leverage LLMs, human inputs, tools, or a combination of them', and can 'simplify and unify complex LLM application workflows as multi-agent conversations' (Wu et al., 2023). Initial experiments show that AutoGen allows humans to engage in activities alongside multiple AI agents in a conversational manner and can produce better performance compared to the standard GPTs (Wu et al., 2023).

Another example of a using multiple agents is the 'Computer use', which is a beta feature from Anthropic that enables the Claude 3.5 Sonnet model to interact with tools that can manipulate a computer desktop environment (Anthropic, 2024a). Using this new feature, Claude can decide to use user-defined *Computer use* tools, and act as an agent to continue to call the *Computer use* tools to determine if more tools use is needed or the task has been completed (Anthropic, 2024b).

While these new features and tools offer better search output, researchers warn that there are several potential ethical considerations that could arise from the development and use of the AutoGen framework, or the 'Computer use' feature, including privacy and data protection, bias and fairness, accountability and transparency, trust and reliance, and various unintended consequences (Wu et al., 2023).

Gen AI and the information services sector

Libraries are social institutions, and users are at the centre of all their activities and *raison d'être*. 'For ILS [information and library science] professionals, human interest is not an add-on or afterthought but rather the reason we do the work at all – it is fundamentally baked into information generation, management, and use', remarks Marchionini (2024). The International Federation of Library Association and Institutions (IFLA) believes that the library and information profession can play a key role in helping users and the public in general to use AI for access to information with minimum risks (IFLA, 2024).

It will be interesting to see how the library and information world adapt to these tools to provide the academic users with the best of both worlds: a conversational tool that: (1) instantaneously provides search results in summary form, with the relevant headings, with supporting data and citations; (2) ensures the quality of the cited items that is ensured by one or more transparent selection criteria for the sources that are used to provide the answer; (3) provides search results with a better understanding of the user needs and contexts, for example, different sets of results for an undergraduate student who needs to write an essay and for a PhD student who requires updated results as the project progresses; and (4) produces search results and summaries that are comprehensive, reliable and consistent.

Large database services that can be accessed remotely appeared more than 50 years ago and they have evolved significantly over the years, and especially over the past 25 years, to meet the demands of the diversity of the content types and formats as well as the emerging technologies and user requirements. Side by side, several open-access digital libraries and repositories have also appeared during this period. All these databases, repositories and digital library services – open-access or commercial – work on the same old paradigm of information access, discussed earlier in this book. In this search environment, the user has to interact with the chosen service through search queries, often through several iterative searches, and finally select the retrieved records, and then read and assimilate the information to address the specific need or problem that triggered the search.

An obvious question here is: how are the Gen AI technologies going to impact the libraries and information services, commercial database services and OA databases and information services such as the ACM Digital Library, Internet Archive and PubMed that over the years have built curated collections of quality information resources on different disciplines and subjects? Some activities, albeit a bit slowly and often by individual institutions rather than sector-wide, are taking place to answer this question. SCONUL, the professional association for academic and research libraries in the UK and Ireland, observes that 'there is a mixed picture across the library support sector in the development of roadmaps for AI products with some providers still appearing to be at the exploratory stage. Others have products in beta testing while some are beginning to offer their products to customers' (SCONUL, 2024).

Some database search services are also adapting some Gen AI tools to develop customised versions for accessing their own collection(s) of scholarly databases. For example:

- Scopus AI is a subscription-based Gen AI tool that generates summaries of topics based on abstracts from the Scopus database (Elsevier, 2025b).
- The Web of Science Research Assistant is a subscription-based generative-AI-powered capability of the Web of Science database for the users to interact with the database to: (a) search for research literature and (b) ask a broad range of questions, such as 'how and why researchers are citing a paper by leveraging enriched cited reference data' or the 'best-fit journal for their manuscript' (Clarivate, 2024a).
- 'ProQuest®, part of Clarivate™, has developed the ProQuest Research Assistant that uses Gen AI technologies to enable people to use conversational inquiry to explore vast, vetted and authoritative content' (Clarivate, 2024b).
- 'Digital Science has announced a closed beta release of Dimensions AI Assistant, which will allow users to achieve their goals quicker by helping them find the most relevant research and receive relevant synopses, leveraging the power of the Dimensions large language model,

Dimensions General Science-BERT, and OpenAI's GPT models' (Dimensions, 2023).

Some open-access repositories and databases are also developing their own version of Gen AI tools. For example, the beta version of JSTOR's Interactive Research Tool uses Gen AI technologies to enable users to:

- **identify relevant material faster** by surfacing key points and arguments from the text being viewed;
- **Discover new topics and content** within the JSTOR corpus, enabling exploration of additional possible paths of inquiry;
- **Be conversational** with a semantic search-powered capability that works better for natural language queries than traditional keyword search.

(JSTOR, 2025)

The JSTOR site reports that these features will 'appear on the content page for journal articles, book chapters, and research reports, and as an option in addition to JSTOR's standard keyword search'.

Many other similar developments are taking place in this space. For example, a SCONUL report says: 'AI augmented student assistants are being developed by Clarivate, and Kortext. Digital Science is developing research management tools which they anticipate will be free to use. Ebsco have user tools in development for augmented discovery and generating article summaries, plus an augmented chat service. Elsevier are developing tools to support editors with review decisions' (SCONUL, 2024, 1).

Knight (2024, 4) provides a brief review of 45 AI-centric projects undertaken within UK higher education institutions (HEIs) that 'reveal a sector engaged in actively exploring the capabilities of generative AI to enhance the educational landscape, focusing on practical applications that benefit students and educators by improving learning processes, teaching methods, and overall educational experiences'. Overall, the rationale for augmented discovery tools being developed by the information service providers, based on defined corpuses of literature, is that this avoids the 'hallucinations' or wrong search outcomes, which occur in large-language models (LLMs). However, alongside the promises and benefits of Gen AI, this approach may lead to some long-term problems for the information services sector. For example, the SCONUL study notes that:

- The responses to an academic query may vary across institutions, depending on the licensed content available at that institution.

- Buying into such tools may create pressure on institutions to maintain subscriptions to particular content deals irrespective of cost. It also clearly raises questions around equity.
- Business models and associated costs to institutions are still being developed, with an emphasis on an approach of additional tools being sold and charged for separately.
- Insufficient attention may be being paid to copyright in some cases.
- There appears to be relatively little work going on in relation to generating or enriching metadata with improved workflows in mind.

(SCONUL, 2024, 1)

These points raise some key questions about the sustainability of the information services sector, especially the higher education and research institutions' information services. It is anticipated that if the costs of these new tools are passed to the information services sector, which is most likely to be the case, then the sector will be forced to find money through efficiency saving or cutting the budget for content or other services.

Summary

Predicting the future is complex, especially in an area as fast-moving as Gen AI. Within a period of two years since the arrival of Chat GPT in November 2022, numerous Gen AI tools have emerged with a range of potential applications, benefits and promises. The growth in Gen AI tools and the diversity of their potential applications show different possibilities:

- Large foundation models like GPT-4o, with many billions of parameters and tokens, are at the leading edge, with multi-modal capabilities that will be necessary to help build more targeted generative apps;
- Multiple agent-based, and combination, models are likely to be commonplace for domain-specific applications that can share the workload across a number of smaller servers or devices for specific tasks to generate the most context-specific and relevant results, while at the same time reducing the financial as well as the energy costs that the large models require.
- Smaller models are being designed to focus on specific applications, for example, 'DeepMind, The Institute of Protein Design, and Facebook have built longer-tail protein structure models to leverage generative capabilities around protein structure and function design.' (McIlwain, 2023).

Gen AI models are also being integrated into widely used cloud services, such as Microsoft 365, and search engines. All these new and emerging tools are likely to cause unanticipated and emergent changes in every field of application, and especially for access to information in everyday life, and for research scholarly activities. There are some mixed views on the use of Gen AI:

> depending on who you are, this is something to be welcomed, and the overall direction of travel is a human-AI hybrid in education and the workplace. An alternative view is that many of these technologies are unscalable due to inherent issues around hallucinations and other 'side-effects' that may prove to be unsolvable.
>
> (Knight, 2024)

Some of the key lessons learnt from the discussions presented in this chapter can be summarised as follows:

1 While the Gen AI tools are quite easy to use for accessing information, the onus is still on the user to ensure that right queries and prompts are created and used to generate successive sets of results to get the most accurate, relevant and reliable information and data supported by the appropriate references.
2 Using any off-the-shelf Gen AI tool may not be the best choice for generating the most exhaustive set of results, as expected in the context of research and scholarly activities, because of some inherent limitations of the LLM-based models. For example, by default, these tools are not linked to the internet – or all the scholarly databases – in a specific domain, and hence the results are likely to be limited by the dataset on which the tool is trained. However, these limitations can be addressed by new technologies like RAG and multi-agent approaches discussed above.
3 Often the search results generated by the Gen AI tools may not be the most representative, accurate and reliable sources of information in a given domain.
4 The results generated by the Gen AI tools may be difficult to reproduce because of their reliance on some information sources and challenges that are more popular, rather than curated and hence the most relevant and trustworthy sources.
5 Gen AI search results are not always consistent. As discussed earlier in this chapter, search output generated by the same tool may be different for the same search conducted at different times of a day, let alone on different days. This may have several negative consequences for

information seeking in any area, and especially where understanding and monitoring the growth and trends of research in a field or domain is paramount, for example for research and scholarly activities.

6 As discussed earlier in the chapter, the cited items in the output are not always very relevant. Therefore, the suitability of the results for the intended purpose of the search, and the overall ethos of research and scholarly information – that is, to find the most relevant, reliable, recent and authentic information on a given topic – raises questions.

In light of all of these lessons, and many more discussed earlier in this book, it is quite evident that users should be cautious about over-reliance on Gen AI tools for information-intensive activities such as education, research and healthcare. The various benefits and opportunities offered by Gen AI tools for undertaking information search activities should be balanced with the conventional approaches to seeking and accessing information using curated databases and specialised database search services. The next chapter discusses the implications of this for the future of education, research and professional practices in information science.

CHAPTER 9

Gen AI for Information Access: Teaching, Research and Professional Practices

Introduction

The rapid growth in Gen AI technologies and tools, and their adoption by search engines for developing AI-driven search tools – like Copilot by Microsoft, and Gemini by Google – make it evident that Gen AI technologies are going to become an integral part of information access in every sphere of life, and especially in education and research. A UK government report suggests that AI, and especially Gen AI, technologies 'can facilitate access to information, education and training' (UK Parliament, 2023). The Russell Group universities in the UK recommends that university students and staff should be prepared to use the AI tools effectively and appropriately (Russell Group, n.d.). The Microsoft *New Future of Work Report 2023* points out: 'Information search as well as content production (manually typing, writing code, designing images) is greatly enhanced by AI, so general information work may shift to integrating and critically analysing retrieved information' (Butler et al., 2023).

Examples of the use of Gen AI tools for access to information, presented in Chapters 4, 5 and 6, and the follow-up discussions in this book, indicate that the emerging AI technologies are having significant benefits as well as challenges for access to information. Some researchers speak in favour of the Gen AI technologies, arguing that:

- just as word processor functions for spell checking, grammar, etc., have become accepted and integrated into our everyday writing practices, so too will the generative AI technologies (McKnight, 2022)
- focusing on how people use Gen AI rather than whether they use it will make people better prepared for a world where AI is likely to be ubiquitous (Mollick, 2023).

Some people call for more debates and discussions, for example:

- 'given the complexity of the ethical, legal and social issues that LLMs touch upon, we need collaborative processes to seek clarity' (Mills, 2023)
- 'just as society reached a consensus about the role of calculators, a similar discourse is urgently needed for integrating LLM technologies like ChatGPT into educational settings' (Park and Ahn, 2024)
- 'It is vital for librarians to work proactively with tech firms to address the limitations and biases of the likes of ChatGPT' (Times Higher Education, 2023).

All of these raise a key question: are these transformative technologies and tools going to significantly reshape, or worse, replace, the existing library and information services for access to information for everyday life and living, and/or for academic, research and scholarly activities?

Some issues that the ongoing discussions need to address in the context of access to information are:

1. How can the Gen AI tools be trained to select the most reliable and peer-reviewed sources and summarise data and information that are most relevant to a user's needs and context?
2. What new skills do the users need to acquire to be able to make optimum use of these tools to access information and data required for specific education and research activities?
3. What role should libraries and educational institutions play to impart this new set of skills to their students and researchers?
4. How may libraries and information services adapt these tools to improve access to information and data?

Based on the findings of the searches conducted using the Gen AI tools discussed in Chapters 4 and 5, and recent research and development around Gen AI and information access, this chapter presents some ideas for addressing such questions. Implications of these recent developments for teaching, research and professional practices in information science are also discussed.

Is Gen AI empowering users?

Since the first appearance of ChatGPT in November 2022, several Gen AI tools have appeared in the marketplace with a promise that they are going to make it easier for people to access information, and transform, if not revolutionise, the ways people use information in everyday life, work, education, research and scholarly activities. So, are the Gen AI tools empowering people in the context of accessing and using information?

The case studies shown in Chapters 4, 5 and 6, and the associated discussions in the other chapters in this book, clearly show that Gen AI tools can facilitate access to information and reduce the burden that users normally face while accessing information through conventional libraries and databases. Gen AI tools allow people to interact in natural language conversational format to ask or prompt for some information, and the tools produce information summarised by assimilating text and data from the retrieved items. These technologies are also being adapted by conventional search engines like Copilot and Gemini, and these tools are used by almost everyone for access to information. So, what implications are these Gen AI-powered search tools, embedded in commonly used search engines, or as specially designed tools for access to research and scholarly information like Consensus, Scholar GPT and Scholar AI, going to have for the knowledge and information ecosystem and its stakeholders like publishers, libraries, databases, and of course the users and their information behaviour and information practices?

Gen AI for information access: a paradigm shift?

Libraries and database search services require their users to choose some specific search terms to formulate queries, using a structured search interface to retrieve documents that match the search terms. These services evolved over time, and they offer various useful features and support for conducting the search – for example, using a simple or an advanced search interface that offers different ways of combining search terms for formulating a complex search expression, selecting one or more fields of the databases to search, and so on. Database services also offer various features for filtering and ranking of the search results, such as by citation, date, relevance, time, author, institutions, etc. The key activities to be performed by the user in a conventional information access scenario can be summarised as follows:

1. decomposing the search goals into queries
2. choosing the right words and phrases
3. conducting the searches using the search interface of the chosen search service
4. retrieving the relevant items
5. reading, analysing and synthesising content and data from the retrieved documents.

The onus is still on the users for conducting a successful search, because all the activities, listed above, require a significant number of skills, time and resources. Furthermore, these activities could be quite challenging for new or novice users, and especially for searches on a topic which is unknown to the user. The user needs some prior knowledge of the subject or discipline for determining the relevance of the search output, accuracy, currency and reliability of the sources.

These responsibilities on the users, can be significantly reduced by the Gen AI tools for accessing information because these search tools take a conversational approach where:

- users can enter a question, a request or a prompt, in a natural language;
- the tool selects and searches some sources or databases;
- the tool fuses information from multiple documents;
- the tool presents the results that address the question or the prompt in an easy-to-read summary format, often with the supporting data and relevant references; and
- all these happen almost instantaneously.

This clearly shows the ease of use, and thus a huge potential for the use of, Gen AI tools for access to information. Findings of the case studies presented in Chapters 4–6 show that the data and information provided by these search tools need to be scrutinised by the user before using them. It is also imperative for the information services sector to 'understand and embrace these technologies and their myriad uses, to acknowledge their limitations and ethical issues, and to recognize why these tools, at least for now, cannot replace humans' (Houston and Corrado, 2023). Users should be advised to divide the search tasks into small sub-tasks and engage with the right Gen AI search tool to find the relevant data and information. The right approach to conversation and prompting the Gen AI tool clearly is also essential. Choice of the search tool is also important since, as discussed in Chapters 4, 5 and 6, search results on the same query may vary significantly from one tool to another. Furthermore, not each Gen AI tool, and/or every feature of a tool, is free at the point of use.

Research shows that Gen AI tools produce information by repackaging sources unknown to the user, making it difficult to ensure the credibility and accountability of information (Graham, 2023; Haggart, 2023). It is imperative that the user reads and verifies the search output and the cited items in relation to the specific search context. As the discussions in Chapters 4, 5 and 6 show, some answers are supported by full citations or links, others aren't; and so, answers that provide full citations or links should be preferred, and the cited items should be checked for the accuracy of the information, and for the reputation and reliability of the sources.

Libraries and database search services ensure the quality of the information sources through a selection process, and they also provide a number of tools for ranking and filtering the research results, such as by date, authors and institutions, number of citations, and so on. As some of the findings from the searches discussed in this book show, it is difficult for the user to know how the recommended items are selected by the chosen search tools, especially when asked for the best or the most important research works on a topic. Also, as discussed in Chapter 8, sometimes it is difficult to find out the most relevant and most cited items (see for example, Figures 8.8 and 8.9).

It should also be noted that not all the Gen AI search tools are designed only for providing research and scholarly information as such, and hence academic users should choose the right tool. Some tools are specifically designed for research and scholarly information search, for example, Consensus, Scholar GPT and Scholar AI. As shown in Chapter 6, these tools often produce better results, especially when recommendations for research literature are asked for. However, it is impossible to know the exhaustivity of a search. Also, because the Gen AI tools have a limitation of the volume of content they can generate, it becomes a key challenge for generating exhaustive sets of relevant search results. As shown in Chapters 5 and 6, some tools recommend where and how to find more relevant items relevant for the query, and some ask the user to specify where to search, for example, PubMed, Google Scholar, JSTOR, and arxiv.org.

Tools that support users to find results with very high recall and precision rank the results in a way that benefits users and, at the same time, providing societal relevance is paramount, and yet this is also extremely complex, consequential and contentious (Lewandowski, Haider and Sundin, 2024). *Recall* and *Precision* are the two classic measures used to determine the level of success of a search. *Recall* is a measure that shows the proportion of the relevant items, in a collection or a database, that is retrieved in a search; and *Precision* is a measure of the proportion of the retrieved items, in a search, that is relevant (Chowdhury, G. G., 2010). As discussed in Chapters 5 and 6, in most cases the user does not have any idea of the resources or databases that the Gen AI tool searches, and the criteria that the tool uses to determine which of the retrieved items are relevant, and how the content is summarised and presented as the output. Therefore, it is obvious that new research is needed to ensure that the user has a say in getting the most exhaustive set of documents (high recall) that are most relevant (high precision) for a specific search context.

Unintended consequences of Gen AI

A UK Government report (2024) notes that 'teachers and experts acknowledge that GenAI could have a transformative impact on education', but 'at the same time, there is considerable concern about the risks it presents, as well as scepticism about whether these can be mitigated' (UK Department of Education, 2024, 4). The UK House of Commons, Science, Innovation and Technology Committee (2024) points out 'perhaps the most far-reaching of the challenges that AI poses is how to deal with a technology which – in at least some of its variants –operates as a "black box". That is to say, the basis of and reasoning for its recommendations may be strictly unknowable' (UK House of Commons, Science, Innovation and Technology Committee, 2024, 3).

Researchers and national and international organisations point out several unintended consequences of Gen AI technologies, such as the following:

1. AI systems pose risks to privacy, safety, security and human autonomy, and therefore governance is essential to ensure AI development and deployment are safe, secure and trustworthy, with policies and regulation that foster innovation and competition (OECD, n.d.)
2. AI technologies pose 'critical societal and policy challenges that policy makers must confront: potential shifts in labour markets, copyright uncertainties, and risk associated with the perpetuation of societal biases and the potential for misuse in the creation of disinformation and manipulated content' (Lorenz, Perset and Berryhill, 2023)
3. 'the capabilities of AI create a "jagged technological frontier" where some tasks are easily done by AI, while others, though seemingly similar in difficulty level, are outside the current capability of AI' (Dell'Acqua et al., 2023)
4. 'generative AI and the synthetic content it produces with varying quality and accuracy can exacerbate challenges. This content proliferates in digital spaces where it is used to train generative AI models, resulting in a vicious negative cycle in the quality of online information' (Lorenz, Perset and Berryhill, 2023)
5. generative AI 'raises concerns about automated and personalised cyber-attacks, surveillance and censorship, overreliance on generative systems despite their flaws, academic dishonesty, and concentrations of power and resources' (Lorenz, Perset and Berryhill, 2023)
6. 'many large language models have been trained, without permission or credit, on the creative and expressive works of multiple knowledge sectors, from art to literature to journalism to the academy. This is a labour question as much as it is a question about intellectual creativity' (Cambridge University, School of the Humanities and Social Sciences, 2024)

7 Use of Gen AI to summarise readings, to suggest answers to questions, draft structures or write answers for questions or essays may in the long run damage the learning and critical thinking skills of students and researchers (Cambridge University, School of the Humanities and Social Sciences, 2024)
8 As well as being fictitious or fabrication (also called hallucination), Gen AI responses may reflect 'historically dominant perspectives about religion, gender or race, or will not be informed by writing about relevant experiences or outlooks that has been suppressed or marginalized in the written record which feeds the training data' (Dempsey, 2023).

Evidence shows that the use of Gen AI creates a number of social issues; for example, according to OECD, 'between 2022 and 2023, the number of AI incidents reported increased by approximately 1278%, coinciding with the mainstreaming of generative AI' (OECD, n.d.). Consequently, effective governance is essential to ensure AI development and deployment are safe, secure and trustworthy, with policies and regulation that foster innovation and competition' (OECD, n.d.).

Sun et al. (2024) show that users' prior knowledge, the style of information presentation and the interactive manner of using search agents are key determinants of trust in health-related information. Use of Gen AI tools for access to information, especially for research and scholarly activities, may have some unintended consequences, especially if the users cannot select the sources – that is, where to search, e.g. databases, websites and digital libraries – and/or cannot control the criteria for deciding the relevance of the retrieved documents, and do not have any control of the way content is created and/or summarised based on the retrieved items. Gen AI tools do not provide reasoning for the output they generate, i.e. why and how they decided to select the documents that they did to generate the answer, how they summarised the content, and so on.

AI governance

Search engines like Google and Microsoft are using Gen AI as part of their search engines that are used by people in most parts of the world for access to information in every walk of life. Chat GPT can now remember previous interactions/conversations with a user which can have both positive and negative consequences (OpenAI, 2024b). Google has created the NotebookLM, a personalised AI research assistant, powered by Google's Gemini 1.5 Pro, which can be used to summarise a research paper, prepare a trend report, and much more, and this offers a tremendous opportunity for users in the context of research and scholarly activities (NotebookLM, 2023). While they revolutionise the process of access to information, these technologies may unintentionally become a potential barrier to achieving one of the key aims of research and scholarship: to acquire critical thinking, and analytical and assimilation skills for spotting trends of, and gaps in, research in an area.

On a positive note, the emerging technologies mentioned above can improve the results based on the specific knowledge of a user and their context. However, this may also mean that the search tool, and the company behind it, will have access to a lot of personal information about the user, and unless the user is very careful, their personal data protection and security may be at risk. Furthermore, content that aligns with the user's existing views or preferences may 'create "echo chambers" or "filter bubbles", where users are isolated in their own informational environment and their exposure to alternative viewpoints may be limited' (Meakin, 2024). International agencies like the OECD express concerns over the potential unintended consequences of the unregulated use of Gen AI technologies. For example, OECD notes that the speed of AI technology development and its widespread impact on people and society 'requires diverse policy ecosystems to work more cohesively' (OECD, 2024), and that the OECD and the UN will 'work together with all stakeholders, including leading scientists and academic centres from around the globe, to realise this goal'.

National governments are also proposing similar measures. Five high-level principles – 'safety, security and robustness; appropriate transparency and explainability; fairness; accountability and governance; and contestability and redress' – underpin the UK Government's approach to regulate AI development and applications (UK House of Commons, Science, Innovation and Technology Committee, 2024). The document identifies the following challenges that need to be addressed through regulations:

1. **The Bias Challenge**. Developers and deployers of AI models and tools must not merely acknowledge the presence of inherent bias in datasets, they must take steps to mitigate its effects.
2. **The Privacy Challenge**. Privacy and data protection frameworks must account for the increasing capability and prevalence of AI models and tools, and ensure the right balance is struck.
3. **The Misrepresentation Challenge**. Those who use AI to misrepresent others, or allow such misrepresentation to take place unchallenged, must be held accountable.

4 **The Access to Data Challenge**. Access to data, and the responsible management of it, are prerequisites for a healthy, competitive and innovative AI industry and research ecosystem.
5 **The Access to Compute Challenge**. Democratising and widening access to compute is a prerequisite for a healthy, competitive and innovative AI industry and research ecosystem.
6 **The Black Box Challenge**. We should accept that the workings of some AI models are and will remain unexplainable and focus instead on interrogating and verifying their outputs.
7 **The Open-Source Challenge**. The question should not be 'open' or 'closed', but rather whether there is a sufficiently diverse and competitive market to support the growing demand for AI models and tools.
8 **The Intellectual Property and Copyright Challenge**. The Government should broker a fair, sustainable solution based around a licensing framework governing the use of copyrighted material to train AI models.
9 **The Liability Challenge**. Determining liability for AI-related harms is not just a matter for the courts – Government and regulators can play a role too.
10 **The Employment Challenge**. Education is the primary tool for policymakers to respond to the growing prevalence of AI, and to ensure workers can ask the right questions of the technology.
11 **The International Coordination Challenge**. A global governance regime for AI may not be realistic nor desirable, even if there are economic and security benefits to be won from international co-operation.
12 **The Existential Challenge**. Existential AI risk may not be an immediate concern but it should not be ignored, even if policy and regulatory activity should primarily focus on the here and now.

(UK House of Commons, Science, Innovation and Technology Committee, 2024)

Information science education and research

Research shows that these are the 'early days for LLMs and generative AI in search, and there may yet be development of the critical features we desire for IR systems' (Hersh, 2024). The discussions so far in the book provide some insight into how the teaching and research in information science may need to be revisited in areas around information access, information behaviour, and related areas. The knowledge and discourse for teaching and research in information science have evolved with the conventional library and scholarly databases and internet search services, with a focus on how the users formulate their questions, and how the search systems interpret those queries to produce the relevant results based on some knowledge of the user contexts, gathered directly – e.g. through the knowledge of the user groups as in the case of a library, a scholarly database or a repository – or indirectly through mining of access data. Use of the Gen AI services for information access needs to be studied closely in different education and research settings to build the required knowledge to inform teaching and research in information science and cognate disciplines around information behaviour, information literacy and information seeking and retrieval.

Specific areas of study for information science education, research and professional development may focus on:

1. How different groups of users – young people, university students, researchers, professionals, and members of the general public – continue to use Gen AI tools for accessing information in different contexts; and whether and how these show any changes in the ways people seek and use information, and what implications these may have for the existing models around information behaviour, information literacy and information seeking and retrieval.
2. Information behaviour and information practices in the context of the use of Gen AI for access to information
3. Information literacy, AI literacy in specific contexts: information for education and research, information for everyday life, and others;
4. Collaborative research and engagement:
    - with researchers and professionals to successfully use and support users in their use of Gen AI tools for access to information;
    - for collaborative research on AI tools and technologies for promoting information access and use: collaborations amongst the information services sector – libraries and database services/digital libraries, professional associations, etc., to develop customised Gen AI tools for academic and research information;
    - with information systems and services within the higher education sector to develop a sector-wide Gen AI tool for access to information through open acess databases like Google Scholar, JSTOR, Internet Archive (https://web.archive.org), Semantic Scholar, and Exaly.com.

Developments in Gen AI technologies have also opened new areas of research and development in several areas. For example, Lo et al. (2024) have developed the Semantic Reader project that introduces novel user interfaces to augment traditional PDFs to improve reading experiences for scholars, presenting an opportunity for further AI research in scholarly document processing.

Implications for information behaviour and practice

As discussed earlier in this book, especially in Chapters 7 and 8, Gen AI technologies and tools for access to information do not follow the usual processes of query formulation; database selection; retrieval, ranking and filtering of search results; and reading and assimilation of information from the retrieved documents. Thus, it is evident that the increasing use of Gen AI tools for access to information will have profound impact on the ways people seek and use information, and consequently on information behaviour, information practice and information affordances. Researchers comment that 'the capabilities of generative AI systems may drive the construction of information seeking practices toward information creation and modification to meet information needs or to solve problems' (Hirvonen et al., 2024).

Specific areas of study for information science education, research and professional development may focus on:

- how different groups of users – young people, university students, researchers, professionals and members of the general public – use Gen AI tools for accessing information in different contexts
- whether and how these show any changes in the ways people seek and use information, and what implications these may have on the existing models around information behaviour, information literacy, information seeking and information practice
- whether and how the increasing use of Gen AI tools for access to information – for everyday life and living, work, education, research and scholarship – change people's information-seeking behaviour and information practices
- whether new research is needed to model people's information seeking, information behaviour and information practices when they use Gen AI tools for access to information for different categories of users, as well as different purposes and contexts.

Such research will further show whether the existing models of information skills and media and information literacy would be adequate to prepare the users for making the optimum use of Gen AI tools for access to information, or whether new literacy skills have to be developed to prepare the users.

Implications for society

The emergence of generative AI products, represented by ChatGPT, has reshaped the way of information seeking since 2022 (Zhou and Li, 2024). Research shows that Gen AI tools have significant potential:

- in education, and they help provide innovative ways to engage students, adapt content and promote personalised learning (Ruiz-Rojas et al., 2023)
- for enhancing higher education teaching and learning (e.g., Adiguzel, Kaya and Cansu, 2023; Aldosari, 2020; Baidoo-Anu and Owusu Ansah, 2023; Ouyang and Jiao, 2021)
- opportunities and challenges (e.g., Aleedy, Atwell and Meshoul, 2022; Chiu et al., 2023a; Hwang and Chang, 2021; UNESCO, 2021a; Vincent-Lancrin and Van Der Vlies, 2020; Wamba et al., 2021).

However, some researchers argue that 'the benefits and the harms that AI systems contribute to may be specific to certain people or communities' (Hirvonen et al., 2024). Gen AI technologies pose critical societal and policy challenges that policymakers must confront. These include potential shifts in labour markets, copyright uncertainties and risk associated with the perpetuation of societal biases and the potential for misuse in the creation of disinformation and manipulated content (Lorenz, Perset and Berryhill, 2023). Research shows that despite the advances in technologies, and their use for access to information, digital divide, information divide and consequently information poverty still remain some of the major challenges in society, not only in the less developed or developing countries but in the developed countries like the UK, USA and Europe (Chowdhury and Chowdhury, 2024).

'Rigorous scientific and evidence-based assessment must be at the heart of global AI governance. This announcement marks a significant step in that direction by bringing the technical and analytical capabilities of the OECD together with the UN's global reach and complementary efforts to support globally coordinated AI governance.' (OECD, 2024). OECD Deputy Secretary General Knudsen said: 'The OECD's AI Policy Observatory, our extensive work to advance the implementation of the AI Principles and the Global Partnership on AI at the OECD provide a strong foundation for this collaboration. Our joint efforts will help countries to seize all the opportunities of AI while mitigating and better managing the associated risks and disruptions to foster human-centred, safe, secure and trustworthy AI.' (OECD, 2024).

AI literacy

Over-reliance on Gen AI-recommended content may reduce people's capacity to critically evaluate the quality, accuracy or reliability of the information (Meakin, 2024). Research shows that librarian-led information literacy training can assist students in developing more sophisticated understandings of the limitations and use cases for artificial intelligence in inquiry-based coursework (Carroll and Borycz, 2024).

As discussed in Chapter 3, alongside digital literacy, information literacy and media and information literacy (MIL), people now should acquire a new form of literacy, AI literacy. A person would be viewed as being AI-literate 'if they are capable of using AI products proficiently and reasonably' (Wang, Rau and Yuan, 2022). So far limited efforts have been made to promote artificial intelligence (AI) literacy for citizens, but an increasing interest in the area can be noticed (Kong, Cheung and Zhang, 2021, 2023; Kong et al., 2024). Research reveals that 'intrinsic motivation and competence to learn with the chatbot depended on both teacher support and student expertise (i.e. self-regulated learning and digital literacy)' (Chiu et al., 2023b).

Cox (2024) mentions that people need theoretical and practical knowledge as well as experience to use AI effectively, calling for the need for AI literacy for specific professional groups, such as those working directly with AI and also for information professionals. Cox further states that Gen AI can be used to support a large number of cognitive activities, such as brainstorming, structuring ideas, gathering information and writing. Generative AI, such as ChatGPT, poses many challenges, such as ethical issues (Hagendorff, 2024), and therefore, qualifying AI literacy as ethical or responsible becomes essential (Cox, 2024).

Some researchers argue that Gen AI literacy is composed of four types of knowledge: theoretical knowledge, ethical knowledge, pragmatic knowledge and reflective knowledge (Zhao, Cox and Cai, 2024). Some researchers argue that 12 defining competencies of Gen AI literacy offer 'a framework for individuals, policymakers, government officials, and educators to take advantage of the potential of generative AI responsibly' (Annapureddy Fornaroli and Gatica-Perez, 2024).

Gen AI and sustainability of the knowledge ecosystem

While creating new and an enormous number of benefits for the users, Gen AI tools may raise some social sustainability issues around access to, and use of, information. The climate change issue, as in any other field, will also have a significant impact on the digital information market and the usability of information (Chowdhury and Chowdhury, 2011). Increasing use of Gen AI technologies for access to information can lead to some sustainability issues having an impact on the economic, social and environmental sustainability of information systems and services (Chowdhury, 2014; Chowdhury and Koya, 2017; Mensah, 2019).

Research shows that AI models like ChatGPT 'hold considerable potential in sustainable development, their usage must be approached carefully, considering current limitations and ethical implications' (Raman et al., 2024).

For example, so far we have limited knowledge about how the LLMs are trained, i.e. what training data, tuning data and other sources are used by the foundation models. Similarly, we have very limited knowledge of the type and quality of information sources that Gen AI tools are using while answering user questions and prompts. These raise a number of questions around the quality and authenticity of information, and this leads to the issues of information literacy and AI literacy, digital divide, information poverty, uncertainty, information practices, information overload, provenance and copyright issues, risks and privacy and security issues.

Increasing use of the Gen AI tools and technologies can pose some challenges associated with the economic sustainability of the knowledge ecosystem that may affect the key players in the information ecosystem – publishers, databases/service providers, libraries, Gen AI developers and service providers. Gen AI is an expensive business. Soon after the arrival of ChatGPT, Microsoft invested US$10 billion in GPT (Forbes, 2023). Other large tech companies also invested huge amounts of money to stay in the race, and this resulted in the rapid development of new Gen AI models, some of which are proprietary, and some are free at the point of use, but all are equipped with a range of new capabilities. As discussed in Chapter 8, some recent developments related to the adoption of Gen AI technologies in the scholarly database world may also add some financial burden on the information services sector.

Research on climate change and the digital information world will pave the way for the development of future digital information services that are both economically and environmentally sustainable (Chowdhury and Chowdhury, 2024). Research shows that:

- 'while ICT offers opportunities to enable reductions in GHG emissions in other sectors, evidence does not support their ability to achieve the sustained significant carbon savings we require by 2050' (Freitag et al., 2021)
- 'AI in education and AI literacy can be used to help realise some of the sustainable development goals, enhance lifelong learning, and advance equality and inclusion on a global scale' (Kong et al., 2024)
- 'sustainable development embodies not only the tension between innovation and equitable resource distribution but also the tension between serving the needs of the environment, economy and society' (Van Wynsberghe, 2021).

Like any technology, there are some energy and environmental costs of the Gen AI technologies and tools. Researchers argue that:

- GPT technologies have a huge environmental impact (Ludvigsen, 2022)
- the hidden environmental costs and impact of Gen AI models are often overlooked (Kumar and Davenport, 2023).

According to some estimates, to process a single request on ChatGPT takes about 10 times as much electricity as a typical Google search; and AI is likely to increase the data centre power demand by 160% in 2023 (Goldman Sachs, 2024). According to an MIT Technology Review report, using an AI model to generate text is significantly less energy-intensive: for example, creating text 1000 times only uses as much energy as 16% of a full smartphone charge, but making an image with Gen AI uses as much energy as charging a phone (Heikkilä, 2023). Another report shows that a typical conversation with ChatGPT, with 10–50 exchanges, requires a half-litre of water to cool the servers, while asking a large generative AI model to create an image requires as much energy as charging a smartphone's battery (Cambridge University, School of the Humanities and Social Sciences, 2024).

Estimates show that using smaller models has much lower energy and environment costs compared to the large models. For example, using a large Gen AI model to classify movie reviews consumes around 30 times more energy than using a model created specifically for that task; and it takes over 590 million uses to reach the environmental cost of training of the Hugging Face's BLOOM model, but for popular models, such as ChatGPT, it could take just a couple of weeks' usage emissions to exceed its training emission (Heikkilä, 2023).

Researchers argue that:

- 'integrating sustainability in Gen-AI's discourse and policy may inform more balanced and responsible technological progress' (Bashir et al., 2024)
- 'sustainable AI is not about how to sustain the development of AI *per se* but it is about how to develop AI that is compatible with sustaining environmental resources for current and future generations; economic models for societies; and societal values that are fundamental to a given society' (Van Wynsberghe, 2021).

Kumar and Davenport (2023) suggest that companies can take eight steps to make Gen AI technologies greener, such as: (1) use existing large generative models instead of generating a new one; (2) fine-tune and train existing models; (3) use energy-conserving computational methods; (4) use a large model only when it offers significant value; (5) be discerning about when to use generative AI; (6) evaluate the energy sources of the cloud provider or data centre; (7) re-use models and resources; and (8) include AI activity in the carbon monitoring initiatives.

Given the multiple players, stakeholders and technology and infrastructure, Gen AI is becoming increasingly resource-intensive, both economically and environmentally. However, new developments are emerging, such as:

- collaborations by multiple players at each level, so that an organisation may build directly on top of ChatGPT or one of the other services, importing results into their own application (Dempsey, 2023);
- smaller Gen AI tools are appearing in the market that can be used in specific domains and applications at far less energy and environmental cost (Heikkilä, 2023).

Bashir et al. (2024) comment that 'to instil accountability for more sustainable Gen-AI practices, stakeholders must assemble to provide guidance and inform decision-making that weighs societal benefits against societal costs (sustainability and otherwise), to shape further development'.

To address all the sustainability issues, areas of research around the social, economic and environmental sustainability should consider:

- social sustainability: user-focused research to develop and demonstrate positive impact of the use of Gen AI for information, such as in reducing the social divide, alleviation of information poverty, equitable education, health, and other social issues;
- economic sustainability: research on improving collaborations and co-operations among the key players and stakeholders of the knowledge ecosystem – libraries, publishers, information service providers and tech companies – to develop the optimum economic models and framework for a sustainable knowledge economy with the users at the heart of all developments;
- environmental sustainability: research to develop more energy-efficient models – large and small, backed up by energy efficient data centres, for development and use of Gen AI tools for a knowledge society.

Implications for information science education and professional practices

One of the key objectives of education and research institutions is to teach the students and researchers how to think critically to be able to analyse, appraise and apply the existing knowledge to create new knowledge that is manifested in the form of recorded information – text, images, multimedia – that can be communicated, stored and processed to create and maintain the knowledge continuum. Cox (2022) discusses 11 different potential approaches that academic libraries might adopt for AI applications in knowledge discovery, and their potential implications. Gimpel et al. (2023) comment that 'it is not surprising that the advent of Gen AI fundamentally challenges accepted knowledge, assumptions, and behaviors in higher education'. Varsik and Vosberg (2024) encourage 'research on AI tools' implications for equity and inclusion to ensure that AI adoption in education supports a more equitable and inclusive learning environment'. The former Vice President and Chief Strategist of OCLC comments on the impact of Gen AI on information services and professionals as follows: 'given where we have been, and where we are going, empathy, education and appropriate transparency about planning and direction are now even more critical in the workplace' (Dempsey, 2023).

Information literacy, information skills or media and information literacy have long been a core area of research and professional practices in information science. As shown in this book, it is well recognised that the Gen AI and LLM-based tools may produce inaccurate, inappropriate, biased or misleading content (Meakin, 2024), and so users should be prepared to check and judge the quality, accuracy and relevance of the output generated by the Gen AI tools. In other words, information literacy, or more importantly AI literacy, have become ever more important in the context of the use of Gen AI for information access.

AI literacy does not require people to become experts in the underlying theory of and developments related to AI, nor does it require people to have programming or development skills. Instead, it is meant to enable people to understand, use and evaluate AI technologies so that they are able to use AI efficiently, responsibly and ethically. Research shows that:

- Use of Gen AI tools like ChatGPT requires careful integration and ongoing management to realise their full potential (Rahman and Islam, 2024)
- ChatGPT can have a significant impact on information literacy and digital skills (Houston and Corrado, 2023; Giannakos et al., 2024; Wang, Rau and Yuan, 2022)
- AI as an information tool may invoke both positive and negative emotions in information seekers (Seikaly, 2024)

- ChatGPT and similar AI tools are bringing a new set of opportunities for the creative industries, but they also pose a set of challenges for those whose work requires originality (Johnson, 2023).

Thus, in order to be able to use AI tools and technologies effectively, efficiently, responsibly and ethically, people should acquire digital literacy, information literacy and AI literacy.

How should the users be prepared to use Gen AI for access to information?

Discussions in the previous section, and research literature, show that:

- while students have a positive attitude towards Gen AI, they also have concerns about accuracy, privacy, ethical issues and so on (Chan and Hu, 2023)
- although students were engaged with Gen AI for academic work, the information that it produced was not always trustworthy (Deschenes and McMahon, 2024)
- AI literacy programmes can contribute to university students' understanding of major AI concepts, literacy and ethical awareness (Kong, Cheung and Zhang, 2023)
- Librarians can be useful partners with instructors and students when it comes to effectively using Gen AI technologies (Houston and Corrado, 2023).

A UK government office has developed ten core principles to guide government office staff in the use of Gen AI for various government activities (UK Cabinet Office, Central Digital and Data Office, 2024). Those 10 core principles are reproduced below, with additional comments under each one to interpret those in the context of the core theme of this book, Gen AI for information access, and the educational and training needs of information professionals as well as information users:

Principle 1: Know what Gen AI is and what its limitations are

Not all Gen AI applications have access to the live internet and scholarly databases for gathering the latest information and data, and hence the results may be limited, sometimes outdated, biased and skewed, depending on the dataset on which the model was trained. Also, sometimes Gen AI can misinterpret a question or prompt, and generate wrong or inappropriate results. In order to get the best responses, users may need to ask specific questions with some context of the use of the generated output. Information professionals as well as the users should be educated on what Gen AI can and cannot do, its limitations and potential unintended consequences and harms. This calls for user education and especially AI literacy skills. Hirvonen et al. (2024) comment that increasing people's AI literacy, and thus a better understanding of the operations of AI technologies and their potential positive and negative impacts, can prepare them to protect themselves from the potential harms of AI. Deschenes and McMahon (2024) stress that information professionals must know the significant impact that Gen AI technologies may have on information-seeking behaviours and research habits of students, so that they are able to advise the students on how to evaluate AI output critically and incorporate it effectively into their research.

Principle 2: Use Gen AI lawfully, ethically and responsibly

A lot of current research has expressed concerns about the quality of AI's generative capability and the accuracy and reliability of the output (Kimmel, 2024). Farrelly and Baker (2023) emphasise the importance of AI literacy and ethical considerations in adopting AI technologies to ensure equitable access and positive outcomes for all students.

This calls for user education on information law and ethics interpreted appropriately in the context of the use of the content produced by Gen AI. Gen AI tools may use unauthorised content and data, and produce content based on that, which may be unethical or unlawful to use. Also, users should be advised that they should not claim AI-generated content as their own creation or content. Sometimes Gen AI results may be biased or inappropriate for a specific user or context. Information professionals and users should be familiar with the contemporary AI Regulations (e.g. UK Department for Science, Innovation and Technology, 2023).

Principle 3: Know how to keep Gen AI tools secure

This calls for education of the developers at the institutional level – such as universities and library and information services consortia but this also has implications for the information professionals as well as the users. Using Gen AI may involve the use of some sensitive data, and everyone should ensure that private or sensitive data sources are not being used to train Gen AI models without the knowledge and explicit consent of the data owner. Developers and managers of Gen AI at the institutional level should ensure security, data protection and privacy, and build safeguards and put technical controls in place.

Principle 4: Have meaningful human control at the right stage

Gen AI may use sources unknown to the user, making it difficult for the user to ensure the quality, credibility and accountability of the information generated by these systems (Graham, 2023; Haggart, 2023; Hirvonen et al., 2024; Larsson et al., 2023). Users should be educated not to take the content generated by the Gen AI tools blindly; instead, they should apply the standard procedures of checking and verification of the sources, and the justifications for taking a stand based on the supporting data and citations. A mechanism designed to gather user feedback may be useful to improve the user search experience from Gen AI tools.

Principle 5: Understand how to manage the full Gen AI lifecycle

Information professionals should, at the institutional level, be trained on how to integrate the use of Gen AI in the context of the institution's core business – such as education and research, business or general service; how to monitor and mitigate the bias and hallucinations of Gen AI; and how to improve the overall user experience while using Gen AI for information access.

Principle 6: Use the right tool for the job

As discussed throughout this book, many Gen AI tools are currently available in the market, and new ones are appearing regularly. Also, the examples shown in Chapters 4, 5 and 6 show that the results generated by the Gen AI tools vary quite significantly; and some Gen AI tools are designed specifically for assisting users in finding research and scholarly information, for example, Consensus and Scholar GPT. Furthermore, LLMs often limit the maximum number of tokens (roughly equal to the word count) the model can process as a single input prompt. Library and information services are used by people as a source of advice and expertise in different areas, and hence it is quite obvious that given the range of choices, people would ask which AI tool is best suited for their specific information- and data-related tasks. Therefore, it is important that information professionals develop a good understanding of the Gen AI tools that are available, how they work, what they are good for, and what their limitations are. This would enable information professionals to advise users on the right tool for accessing information for their specific needs and context.

Principle 7: Be open and collaborative

A joined-up initiative to develop policies for specific sectors of information services, such as the health, education and research, legal, national and public sectors, should be developed to ensure that everyone follows the best practices and procedures around the use of Gen AI tools for information. Professional bodies and consortia can produce policies and guidelines for awareness, training and policies around the use of Gen AI tools for information access that will inform the information workforce and empower them to provide better services and answer questions from the users about different aspects of Gen AI for access to information. Similarly, a set of policies and guidelines might help information professionals to engage with various stakeholders to engage in informed discussions on the use of Gen AI for various information-related services and tasks. Lo (2023) provides some useful guidelines and recommendations for developing AI policies.

Principle 8: Work with commercial colleagues from the start

The policies, procedures and best practice for the use of Gen AI for information access should be developed in consultation with the relevant commercial and other partners and stakeholders so that everyone can work together to provide the best information services for the target users and communities.

Principle 9: Have the skills and expertise needed to build and use Gen AI

Information professionals and users should know that the output generated by Gen AI tools depends heavily on the prompts, and hence they should acquire an understanding of how best to engage with, or prompt, the Gen AI tools for access to different kinds of information.

Principle 10: Use these principles alongside your organisation's policies and have the right assurance in place

All the above policies and principles should be aligned with the organisation's policies; and therefore information professionals should be trained to develop and use the new skills, mentioned above, in the context of the goals and functions of the parent organisation or institution.

All the above points should form part of the education and training programmes in order to prepare the information workforce that is trained in advising people in effective use of the emerging Gen AI technologies. Some other areas of information science education should also be informed by new research around information retrieval, information behaviour, information seeking and retrieval models and information practice in the light of the increasing use of Gen AI for information access. Alongside the theoretical discussions on these topics, information science students in their taught courses and/or PhD studies should be encouraged to undertake practical research – as part of their assignments, coursework and research activities – to study and critically analyse how people use and interact with Gen AI tools for access to information in different contexts, and the associated issues and challenges, such as relevance, reliability, accuracy, quality, trust, ethics and privacy, related to the information produced by the Gen AI tools. This new knowledge can feed into further research that may result in new or revised models for information retrieval, information seeking and information practices around the use of Gen AI for access to information in different domains and contexts.

Summary

Gen AI technologies and the associated tools are new and are at the early stage of development: 'there are enormous new opportunities and challenges in an AI-augmented world. Be prepared to be awed and disappointed – be realistic. . . . it will require courage and energy to accept the responsibilities and challenges the coming decades will bring' (Marchionini, 2024). However, the fast pace of development and interests in these technologies demonstrate clear signals for their rapid adoption and use in different fields. Examples and discussions in this book demonstrate the potential benefits of the use of Gen AI technologies for information in an everyday life context, as well as in the context of education and research. However, transformative technologies like Gen AI also come with some challenges that need to be understood and addressed in order to make the best use of them. Shah and Bender (2024) argue that Gen AI and LLM-based search systems 'take away transparency and user agency, further amplify the problems associated with bias in IA [information access] systems, and often provide ungrounded and/or toxic answers that may go unchecked by a typical user'.

Given the rapid developments and large corporate investments in this space, we expect to continue to see resources poured into developing and promoting LLM- and chatbot-based AI systems.

It is hoped that the examples, discussions, and recommended areas and professional practices mentioned in this book will be the topics for many upcoming research papers, articles, books, special issues of journals and conferences that will trigger further research, educational and professional practices in information science, computer science and cognate disciplines. This will ensure that people can make use of Gen AI technologies for access to information effectively, efficiently, ethically, responsibly and confidently.

With appropriate measures of user education and literacy, governance structures and economic, social and environmental sustainability measures, these new and emerging technologies will have a transformative impact to the knowledge society.

References

Acar, O. A. (2023) AI Prompt Engineering Isn't the Future, https://hbr.org/2023/06/ai-prompt-engineering-isnt-the-future.

Adiguzel, T., Kaya, M. H., and Cansu, F. K. (2023) Revolutionizing Education with AI: Exploring the Transformative Potential of ChatGPT, *Contemporary Educational Technology*, **15** (3), https://doi.org/10.30935/cedtech/13152.

Agosti, M. (2008) Information Access using the Guide of User Requirements. In Agosti, M. (ed.), *Access Through Search Engines and Digital Libraries*, Springer, 1–12.

Aldosari, S. A. M. (2020) The Future of Higher Education in the Light of Artificial Intelligence Transformations, *International Journal of Higher Education*, **9** (3), 145–51, https://doi.org/10.5430/ijhe.v9n3p145.

Aleedy, M., Atwell, E. and Meshoul, S. (2022) Using AI Chatbots in Education: Recent Advances Challenges and Use Case. In: *Artificial Intelligence and Sustainable Computing*, Proceedings of ICSISCET 2021, 661–75), https://doi.org/10.1007/978-981-19-1653-3_50.

Annapureddy, R., Fornaroli, A. and Gatica-Perez, D. (2024) Generative AI Literacy: Twelve Defining Competencies, *Digital Government: Research and Practice*, https://doi.org/10.1145/3685680.

Anthropic (2024a) Claude 3.5 Sonnet, www.anthropic.com/news/claude-3-5-sonnet.

Anthropic (2024b) Computer Use (Beta), https://docs.anthropic.com/en/docs/build-with-claude/computer-use.

Athukorala, K., Głowacka, D. Jacucci, G., Oulasvirta, A. and Vreeken, J. (2016) Is Exploratory Search Different? A Comparison of Information Search Behavior for Exploratory and Lookup Tasks, *Journal of the Association for Information Science and Technology*, **67** (11), 2635–51.

AWS (2024a) What is Generative AI?, https://aws.amazon.com/what-is/generative-ai.

AWS (2024b) What is LLM (Large Language Model)?, https://aws.amazon.com/what-is/large-language-model.

AWS (2024c) What is RAG (Retrieval-Augmented Generation), https://aws.amazon.com/what-is/retrieval-augmented-generation.

Baeza-Yates, R. and Ribeiro-Neto, B. (1999) *Modern Information Retrieval,* ACM Press.

Baidoo-Anu, D. and Owusu Ansah, L. (2023) Education in the Era of Generative Artificial Intelligence (AI): Understanding the Potential Benefits of ChatGPT in Promoting Teaching and Learning (25 January), *SSRN blog,* https://ssrn.com/abstract=4337484 or http://dx.doi.org/10.2139/ssrn.4337484.

Bashir, N., Donti, P., Cuff, J., Sroka, S., Ilic, M., Sze, V., Delimitrou, C. and Olivetti, E. (2024) The Climate and Sustainability Implications of Generative AI, *An MIT Exploration of Generative AI,* 27 March, https://mit-genai.pubpub.org/pub/8ulgrckc/release/2?readingCollection=9070dfe7.

Bates, M. J. (1974) Speculations on The Sociocultural Context of Public Information Provision in the Seventies and Beyond., In: Cuadra, C.A. and Bates, M. J. (eds), *Library and Information Service Needs of the Nation: Proceedings of a Conference on the Needs of Occupational, Ethnic, and other Groups in the United States. Sponsored by the National Commission on Libraries and Information Science,* US Government Printing Office, 51–76.

Bates, M.J. (1989) The Design of Browsing and Berrypicking Techniques for the Online Search Interface, *Online Review,* **13** (5), 407–24.

Bawden, D. and Robinson, L. (2012) *Introduction to Information Science,* Facet Publishing.

Bell, D. J. and Ruthven, I. (2004) Searcher's Assessments of Task Complexity for Web Searching. In: McDonald, S. and Tait, J. (eds), *Advances in Information Retrieval,* European Conference on Information Retrieval (ECIR 2004), Lecture Notes in Computer Science vol 2997. Springer, https://doi.org/10.1007/978-3-540-24752-4_5.

Blake, C. and Pratt, W. (2006) Collaborative Information Synthesis I: a Model of Information Behaviors of Scientists in Medicine and Public Health, *Journal of the American Society of Information Science and Technology,* **57** (13), 1740–9.

Borgman, C. L. (2012) The Conundrum of Sharing Research Data, *Journal of the American Society for Information Science and Technology,* **63** (6), 1059–78.

Borgman, C.L. (2015) *Big Data, Little Data, No Data: Scholarship in the Networked World,* MIT Press.

Borgman, C.L., Wallis, J. C. and Mayernik, M. S. (2012) Who's Got the Data? Interdependencies in Science and Technology Collaborations, *Computer Supported Cooperative Work,* **21** (6), 485–523.

Buckland, M. (1991) Information as Thing, *Journal of the American Society for Information Science,* **42** (5), 351–60.

Buckland, M. (2012) What Kind of Science can Information Science Be? *Journal of Information Science and Technology,* **63**, (1),: 1-7.

Butler, J., Jaff, S., Baym, N., Czerwinski, M., Iqbal, S., Nowak, K., Rintel, S., Sellen, A., Vorvoreanu, M., Abdulhamid, N. G., Amores, J., Andersen, R., Awori, K., Axmed, M., Boyd, D., Brand, J., Buscher, G., Carignan, D., Chan, M., Coleman,

A., Counts, S., Daepp, M., Fourney, A., Goldstein, D. G., Gordon, A., Halfaker, A. L., Hernandez., J., Hofman, J., Lay-Flurrie, J., Liao, V., Lindley, S., Manivannan, S., McIlwain, C., Nepal, S., Neville, J., Nyairo, S., O'Neill, J., Poznanski, V., Ramos, G., Rangan, N., Rosedale, L., Rothschild, D., Safavi, T., Sarkar, A., Scott, A., Shah, C., Shah, N. P., Shapiro, T., Shaw, R., Simkute, A., Suh, J., Suri, S., Tanase, I., Tankelevitch, L., Troy, A., Wan, M., White, R. W., Yang, L., Hecht, B. and Teevan, J. (2023) *Microsoft New Future of Work Report 2023*, https://aka.ms/nfw2023.

Byström, K. (2002) Information and Information Sources in Tasks of Varying Complexity, *Journal of the American Society for Information Science and Technology*, **53** (7), 581–91.

Byström, K. (2007) Approaches to 'Task' in Contemporary Information Studies, *Information Research*, **12** (4), paper Colis26, https://informationr.net/ir///12-4/colis/colis26.html.

Byström, K. and Hansen, P. (2005) Conceptual Framework for Tasks in Information Studies, *Journal of the American Society for Information Science and Technology*, **56** (10), 1050–61.

Cambridge Dictionary (2017) Cambridge University Press, http://dictionary.cambridge.org/dictionary/english/information-retrieval.

Cambridge University, School of the Humanities and Social Sciences (2024) *Generative AI and Your Learning*, www.cshss.cam.ac.uk/education/generative-artificial-intelligence-ai-and-scholarship/generative-ai-and-your-learning.

Carroll, A. J. and Borycz, J. (2024) Integrating Large Language Models and Generative Artificial Intelligence Tools into Information Literacy Instruction, *Journal of Academic Librarianship*, **50** (4), https://doi.org/10.1016/j.acalib.2024.102899.

Case, D. O. (2010) A Model of the Information Seeking and Decision Making Of Online Coin Buyers, *Information Research*, **15** (4), paper 448, http://InformationR.net/ir/15-4/paper448.html.

Case, D. O. and Given, L. (2016) *Looking for Information: a Survey of Research on Information Seeking, Needs, and Behaviour*, 4th edn, Emerald.

Chan, C. K. Y. and Hu, W. (2023) Students' Voices on Generative AI: Perceptions, Benefits, and Challenges in Higher Education, *International Journal of Educational Technology in Higher Education*, **20** (43), https://doi.org/10.1186/s41239-023-00411-8.

Chew, S. W. and Khoo, C. S. G. (2016) Comparison of Drug Information on Consumer Drug Review Sites versus Authoritative Health Information Websites, *Journal of the Association for Information Science and Technology*, **67**, 333–49.

Chiu, T. K. F., Xia, Q., Zhou, X., Chai, C. S. and Cheng, M. (2023a) Systematic Literature Review on Opportunities, Challenges, and Future Research Recommendations of Artificial Intelligence in Education, *Computers and Education: Artificial Intelligence*, **4**, 100118, https://doi.org/10.1016/j.caeai.2022.100118.

Chiu, T. K. F., Moorhouse, B. L., Chai, C. S. and Ismailov, M. (2023b) Teacher Support and Student Motivation to Learn with Artificial Intelligence (AI) Based Chatbot, *Interactive Learning Environments*, **32** (7), 3240–56, https://doi.org/10.1080/10494820.2023.2172044.

Chowdhury, G.G. (2010) *Introduction to Modern Information Retrieval*, 3rd edn, Facet Publishing.

Chowdhury, G. G. (2014) *Sustainability of Scholarly Information*, Facet Publishing.

Chowdhury, G. G. and Chowdhury, S. (2011) *Information Users and Usability in the Digital Age*, Facet Publishing.

Chowdhury, G. G. and Chowdhury, S. (2024) *Information for Sustainable Development: Technology, People and Society*, Facet Publishing.

Chowdhury, G. G. and Foo, S. (2012a) Digital Libraries and Information Access: Introduction. In Chowdhury, G. and Foo, S. (eds), *Digital Libraries and Information Access: Research Perspectives*, Facet Publishing, 1–11.

Chowdhury, G. G. and Foo, S. (2012b) Information Access. In: Chowdhury, G. and Foo, S. (eds), *Digital Libraries and Information Access: Research Perspectives*, Facet Publishing, 47–67.

Chowdhury, G. G. and Koya, K. (2017) Information Practices for Sustainability: Role of iSchools in Achieving the UN Sustainable Development Goals (SDGs), *Journal of the Association for Information Science and Technology*, **68** (9), 2128–38, https://doi.org/10.1002/asi.23825.

Chowdhury, S. (2010) Digital Libraries: a New Paradigm Shift with Some Issues and Challenges, *International Conference on Digital Libraries 2010 (ICDL 2010): Shaping the Information Paradigm*, TERI, 23–26 February, 480–7.

Chowdhury, S. (2012) The Usability of Digital Libraries. In Chowdhury, G. and Foo, S.(eds), *Digital Libraries and Information Access: Research Perspectives*, Facet Publishing, 167–77.

Chowdhury, S., Gibb, F. and Landoni, M. (2014) A Model of Uncertainty and its Relation to Information Seeking and Retrieval (IS&R), *Journal of Documentation*, **70** (4), 575–604, https://doi.org/10.1108/JD-05-2013-0060.

Chu, H. (2010) *Information Representation and Retrieval in the Digital Age*, 2nd edn, Information Today.

Chui, M., Roberts, R. and Yee, L. (2022) *Generative AI is Here: How Tools Like ChatGPT Could Change Your Business*, McKinsey & Company, www.mckinsey.com/~/media/mckinsey/business%20functions/quantumblack/our%20insights/generative%20ai%20is%20here%20how%20tools%20like%20chatgpt%20could%20change%20your%20business/generative-ai-is-here-how-tools-like-chatgpt-could-change-your-business.pdf .

CILIP (2018) *Information Literacy*, https://infolit.org.uk/ILdefinitionCILIP2018.pdf.

Clarivate (2024a) Beyond Discovery: AI and the Future of the Web of Science, https://librarytechnology.org/pr/30040.

Clarivate (2024b) ProQuest, Part of Clarivate, Launches AI-powered Research Assistant, https://about.proquest.com/en/blog/2024/proquest-part-of-clarivate-launches-ai-powered-research-assistant.

Clarivate (2025) Web of Science Platform, https://clarivate.com/products/scientific-and-academic-research/research-discovery-and-workflow-solutions/webofscience-platform.

Collins English Dictionary (2017) Definition of 'Information Retrieval System', www.collinsdictionary.com/dictionary/english/information-retrieval-system.

Cool, C. and Belkin, N. J. (2011) Interactive Information Retrieval: History and Background. In Ruthven, I. and Kelly, D. (eds), *Interactive Information Seeking, Behaviour and Retrieval,* Facet Publishing, 1–14.

Cornell University Research & Innovation (2023) Generative AI in Academic Research: Perspectives and Cultural Norms, https://research-and-innovation.cornell.edu/generative-ai-in-academic-research.

Cox, A. (2022) How Artificial Intelligence Might Change Academic Library Work: Applying the Competencies Literature and the Theory of the Professions, *Journal of the Association for Information Science and Technology,* **74** (3), 367–80, https://doi.org/10.1002/asi.24635.

Cox, A. (2024) Algorithmic Literacy, AI Literacy and Responsible Generative AI Literacy, *Journal of Web Librarianship,* 1–18, https://doi.org/10.1080/19322909.2024.2395341.

Croft, W. B. (1986) Boolean Queries and Term Dependencies in Probabilistic Retrieval Models, *Journal of the American Society for Information Science,* **37** (2), 71–77, https://doi.org/10.1002/(SICI)1097-4571(198603)37:2<71::AID-ASI3>3.0.CO;2-4.

Cuconasu, F., Trappolini, G., Siciliano, F., Filice, S., Campagnano, C., Maarek, Y., Tonellotto, N. and Silvestri, F. (2024) The Power of Noise: Redefining Retrieval for RAG Systems. In *47th International ACM SIGIR Conference on Research and Development in Information Retrieval, SIGIR 2024,* 719–29, https://doi.org/10.1145/3626772.3657834.

Dell'Acqua, F., McFowland III, E., Mollick, E. R., Lifshitz-Assaf, H., Kellogg, K., Rajendran, S., Krayer, L., Candelon, F. and Lakhani, K. R. (2023) Navigating the Jagged Technological Frontier: Field Experimental Evidence of the Effects of AI on Knowledge Worker Productivity and Quality, Harvard Business School Technology & Operations Mgt. Unit Working Paper No. 24-013, 15 September, The Wharton School Research Paper, https://ssrn.com/abstract=4573321.

Dempsey, L. (2023) Generative AI and Libraries: Seven Contexts, www.lorcandempsey.net/generative-ai-and-libraries-7-contexts.

Deschenes, A. and McMahon, M. (2024) A Survey on Student Use of Generative AI Chatbots for Academic Research, *Evidence Based Library and Information Practice,* **19** (2), 2–22.

Dimensions (2023) Powering Research with Dimensions AI Assistant, www.dimensions.ai/blog/powering-research-with-dimensions-ai-assistant.

Ellis, D. (1989) A Behavioural Approach to Information Retrieval System Design, *Journal of Documentation*, **45** (3), 171–212, https://doi.org/10.1108/eb026843.

Elsevier (2025a) Scopus Content, www.elsevier.com/products/scopus/content.

Elsevier (2025b) Scopus AI, www.elsevier.com/en-gb/products/scopus/scopus-ai.

Encyclopedia.com (2019) Information Access, www.encyclopedia.com/computing/news-wires-white-papers-and-books/information-access.

Fairthorne, R. (1961) *Towards Information Retrieval,* Butterworth.

Fan, W., Ding, Y., Ning, L., Wang, S., Li, H., Yin, D., Chua, T-S. and Li, Q. (2024) A Survey on RAG Meeting LLMs: Towards Retrieval-Augmented Large Language Models. In *Proceedings of the ACM SIGKDD International Conference on Knowledge Discovery and Data Mining, ACM SIGKDD Conference on Knowledge Discovery and Data Mining*, KDD 2024, Barcelona, 25–29 August, 6491 – 6501.

Farrelly, T. and Baker, N. (2023) Generative Artificial Intelligence: Implications and Considerations for Higher Education Practice, *Education Sciences*, **13** (11), 1109.

Forbes (2023) Microsoft Confirms $10 Billion Investment into ChatGPT, Changing How Microsoft Competes with Google, Apple, and Other Tech Giants, *Forbes*, 27 January, www.forbes.com/sites/qai/2023/01/27/microsoft-confirms-its-10-billion-investment-into-chatgpt-changing-how-microsoft-competes-with-google-apple-and-other-tech-giants.

Freitag, C., Berners-Lee, M., Widdicks, K., Knowles, B., Blair, G. S. and Friday, A. (2021) The Real Climate and Transformative Impact of ICT: a Critique of Estimates, Trends, and Regulations, *Patterns*, **2** (9), 100340, https://doi.org/10.1016/j.patter.2021.100340.

Giannakos, M., Azevedo, R., Brusilovsky, P., Cukurova, M., Dimitriadis, Y., Hernandez-Leo, D., Järvelä, S., Mavrikis, M. and Rienties, B. (2024) The Promise and Challenges of Generative AI in Education, *Behaviour & Information Technology*, 1–27, https://doi.org/10.1080/0144929X.2024.2394886.

Gimpel, H., Hall, K., Decker, S., Eymann, T., Lämmermann, L., Mädche, A., Röglinger, M., Ruiner, C., Schoch, M., Schoop, M., Urbach, N. and Vandirk, S. (2023) *Unlocking the Power of Generative AI Models and Systems such as GPT-4 and ChatGPT for Higher Education: a Guide for Students and Lecturers*, University of Hohenheim, 20 March, www.econstor.eu/bitstream/10419/270970/1/1840457716.pdf.

Given, L., Case, D. and Wilson, R. (2023) *Looking for Information: Examining Research on How People Engage with Information*, 5th edn, Emerald.

Goldman Sachs (2024) AI is Poised to Drive 160% Increase in Data Center Power Demand, 14 May, www.goldmansachs.com/insights/articles/AI-poised-to-drive-160-increase-in-power-demand?.

González-Teruel, A. and Pérez-Pulido, M. (2020) The Diffusion and Influence of Theoretical Models of Information Behaviour: the Case of Savolainen's ELIS Model, *Journal of Documentation*, **76** (5), 1069–89, https://doi.org/10.1108/JD-10-2019-0197.

Google (2023) Introducing Gemini: our largest and most capable AI model, https://blog.google/technology/ai/google-gemini-ai/#capabilities.

GPTStore.ai (n.d.) https://gptstore.ai/plugins/scholar-ai-net.

Graf, B. and Antoni, C. H. (2022) Drowning in the Flood of Information: a Meta-Analysis on the Relation between Information Overload, Behaviour, Experience, and Health and Moderating Factors, *European Journal of Work and Organizational Psychology*, **32** (2), 173–98, https://doi.org/10.1080/1359432X.2022.2118051.

Graham, M. (2023) ChatGPT Can't Lie to You, but You Still Shouldn't Trust It, *The Conversation*, 9 March, https://theconversation.com/chatgpt-cant-lie-to-you-but-you-still-I-trust-it-201127.

Grossman, D. A. and Frieder, O. (2004) *Information Retrieval: Algorithms and Heuristics*, 2nd edn, Springer.

Guo, M., Zhou, Z., Gotz, D. and Wang, Y. (2023) GRAFS: Graphical Faceted Search System to Support Conceptual Understanding in Exploratory Search, *ACM Transactions on Interactive Intelligent Systems*, **13** (2), Article 9, 36, https://doi.org/10.1145/3588319.

Hagendorff, T. (2024) Mapping the Ethics of Generative AI: a Comprehensive Scoping Review, *Minds and Machines (Dordrecht)*, **34** (4), https://doi.org/10.1007/s11023-024-09694-w.

Haggart, B. (2023) Here's Why ChatGPT Raises Issues of Trust, *World Economic Forum*, 6 February, www.weforum.org/ agenda/2023/02/why-chatgpt-raises-issues-of-trust-ai-science.

Halpern, D. F. and Dunn, D. S. (2021) Critical Thinking: a Model of Intelligence for Solving Real-world Problems, *Journal of Intelligence*, **9** (2), 22, https://doi.org/10.3390/jintelligence9020022.

Hearst, M. (1999) User Interface and Visualization. In Baeza-Yates, R. and Riberio-Neto, B. (eds), *Modern Information Retrieval*, 257–89, Addison-Wesley Longman Publishing, https://www2.dcc.ufmg.br/livros/irbook/10/node8.html.

Heikkilä, M. (2023) Making an Image with Generative AI Uses As Much Energy as Charging Your Phone, *MIT Technology Review*, 1 December, www.technologyreview.com/2023/12/01/1084189/making-an-image-with-generative-ai-uses-as-much-energy-as-charging-your-phone.

Hektor, A. (2001) *What's the Use? Internet and Information Behaviour in Everyday Life*, Linköping University.

Hersh, W. (2024) Search Still Matters: Information Retrieval in the Era of Generative AI, *Journal of the American Medical Informatics Association*, **31** (9), 2159–61, https://doi.org/10.1093/jamia/ocae014.

Hirvonen, N., Jylhä, V., Lao, Y. and Larsson, S. (2024) Artificial Intelligence in the Information Ecosystem: Affordances for Everyday Information Seeking, *Journal of the Association for Information Science and Technology*, **75** (10), 1152–65, https://doi.org/10.1002/asi.24860.

Houston, A. B. and Corrado, E. M. (2023) Embracing ChatGPT: Implications of Emergent Language Models for Academia and Libraries, *Technical Services Quarterly*, **40** (2), 76–91, https://doi.org/10.1080/07317131.2023.2187110.

Hwang, G. J. and Chang, C. Y. (2021) A Review of Opportunities and Challenges of Chatbots in Education, *Interactive Learning Environments*, 18 July, https://doi.org/10.1080/10494820.2021.1952615 .

IBM (2025a) What is Prompt Engineering?, www.ibm.com/topics/prompt-engineering.

IBM (2025b) What is generative AI?, https://research.ibm.com/blog/what-is-generative-AI.

IFLA (2024). Information Access: the Internet and AI, https://www.ifla.org/news/information-access-the-internet-and-ai.

Ingwersen , P.and Jarvelin, P. (2005) *The Turn: Integration of Information Seeking and Retrieval in Context, Springer.*

Johnson, C. (2023) Action Learning in an Uncertain World, *Action Learning: Research and Practice*, **20** (1), 3–4, https://doi.org/10.1080/14767333.2023.2171528.

Jones, B. M. (2023) How Generative AI Tools Help Transform Academic Research, *Forbes*, 28 September, www.forbes.com/sites/beatajones/2023/09/28/how-generative-ai-tools-help-transform-academic-research.

JSTOR (2025) JSTOR's Interactive Research Tool, https://about.jstor.org/gen-ai/#about.

Kimmel, S. (2024) AI Facilitated Critical Thinking in an Undergraduate Project Based Service-Learning Course, *Journal of Behavioral and Applied Management*, **24** (2), 123–30, https://doi.org/10.21818/001c.122149.

Knight, C. (2024) AI Garage Overview: a Short Commentary to Submitted Generative AI Cases, *AdvanceHE*, 23 April, www.advance-he.ac.uk/news-and-views/ai-garage-snapshots-practice, 4–5.

Kong, S.-C., Cheung, W. M.-Y. and Zhang, G. (2021) Evaluation of an Artificial Intelligence Literacy Course for University Students with Diverse Study Backgrounds, *Computers and Education: Artificial Intelligence*, **2**, https://doi.org/10.1016/j.caeai.2021.100026.

Kong, S.-C., Cheung, W. M.-Y. and Zhang, G. (2023) Evaluating an Artificial Intelligence Literacy Programme for Developing University Students' Conceptual Understanding, Literacy, Empowerment and Ethical Awareness, *Educational Technology A Society*, **26** (1), 16–30, www.jstor.org/stable/48707964.

Kong, S. C., Korte, S. M., Burton, S., Keskitalo, P., Turunen, T., Smith, D., Wang, L., Lee, J. C. K. and Beaton, M. C. (2024) Artificial Intelligence (AI) Literacy–an

Argument for AI Literacy in Education, *Innovations in Education and Teaching International*, 1–7, https://doi.org/10.1080/14703297.2024.2332744.

Kuhlthau, C. (1988) Longitudinal Case Studies of the Information Search Process of Users in Libraries, *Library and Information Science Research*, **10**, 257–304.

Kuhlthau, C. (1991) Inside the Search Process: Information Seeking from the User's Perspective, *Journal of the American Society for Information Science*, **42** (5), 361–71.

Kuhlthau, C. (1993) A Principle of Uncertainty for Information Seeking, *Journal of Documentation*, **49** (4), 339–55.

Kuhlthau, C. (1999a) Accommodating the User's Information Search Process: Challenges for Information Retrieval System Designers, *Bulletin of the American Society for Information Science and Technology*, **25** (3), 12–16.

Kuhlthau, C. (1999b) The Role of Experience in the Information Search Process of an Early Career Information Worker: Perceptions of Uncertainty, Complexity, Construction, and Sources, *Journal of the American Society for Information Science*, **50** (5), 399–412.

Kuhlthau, C. (2018) Longitudinal Evidence of the Influence of the ISP on Information Workers, ASIS&T SIG-Use, https://wp.comminfo.rutgers.edu/ckuhlthau/wp-content/uploads/sites/185/2019/03/Asist-siguse-2018.pdf

Kuhlthau, C., Heinstrom, J. and Todd, R. (2008) The 'Information Search Process' Revisited: is the Model Still Useful? *Information Research*, **13** (4), https://informationr.net/ir/13-4/paper355.html.

Kumar, A. and Davenport, T. (2023) *How to Make Generative AI Greener?*, 20 July, *Harvard Business Review*, https://hbr.org/2023/07/how-to-make-generative-ai-greener.

Larsson, S., Haresamudram, K., Högberg, C., Lao, Y., Nyström, A., Söderlund, K. and Heintz, F. (2023) Four Facets of AI Transparency. In Lindgren, S. (ed.), *Handbook of Critical Studies of Artificial Intelligence*, Edward Elgar Publishing.

Lewandowski, D., Haider, J. and Sundin, O. (2024) JASIST Special Issue Editorial: Re-orienting Search Engine Research in Information Science, *Journal of the Association for Information Science and Technology*, **75** (5), 503–11, https://doi.org/10.1002/asi.24845.

Lewis, P., Perez, E., Piktus, A., Petroni, F., Karpukhin, V., Goyal, N., Küttler, H., Lewis, M., Yih, W.-T., Rocktäschel, T., Riedel, S. and Kiela, D. (2021) Retrieval-Augmented Generation for Knowledge-Intensive NLP Tasks, *arXiv*, https://arxiv.org/abs/2005.11401.

Liu, Y., Qin, C., Wang, Y.and Ma, X. (2024) Exploratory Search in Information Systems: a Systematic Review, *Electronic Library*, **42** (2), 308–39, https://doi.org/10.1108/EL-11-2023-0264.

Lo, K., Chang, J. C., Head, A., Bragg, J., Zhang, A. X., Trier, C., Anastasiades, C., August, T., Authur, R., et al. (2024) The Semantic Reader Project: Augmenting

Scholarly Documents Through AI-powered Interactive Reading Interfaces, *Communications of the ACM*, **67** (10), 50–61, https://doi.org/10.1145/3659096.

Lo, L. S. (2023) AI Policies Across the Globe: Implications and Recommendations for Libraries, *IFLA Journal*, **49** (4), 645–9, https://doi.org/10.1177/03400352231196172.

Lorenz, P., Perset, K. and Berryhill, J. (2023) *Initial Policy Considerations for Generative Artificial Intelligence*, OECD Artificial Intelligence Papers, No. 1, OECD Publishing, https://doi.org/10.1787/fae2d1e6-en.

Luccioni, S., Jernite, Y. and Strubell, E. (2024) Power Hungry Processing: Watts Driving the Cost of AI Deployment?. In *Proceedings of the 2024 ACM Conference on Fairness, Accountability, and Transparency (FAccT '24)*, Association for Computing Machinery, 85–99, https://doi.org/10.1145/3630106.3658542.

Ludvigsen, K. (2022) The Carbon Footprint of Chat GPT, *Towards Data Science*, 21 December, updated 20 March 2023, https://towardsdatascience.com/the-carbon-footprint-of-chatgpt-66932314627d.

McIlwain, M. (2023) Game on in the Generative AI Stack, *Madrona*, 20 March, www.madrona.com/game-on-in-the-generative-ai-stack.

McKnight, L. (2022) Eight Ways to Engage with AI Writers in Higher Education, *Times Higher Education*, www.timeshighereducation.com/campus/eight-ways-engage-ai-writers-higher-education.

Manning, C., Raghavan, P. and Schütze, H. (2009) *An Introduction to Information Retrieval*, Cambridge University Press, https://nlp.stanford.edu/IR-book/pdf/irbookonlinereading.pdf.

Marchionini, G. (2006) Exploratory Search: from Finding to Understanding, *Communications of the ACM*, **49** (4), 41–6, https://doi.org/10.1145/1121949.1121979.

Marchionini, G. (2024) Information and Library Professionals' Roles and Responsibilities in an AI-augmented World, *Journal of the Association for Information Science and Technology*, **75** (8), 865–8, https://doi.org/10.1002/asi.24930.

Martineau, K. (2023) What is Generative AI?, IBM Blog, 20 April, https://research.ibm.com/blog/what-is-generative-AI.

Meakin, L. (2024) Exploring the Impact of Generative Artificial Intelligence on Higher Education Students' Utilization of Library Resources: a Critical Examination, *Information Technology and Libraries*, **43** (3), 1–13, https://doi.org/10.5860/ital.v43i3.17246.

Meho, L. and Tibbo, H. (2003) Modeling the information-seeking Behavior of Social Scientists: Ellis's Study Revisited, *Journal of the American Society for Information Science and Technology*, **54** (6), 570–87, https://doi.org/10.1002/asi.10244.

Mensah, J. (2019) Sustainable Development: Meaning, History, Principles, Pillars, and Implications for Human Action: Literature Review, *Cogent Social Sciences*, **5** (1), https://doi.org/10.1080/23311886.2019.1653531.

Microsoft (2023) Introducing Microsoft 365 Copilot – Your Copilot for Work, https://blogs.microsoft.com/blog/2023/03/16/introducing-microsoft-365-copilot-your-copilot-for-work.

Microsoft (2024) Retrieval Augmented Generation (RAG) in Azure AI Search, https://learn.microsoft.com/en-us/azure/search/retrieval-augmented-generation-overview.

Mills, A. (2023) Seeing Past the Dazzle of ChatGPT, *Inside Higher Ed.*, 18 January, www.insidehighered.com/advice/2023/01/19/academics-must-collaborate-develop-guidelines-chatgpt-opinion.

MIT Sloan Teaching & Learning Technologies (2025) Effective Prompts for AI: the Essentials, https://mitsloanedtech.mit.edu/ai/basics/effective-prompts.

Mollick, E. (2023) My Class Required AI. Here's What I've Learned So Far, *One Useful Thing*, 17 February, https://oneusefulthing.substack.com/p/my-class-required-ai-heres-what-ive.

Mooers, C.N. (1950) Information Retrieval Viewed as Temporal Signalling, *Proceedings of the International Congress of Mathematicians, Cambridge, MA, August 30-September 6*, 1950, American Mathematical Society, 572–3, www.mathunion.org/ICM/ICM1950.1/ICM1950.1.ocr.pdf.

Najork , M. (2023) Generative Information Retrieval, keynote paper, ACMSIGIR 2023 Conference, https://dl.acm.org/doi/10.1145/3539618.3591871.

NotebookLM (2023) Welcome to NotebookLM, https://notebooklm.google.com/?_gl=1*zjzrg1*_up*MQ..*_ga*NjQ0NjkzNDY5LjE3MjczNTMxMTk.*_ga_W0LDH41ZCB*MTcyNzM1MzExOC4xLjAuMTcyNzM1MzExOC4wLjAuMA..&original_referer=https:%2F%2Fnotebooklm.google%23&pli=1.

OECD (2023) *OECD Employment Outlook 2023: Artificial Intelligence and the Labour Market*, OECD Publishing, https://doi.org/10.1787/08785bba-en.

OECD (2024) OECD and UN Announce Next Steps in Collaboration on Artificial Intelligence, Press release, 22 September, www.oecd.org/en/about/news/press-releases/2024/09/oecd-and-un-announce-next-steps-in-collaboration-on-artificial-intelligence.html.

OECD (n.d.) Artificial Intelligence, www.oecd.org/en/topics/artificial-intelligence.html.

OpenAI (2023) The OpenAI Cookbook, https://cookbook.openai.com/examples/vector_databases/readme.

OpenAI (2024a) Retrieval Augmented Generation (RAG) and Semantic Search for GPTs, https://help.openai.com/en/articles/8868588-retrieval-augmented-generation-rag-and-semantic-search-for-gpts.

OpenAI (2024b) Memory and New Controls for ChatGPT, 13 February, https://openai.com/index/memory-and-new-controls-for-chatgpt.

OpenAI (2024c) Introducing the GPT Store, https://openai.com/index/introducing-the-gpt-store.
OpenAI Platform (2024) Models, https://platform.openai.com/docs/models/gpt-4o.
OpenAI Platform (2025) Prompt Engineering: Six Strategies for Getting Better Results, https://platform.openai.com/docs/guides/prompt-engineering/six-strategies-for-getting-better-results.
Ouyang, F. and Jiao, P. (2021) Artificial Intelligence in Education: the Three Paradigms, *Computers & Education: Artificial Intelligence*, **2**, 100020, https://doi.org/10.1016/j.caeai.2021.100020.
Oxford University (2025) Use of Generative AI tools to Support Learning, www.ox.ac.uk/students/academic/guidance/skills/ai-study.
Park, H. and Ahn, D. (2024) The Promise and Peril of ChatGPT in Higher Education: Opportunities, Challenges, and Design Implications. In *Proceedings of the CHI Conference on Human Factors in Computing Systems (CHI '24), May 11–16, Honolulu*, ACM, https://doi.org/10.1145/3613904.3642785 .
Parvez, M. R., Ahmad, W. U., Chakraborty, S., Ray, B. and Chang, K.-W. (2021) Retrieval Augmented Code Generation and Summarization, *arXiv*, https://arxiv.org/abs/2108.11601.
Petras, V. (2024) The Identity of Information Science, *Journal of Documentation*, **80** (3), 579–96, https://doi.org/10.1108/JD-04-2023-0074.
Prasetyo, Y. A., Dedi, B. and Ngadiran, A. (2024) Critical Thinking and Artificial Intelligence in Tandem: a Nursing Perspective, *Journal of Healthcare Administration*, **3** (1), 72–81, https://doi.org/10.33546/joha.3352.
Proquest (2025) LISA: Library and Information Science Abstracts, https://about.proquest.com/en/products-services/lisa-set-c.
Rahman, M. H. and Islam, M. N. (2024) The Impact of ChatGPT for Enhancing Knowledge Management in University Libraries, *Journal of Web Librarianship*, 1–20, https://doi.org/10.1080/19322909.2024.2391907.
Raman, R., Lathabai, H. H., Mandal, S., Das, P., Kaur, T. and Nedungadi, P. (2024) ChatGPT: Literate or Intelligent about UN Sustainable Development Goals? *PloS One*, **19** (4), e0297521–e0297521, https://doi.org/10.1371/journal.pone.0297521.
Ruiz-Rojas, L. I., Acosta-Vargas, P., De-Moreta-Llovet, J. and Gonzalez-Rodriguez, M. (2023) Empowering Education with Generative Artificial Intelligence Tools: Approach with an Instructional Design Matrix, *Sustainability*, **15** (15), NA, http://dx.doi.org/10.3390/su151511524.
Ruotsalo, T., Jacucci, G. and Kaski, S. (2020) Interactive Faceted Query Suggestion for Exploratory Search: Whole-session Effectiveness and Interaction Engagement, *Journal of the Association for Information Science and Technology*, **71** (7), 742–56, https://doi.org/10.1002/asi.24304.
Russell Group (n.d.) *Russell Group Principles on the Use of Generative AI Tools in Education*, https://russellgroup.ac.uk/media/6137/rg_ai_principles-final.pdf.

Saenko, K. (2023) A Computer Scientist Breaks Down Generative AI's Hefty Carbon Footprint: is Generative AI Bad for the Environment? A Computer Scientist Explains the Carbon Footprint of ChatGPT and its Cousins – and How to Reduce It, 25 May, www.scientificamerican.com/article/a-computer-scientist-breaks-down-generative-ais-hefty-carbon-footprint.

Salton, G., and Yang, C. S. (1973) On the Specification of Term Values in Automatic Indexing, *Journal of Documentation*, **29** (4), 351–72.

Savolainen, R. (1995) Everyday Life Information Seeking: Approaching Information Seeking in the Context of 'Way of Life', *Library and Information Science Research*, **17** (3), 259–94.

Savolainen, R. (1998) Seeking and Using Information from the Internet. The Context of Non-work Use. In Wilson, T. D. and Allen, D. K. (eds), *Exploring the Contexts of Information Behaviour, Proceedings of the 2nd International Conference on Research in Information Needs, Seeking and Use in Different Contexts, Sheffield, UK, August 13–15*, Taylor Graham, 356–70.

Savolainen, R. (1999) The Role of the Internet in Information Seeking: Putting the Networked Services in Context: Information Seeking in Context (ISIC), *Information Processing & Management*, **35** (6), 765–82.

Savolainen, R. (2006) Everyday Life Information Seeking. In Fisher, K., Erdelez, S. and McKechnie, L. (eds), *Theories of Information Behavior*, Information Today, 143–8.

Savolainen, R. (2008) *Everyday Information Practices: a Social Phenomenological Perspective*, Scarecrow Press.

Savolainen, R. (2010) Everyday Life Information Seeking. In *Encyclopaedia of Library and Information Sciences*, 3rd edn, 1778–89, https://infocom.hyperlib.sjsu.edu/wp-content/uploads/2018/08/Everyday-Information-Seeking_Savolainen.pdf.

Savolainen, R. and Kari, J. (2004) Placing the Internet in Information Source Horizons: a Study of Information Seeking by Internet Users in the Context of Self-development, *Library & Information Science Research*, **26** (4), 415–33, https://doi.org/10.1016/j.lisr.2004.04.004.

Savolainen, R. and Kari, J. (2006a) Facing and Bridging Gaps in Web Searching, *Information Processing & Management*, **42** (2), 519–37.

Savolainen, R. and Kari, J. (2006b) User-defined Relevance Criteria in Web Searching, *Journal of Documentation*, **62** (6), 685–707, https://doi.org/10.1108/00220410610714921.

Savolainen, R. and Thomson, L. (2022) Assessing the Theoretical Potential of an Expanded Model for Everyday Information Practices, *Journal of the Association for Information Science and Technology*, **73** (4), 511–27, https://doi.org/10.1002/asi.24589.

ScholarAI (n.d.) https://scholarai.io/why-scholarai.

SCONUL (2024) *Technology and Markets Strategy Group: AI project – AI roadmap meetings*, www.sconul.ac.uk/SCONULDownloadController/Download?iType=1&iID=2282&cGUID=65e7869a-48f8-403c-8eb6-3766c526d926&cTempLocation=.

Seikaly, K. (2024) ChatGPT, How Do People Feel About You?: Emotions, Artificial Intelligence, and Information Behavior, *Journal of Web Librarianship*, **18** (3),1–16, https://doi.org/10.1080/19322909.2024.2382689.

Shah, C. (2024) AI Search Answers are the Fast Food of Your Information Diet – Convenient and Tasty, but No Substitute for Good Nutrition, *The Conversation*, 7 June, https://theconversation.com/ai-search-answers-are-the-fast-food-of-your-information-diet-convenient-and-tasty-but-no-substitute-for-good-nutrition-230759.

Shah, C. and Bender, E. (2024) Envisioning Information Access Systems: What Makes for Good Tools and a Healthy Web?, *ACM Transactions on the Web*, **18** (3), 1–24, https://doi.org/10.1145/3649468.

Shah, C., White, R. W., Thomas, P., Mitra, B, Sarkar, S. and Belkin, N. (2023) Taking Search to Task. In *ACM SIGIR Conference on Human Information Interaction and Retrieval (CHIIR '23), March 19–23*, https://doi.org/10.1145/3576840.3578288.

Sparck Jones, K. (1972) A Statistical Interpretation of Term Specificity and its Application in Retrieval, *Journal of Documentation*, **28** (1), 11–21, https://doi.org/10.1108/eb026526.

Sparck Jones, K. and Willett, P. (1997) Overall Introduction. In Sparck Jones, K. and Willett, P. (eds), *Readings in Information Retrieval*, Morgan Kaufmann, 1–7.

Stryker, C. and Scapicchio, M. (2024) What is Generative AI? IBM, 22 March, www.ibm.com/topics/generative-ai.

Suleyman, M. and Bhaskar, M. (2023) *The Coming Wave: AI, Power and the Twenty-first Century's Greatest Dilemma*, Bodley Head.

Sun, X., Ma, R., Zhao, X., Li, Z., Lindqvist, J., Ali, A. E. and Bosch, J. A. (2024) Trusting the Search: Unraveling Human Trust in Health Information from Google and ChatGPT, ACM, https://arxiv.org/pdf/2403.09987.

Times Higher Education (2023) Universities Need to Help Improve AI-driven Internet Searches, *Times Higher Education*, www.timeshighereducation.com/blog/universities-need-help-improve-ai-driven-internet-searches.

Tru, A. (2024) Discover the New Multi-Lingual, High-Quality Phi-3.5 SLMs, https://techcommunity.microsoft.com/blog/azure-ai-services-blog/discover-the-new-multi-lingual-high-quality-phi-3-5-slms/4225280.

Tunjungsari, H. and Takwin, B. (2021) Understanding Critical Thinking Practice in Everyday Life Through Stages of Critical Thinking Skills and Disposition, *Mind, Brain, and Education*, **15**, 225–31, https://doi.org/10.1111/mbe.12279.

UK Cabinet Office, Central Digital and Data Office (2024) *Generative AI Framework for HMG*, www.gov.uk/government/publications/generative-ai-framework-for-hmg/generative-ai-framework-for-hmg-html.

UK Department for Science, Innovation and Technology (2023), *A Pro-innovation Approach to AI Regulation*, www.gov.uk/government/publications/ai-regulation-a-pro-innovation-approach/white-paper.

UK Department of Education (2024) *Generative AI in Education: Educator and Expert Views*,
https://assets.publishing.service.gov.uk/media/65b8cd41b5cb6e000d8bb74e/DfE_GenAI_in_education_-_Educator_and_expert_views_report.pdf .

UK House of Commons, Science, Innovation and Technology Committee (2024) *Governance of Artificial Intelligence (AI) Report: Third Report of Session 2023–24*, https://publications.parliament.uk/pa/cm5804/cmselect/cmsctech/38/report.html.

UK Parliament (2023) *Artificial Intelligence: Development, Risks and Regulation*, House of Lords Library, 18 July, https://lordslibrary.parliament.uk/artificial-intelligence-development-risks-and-regulation.

UNESCO (2021a) *Media and Information Literate Citizens: Think Critically, Click Wisely*! https://unesdoc.unesco.org/ark:/48223/pf0000377068.

UNESCO (2021b) *Artificial Intelligence in Education: Opportunities, Challenges and Risks*, www.unesco.org/en/digital-education/artificial-intelligence.

UNESCO (2023) Global Media and Information Literacy Week 2022, www.unesco.org/en/articles/global-media-and-information-literacy-week-2022.

Vakkari, P. (2003) Task-based Information Searching, *Annual Review of Information Science and Technology*, **37** (1), 413–64, https://doi.org/10.1002/aris.1440370110.

Van Wynsberghe, A. (2021) Sustainable AI: AI for Sustainability and the Sustainability of AI, *AI and Ethics*, **1**, 213–18, https://doi.org/10.1007/s43681-021-00043-6.

Varsik, S. and Vosberg, L. (2024) *The Potential Impact of Artificial Intelligence on Equity and Inclusion in Education*, OECD Artificial Intelligence Papers, No. 23, OECD Publishing, https://doi.org/10.1787/15df715b-en.

Vincent-Lancrin, S. and Van Der Vlies, R. (2020) *Trustworthy Artificial Intelligence (AI) in Education: Promises and Challenges*, OECD Education Working Papers, 218, OECD Publishing, https://doi.org/10.1787/a6c90fa9-en.

Vuong, T. and Ruotsalo, T. (2024) Predicting Representations of Information Needs from Digital Activity Context, *ACM Transactions on Information Systems*, **42** (4), article no. 95. 1–29, https://doi.org/10.1145/3639819.

Wamba, S., Bawack, R. E., Guthrie, C., Queiroz, M. M. and Carillo, K. D. A. (2021) Are We Preparing for a Good AI Society? A Bibliometric Review and Research Agenda, *Technological Forecasting & Social Change*, **164**, 120482, https://ssrn.com/abstract=3735322 or http://dx.doi.org/10.2139/ssrn.3735322.

Wang, B., Rau, P. L. P. and Yuan, T. (2022) Measuring User Competence in Using Artificial Intelligence: Validity and Reliability of Artificial Intelligence Literacy Scale, *Behaviour & Information Technology*, **42** (9), 1324–37, https://doi.org/10.1080/0144929X.2022.2072768.

Wang, L. L. (2024) Generative AI for Scholarly Information Access, *Charleston Hub*, www.charleston-hub.com/2024/07/generative-ai-for-scholarly-information-access.
White, R. W. (2016) *Interactions with Search Systems*, Cambridge University Press.
White, R. W. (2024) Advancing the Search Frontier with AI Agents: AI Agents are Extending the Capabilities of Traditional Search Engines to Help Users Tackle Complex Tasks, *Communications of the ACM*, 20 August, https://cacm.acm.org/research/advancing-the-search-frontier-with-ai-agents.
White, R. W. and Roth, R. A. (2009) Exploratory Search: Beyond the Query-Response Paradigm, *Synthesis Lectures on Information Concepts, Retrieval, and Services*, **1** (1), 1–98, https://doi.org/10.2200/S00174ED1V01Y200901ICR003.
Wilson, T. D. (1999) Models in Information Behaviour Research, *Journal of Documentation*, **55** (3), 249–70, https://doi.org/10.1108/EUM0000000007145.
Wilson, T. D. (2000) Human Information Behaviour, *Informing Science*, **3** (2), 49–55, https://doi.org/10.28945/576.
Wilson, T. D. (2006) On User Studies and Information Needs, *Journal of Documentation*, **62** (6), 658–70, http://dx.doi.org/10.1108/00220410610714895.
Wilson, T.D. (2007) Evolution in Information Behavior Modeling: Wilson's Model. In Fisher, K., Erdelez, S. and L. McKechnie, (eds) *Theories of Information Behavior*, Information Today, 31–6. [Slightly revised and updated October 2007]. http://InformationR.net/tdw/publ/papers/2005SIGUSE.html.
Wu, Q., Bansal, G., Zhang, J., Wu, Y., Li, B., Zhu, E., Jiang, L., Zhang, X., Zhang, S., Liu, J., Awadallah, A. H., White, R. W., Burger, D. and Wang, C. (2023) AutoGen: Enabling Next-Gen LLM Applications via Multi-Agent Conversation, *arXiv*, https://arxiv.org/abs/2308.08155.
Yi, Y. (2021) Establishing the Concept of AI Literacy, *Jahr – European Journal of Bioethics*, **12** (2), 353–68, https://doi.org/10.21860/j.12.2.8.
Zewe, A. (2023) Explained: Generative AI: How Do Powerful Generative AI Systems Like ChatGPT Work, and What Makes Them Different from Other Types of Artificial Intelligence?, *MIT News*, 9 November, https://news.mit.edu/2023/explained-generative-ai-1109.
Zhao, X., Cox, A. and Cai, L. (2024) ChatGPT and the Digitisation of Writing, *Humanities and Social Sciences Communications*, **11**, 1–9, https://doi.org/10.1057/s41599-024-02904-x.
Zhou, T. and Li, S. (2024) Understanding User Switch of Information Seeking: from Search Engines to Generative AI, *Journal of Librarianship and Information Science*, https://doi.org/10.1177/09610006241244800.

Index

The manufacturer's authorised representative in the EU for product
safety is Logos Europe, 9 rue Nicolas Poussin, 17000 La Rochelle,
France (contact@logoseurope.eu, www.logoseurope.eu)
GPSR Authorized Representative: Easy Access System Europe—Mustamäe
tee 50, 10621 Tallinn, Estonia, gpsr.requests@easproject.com
Printed and bound by CPI Group (UK) Ltd, Croydon, CR0 4YY
27/08/2026
02205294-0002